Network Functions Virtualization (NFV) with a Touch of SDN

Network Functions Virtualization (NFV) with a Touch of SDN

Rajendra Chayapathi CCIE® No. 4991,
Syed Farrukh Hassan CCIE® No. 21617,
Paresh Shah

✦✦ Addison-Wesley

Boston • Columbus • Indianapolis • New York • San Francisco
Amsterdam • Cape Town • Dubai • London • Madrid • Milan
Munich • Paris • Montreal • Toronto • Delhi • Mexico City
São Paulo • Sidney • Hong Kong • Seoul • Singapore • Taipei • Tokyo

For information about buying this title in bulk quantities, or for special sales opportunities (which may include electronic versions; custom cover designs; and content particular to your business, training goals, marketing focus, or branding interests), please contact our corporate sales department at corpsales@pearsoned.com or (800) 382-3419.

For government sales inquiries, please contact governmentsales@pearsoned.com.

For questions about sales outside the U.S., please contact intlcs@pearson.com.

Visit us on the Web: informit.com/aw

Library of Congress Control Number: 2016952060

ISBN-13: 978-0-13-446305-6
ISBN-10: 0-13-446305-6

1 16

Editor-in-Chief
Mark Taub

Product Line Manager
Brett Bartow

Development Editor
Marianne Bartow

Managing Editor
Sandra Schroeder

Project Editor
Mandie Frank

Copy Editor
Warren Hapke

Indexer
Cheryl Lenser

Proofreader
Sasirekha

Technical Reviewers
Mark Cohen
Krishna Doddapaneni

Editorial Assistant
Vanessa Evans

Designer
Chuti Prasertsith

Compositor
codeMantra

I would like to dedicate this book to all the curious minds out there whose interest in NFV is the inspiration for this book. I would also like to dedicate this book to my ever supportive and loving family, for without their encouragement, support, and help, this endeavor wouldn't have been possible. Thanks to all who have supported me to write this book.

— Rajendra Chayapathi

I would like to dedicate this book to my wife and children for their love, patience, and especially for their strong support to me while writing this book. Thanks to them for letting me sacrifice many weekends and weeknights of family time. I would also like to thank my parents for their continued support, encouragement, and for guiding me through their wisdom.

— Syed F. Hassan

I would like to dedicate this book to my family, friends, and parents. I especially thank my wife, who filled in for me by taking care of the kids and keeping them busy to not slow me down. I also give a big thank you to my two adorable daughters, who excused me from spending time with them. Lastly I would like to acknowledge the support from my parents for motivating me to think different and share the knowledge with others, which translated to writing this book. Without their support, this book wouldn't have been possible.

— Paresh Shah

And most importantly, all of us would like to thank God for all His blessings in our lives!

Contents

Preface

Register your copy of *Network Functions Virtualization (NFV) with a Touch of SDN* at informit.com for convenient access to downloads, updates, and corrections as they become available. To start the registration process, go to informit.com/register and log in or create an account. Enter the product ISBN 9780134463056 and click Submit. Once the process is complete, you will find any available bonus content under "Registered Products."

Acknowledgments

We would like to say a very special thanks to the technical reviewers, Nicolas Fevrier and Alexander Orel. They took up the challenge of reviewing and correcting the technical inaccuracies and shared their expert opinions by providing us with helpful recommendations. Their expertise, suggestions, and guidance helped us to navigate presenting the content in the right direction and keep it at an appropriate depth.

We would like to thank Brett and Marianne Bartow at Addison-Wesley Professional for bearing with us throughout the process of putting this book together and guiding us through each step. Finally, we would like to thank our colleagues and peers for giving us the inspiration and encouragement to share our knowledge through this book.

About the Authors

Rajendra Chayapathi is a Senior Solution Architect in Cisco's professional and consulting services organization. His most recent work has been on emerging technologies such as NFV, SDN, programmability and network orchestration and its adoption in the industry. He has over twenty years of experience in networking technologies, customer interaction, and networking products; his focus is on network design and architecture. He has previously worked in Cisco's engineering teams where he was involved on various network operating systems and product development. Before his employment at Cisco, he provided consultancy services to AT&T and financial institutions for the design and deployment of IP core network technologies. He has been a regular speaker at multiple technology conferences such as Cisco Live, Cisco Connect and NANOG. Rajendra has a CCIE (#4991) in Routing and Switching and also holds a Bachelor's degree in Electronics and Communication from University of Mysore, India and a Masters' degree in Business Administration with a focus on technology Management from University of Phoenix, USA.

Syed Farrukh Hassan has been in the networking industry for fifteen years, and is currently a Senior Solutions Architect in Cisco's professional and consulting services organization. He has worked with various Internet and cloud service providers, helping them in adoption of innovative network technologies and supporting them in design and deployment of new architectures. In his current role, Syed is involved in SDN and NFV adoption, providing guidance, future strategy, and planning to service provider, enterprise, and data center customers. Syed has previously been part of engineering teams within Cisco and has been an active contributor towards design and innovation of network products and solutions. Syed has been a regular speaker in public forums and conferences and is recognized as a Cisco Live Distinguished Speaker. Syed is a double CCIE in Service Provider and Data Center technologies (#21617) and also a VMware Certified Network Virtualization Professional (VCP-NV). He holds a Bachelors' degree in Engineering from NED University, Pakistan, and a Masters' degree in Engineering from the University of Florida, Gainesville, USA.

Paresh Shah has been in the network industry for more than twenty years and currently working as a Director in Cisco's professional and consulting services organization. He is responsible for bringing to market new disruptive services based on cutting-edge technologies and solutions to achieve successful deployment in customer networks. Paresh has led various global engineering and customer-facing groups in the service provider market and is a veteran of the high-end routing, service provider, enterprise, and cloud segments. He started his career as an engineer in 1996 building one of the first high-speed multi-services routers in the industry and was responsible for adoption of new technologies then, like MPLS, BGP, and L2/L3 VPN and new operating systems like IOS-XR. Paresh is leading the adoption of NFV, SDN, and segment routing consultancy services and driving the solutions for cloud-providers, traditional service providers, and enterprises that are looking to adopt these new technologies. Paresh is a regular speaker at industry conferences such as Cisco Live, NANOG, and SANOG, with a pulse on the latest trends in the industry. He has a Bachelors' degree in Electrical Engineering from University of Pune, India and a Masters' degree focusing in Networking and Telecommunications from University of Missouri-Kansas City, USA.

About the Technical Reviewers

Nicolas Fevrier is a Technical Leader in Cisco's Service Provider team. He is a networking veteran and during his twelve years at Cisco he has taken up positions for technology validation, consultancy services, and most recently Technical Marketing. He has traveled around the world to deploy, support and promote various IOS XR routing platforms. Currently Nicolas focus is towards driving and facilitating the adoption of the cutting-edge technologies focused on IOS XR products. He is also heavily engaged in providing guidance on network services such as services for securing network, mitigation of distributed Denial of Service, and services for network transformation using Carrier Grate NAT. Nicolas has strong interest in NFV and SDN areas, and has been part of technical marketing team for Cisco's service provider business. He is a regular speaker at technical conferences and a distinguished Cisco Live speaker. Nicolas holds a CCIE in Routing and Switching (#8966).

Alexander Orel has more than fifteen years of experience in networking field. He has worked in multi-vendor environments for various Internet service providers and network consulting companies. Currently Alexander works as a Solutions Architect in Cisco Professional and consulting services team, where he works with global service providers and enterprises, ratifying their requirements, and helping them plan and supporting the deployment of Next-Generation network products and technologies. His specialization is IOS XR-based platforms and NFV technologies. Alexander has a Master's degree in applied physics from Moscow Institute of Physics and Technology and currently holds CCIE certification #10391 in R&S and DC. Alexander has been a frequent presenter at various technology conferences such as Cisco Live and Cisco Connect. Alexander lives and works in Ottawa, Canada.

Introduction

Network functions virtualization (NFV) is significantly influencing the world of networking and changing how networks are designed, deployed, and managed.

NFV gives network service providers freedom of choice and allows separating the networking software from the hardware. This decoupling brings advantages such as cost savings in deploying and operating the network, rapid on-demand provisioning of new network functions, increased efficiency, and agile network scalability. These advantages open the door for new business opportunities, bring new services to market quicker and have been attracting tremendous interest from cloud and Internet service providers, mobile operators, and enterprise market segments.

Who Should Read This Book?

The book is targeted towards network engineers, architects, planners, and operators with any level of experience in networking technologies who are ready to enter the world of network functions virtualization. It assumes basic networking knowledge but is meant to be an entry-level book when it comes to understanding NFV architecture, deployment, management, and associated technologies.

Goals and Methods—How This Book Is Organized

It is critical to understand NFV (like any other disruptive technology) to maximize the benefits that it offers as well as to use it effectively and efficiently. This understanding of NFV requires learning new concepts and technologies and involves a learning curve for the engineers, architects, planners, designers, operators, and managers of today's networks. The motivation to write this book comes from the desire to facilitate learning about NFV technologies.

The goal of the book is to enable the reader to get a firm grasp on the NFV technologies and its building blocks. With the adaption of NFV, the roles in the networking industry will evolve significantly. This book gets readers ready to enter the NFV era, arming them with the knowledge to design, deploy, monetize, and make informed decisions about adopting NFV solutions in their networks.

The book takes the approach of building the concepts bottom-up, starting with the basic NFV concepts and discussing the advantages and design principles in depth, based on its applications. It gets the reader familiar with NFV orchestration, management, and use cases, then follow this with a discussion on the related technology of software-defined networking (SDN). It finishes with a discussion of the advanced NFV topics that glue everything together to complete the NFV canvas. The discussion is split into six chapters, each with its own goals.

Chapter 1: The Journey to Network Functions Virtualization (NFV) Era

The goal of this chapter is to understand the benefits of NFV and the market drivers that are enabling its adaption. The chapter starts the journey towards NFV by analyzing the network evolution over the past decades. This chapter also focuses on building the foundation knowledge of NFV by introducing the architectural framework and its components.

Chapter 2: Virtualization Concepts

This chapter focuses on the key technology that makes NFV possible—virtualization. The goal of this chapter is to get the reader very well acquainted with virtualization technologies and how they relate to NFV.

Chapter 3: Virtualization of Network Functions

This chapter takes a closer look at the design and deployment considerations for an NFV based network. The chapters also discuss the technical challenges that are expected when transforming today's networks to adapt NFV. The chapter closes with a discussion of network functions and services that are adapting or can adapt NFV.

By the end of the first three chapter, the reader should be familiar with planning an NFV deployment, foreseeing the challenges and design issues that will need to be considered, and evaluating the advantages that this transformation will bring and how those advantages can be maximized.

Chapter 4: NFV Deployment in the Cloud

With the foundations and design challenges already laid out and discussed in the previous chapters, this chapter takes those concepts and applies them towards orchestrating, building, and deploying NFV networks and services. The chapter also visits the management and orchestration solutions available, both through vendors and the open source community.

By the end of this chapter, the reader should have a through understanding of the tools and techniques that can be used to deploy and manage an NFV network.

Chapter 5: Software Defined Networking (SDN)

This chapter shifts to new topic and touches upon the concepts of SDN. The chapter covers the fundamentals of SDN and describes its correlation with NFV.

Chapter 6: Stitching It All Together

This chapter consolidates the knowledge gained from the previous chapters. Important considerations in an NFV network, such as security, programmability, performance, and function chaining, are discussed in this chapter. It also gives insight into the evolving NFV concepts that will shape the future of this technology.

Chapter 1

The Journey to Network Functions Virtualization (NFV) Era

Network functions virtualization (NFV) is a fast-emerging technology area that is heavily influencing the world of networking. It is changing the way networks are designed, deployed, and managed, transforming the networking industry towards a virtualization approach and moving away from customized hardware with prepackaged software.

This chapter walks you through the NFV journey and the market drivers behind it. It allows you to get acquainted with the concepts of NFV and examines the ongoing efforts towards standardization. It lays the foundation which is instrumental in understanding networking industry transition to NFV. It explains how the industry is evolving from a hardware centric approach to a virtualized and software—based network approach in the effort to meet the need and feed of cloud-based services which demand open, scalable, elastic and agile networks.

The main topics covered in this chapter are:

- Evolution from traditional network architecture to NFV

- NFV standardization efforts and an overview of the NFV architectural framework

- Benefits and market drivers behind NFV

The Evolution of Network Architecture

To appreciate the motivation and need behind the networking industry's fast adoption of NFV, it's helpful to take a look at the history of networking and the challenges that it faces today. Data communication networks and devices have evolved and improved over time. But while networks have become faster and more resilient with higher capacity, they still struggle to cope with the demands of the changing market. The networking industry is being driven by a new set of requirements and challenges brought forward by cloud-based services such as infrastructure to support those services and demands to make them work more efficient. Mega-scale data centers hosting computing and storage, a factorial increase in data-enabled devices, and Internet of Things (IoT) applications are just some of examples of areas that need to be addressed for improved throughput and latency in existing networks.

This section examines traditional networks and networking devices and identifies the reasons they have been unable to cope with the new types of demands. It also takes a look at the way NFV brings a fresh perspective and different solution to these market-driven needs.

Traditional Network Architecture

The traditional phone network and perhaps even telegram networks are examples of the earliest data transport networks. Early on, the design criteria and quality benchmark by which networks were judged were latency, availability, throughput, and the capacity to carry data with minimal loss.

These factors directly influenced the development and requirements for the hardware and equipment to transport the data (text and voice, in this case). Additionally, hardware systems were built for very specific use cases and targeted functions, ran tightly coupled proprietary operating systems on them, and were meant to perform only specific functions. With the advent of data transport networks, the requirements and factors that influence the network's design and the devices' efficiency stayed unchanged (for example, the network design should achieve highest throughput with minimum latency and jitter over extended distances with minimal loss).

All the traditional networking devices were made for specific functions, and the data networks built were tailored and customized to meet these efficiency criteria effectively. The software or code running on these custom-designed hardware systems was tightly coupled to it, closely integrated with the silicon Field Programmable and Customized Integrated Circuits and focused exclusively on performing the specific functions of the device.

Figure 1-1 illustrates some of the characteristics of traditional network devices deployed today.

With the exponential increase in bandwidth demand, heavily driven by video, mobile, and IoT applications, service providers are constantly looking for ways to expand and scale their network services, preferably without significant increase in costs. The characteristics of traditional devices present a bottleneck to this requirement and create many constraints that limit the scalability, deployment costs, and

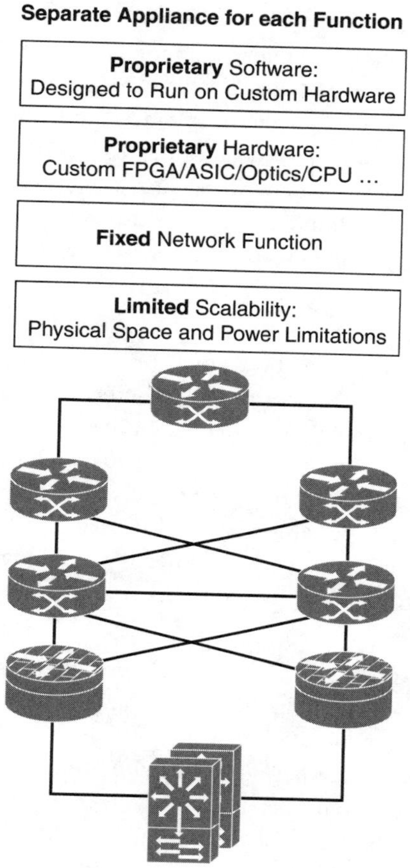

Separate Appliance for each Function

Proprietary Software:
Designed to Run on Custom Hardware

Proprietary Hardware:
Custom FPGA/ASIC/Optics/CPU ...

Fixed Network Function

Limited Scalability:
Physical Space and Power Limitations

Figure 1-1 *Traditional Network Devices*

operational efficiency of the network. This situation forces the operators to consider alternatives that can remove the limitations. Let's examine some of these limitations.

Flexibility Limitations

Vendors design and develop their equipment with a generic set of requirements and offer the functionality as a combination of specific hardware and software. The hardware and software are packaged as a unit and limited to the vendor's implementation. This restricts the choices of feature combinations and hardware capabilities that can be deployed. The lack of flexibility and customization to meet fast-changing requirements results in inefficient use of resources.

Scalability Constraints

Physical network devices have scalability limitations in both hardware and software. The hardware requires power and space, which can become a constraint in densely populated areas. The lack of these resources may limit the hardware that can be deployed. On the software side, these traditional devices may not be able to keep up with the scale of changes in the data network, such as number of routes or labels. Each device is designed to handle a limited multi-dimensional scale, and once that ceiling is hit, the operator has a very limited set of options aside from upgrading the device.

Time-to-Market Challenges

As requirements grow and change over time, equipment isn't always able to quickly keep up with these changes. Service providers often delay offering new services to meet the shift in the market requirements. Implementing new services requires upgrading the networking equipment. This leads to complex decisions to choose the appropriate migration path. This route may imply re-evaluation of new equipment, redesign of the network, or possibly new vendors that may be more suitable to meet the new needs. This increases the cost of ownership and longer timeline to offer new services to customers, resulting in loss of business and revenue.

Manageability Issues

Monitoring tools employed in the networks implement standardized monitoring protocols such as a Simple Network Management Protocol (SNMP), NetFlow, syslog, or similar systems for gathering device state and information. However, for monitoring vendor-specific parameters, relying on standard protocols may not suffice. For example, a vendor may be using nonstandard MIB or vendor-defined syslog messages. For such in-depth level of monitoring and control the management tools become very specific and tailored for the vendor's implementation. Whether these management tools are built in-house or offered directly by the vendors, it is sometimes not feasible to port these to a different vendor's devices.

High Operational Costs

The operational costs are high because of the need to have highly trained teams for each vendor-specific system being deployed in the network. This also tends to lock the provider into a specific vendor, because switching to a different vendor would mean additional costs to retrain operational staff and revamp operational tools.

Migration Considerations

Devices and networks need to be upgraded or reoptimized over a period of time. This requires physical access and on-site personnel to deploy new hardware, reconfigure physical connectivity, and upgrade facilities at the site. This creates a cost barrier for migration and network upgrade decisions, slowing down the offering of new services.

Capacity Over-Provisioning

Short- and long-term network capacity demands are hard to predict, and as a result networks are built with excess capacity and are often more than 50% undersubscribed. Underutilized and overprovisioned networks result in lower return on investment.

Interoperability

For faster time to market and deployment, some vendors try to implement new networking functionality before it is fully standardized. In many cases, this implementation becomes proprietary, which creates inter-operability challenges that require service providers to validate interoperability before deploying it in production environment.

Introducing NFV

In data centers, the server virtualization approach is already proven technology, where stacks of independent server hardware systems have mostly been replaced by virtualized servers running on shared hardware.

NFV builds on this concept of server virtualization. It expands the concept beyond servers, widening the scope to include network devices. It also allows the ecosystem to manage, provision, monitor, and deploy these virtualized network entities.

The acronym NFV is used as a blanket term to reference the overall ecosystem that comprises the virtual network devices, the management tools, and the infrastructure that integrates these software pieces with computer hardware. However, NFV is more accurately defined as the method and technology that enables you to replace physical network devices performing specific network functions with one or more software programs executing the same network functions while running on generic computer hardware. One example is replacing a physical firewall appliance with a software-based virtual machine. This virtual machine provides the firewall functions, runs the same operating system, and has the same look and feel—but on non-dedicated, shared, and generic hardware.

With NFV, the network functions can be implemented on any generic hardware that offers the basic resources for processing, storage, and data transmission. Virtualization has matured to the point that it can mask the physical device, making it possible to use commercial off the shelf (COTS) hardware to provide the infrastructure for NFV.

COTS

Commercial off the shelf (COTS) refers to any product or service that is developed and marketed commercially. COTS hardware refers to general-purpose computing, storage, and networking gear that is built and sold for any use case that requires these resources. It doesn't enforce usage of a proprietary hardware or software.

Figure 1-2 shows the transition from traditional network devices to NFV.

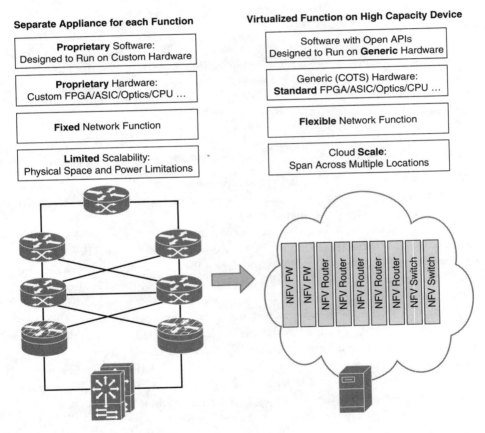

Separate Appliance for each Function

Proprietary Software: Designed to Run on Custom Hardware
Proprietary Hardware: Custom FPGA/ASIC/Optics/CPU ...
Fixed Network Function
Limited Scalability: Physical Space and Power Limitations

Virtualized Function on High Capacity Device

Software with Open APIs Designed to Run on **Generic** Hardware
Generic (COTS) Hardware: **Standard** FPGA/ASIC/Optics/CPU ...
Flexible Network Function
Cloud **Scale**: Span Across Multiple Locations

Figure 1-2 *Transition to NFV*

In traditional network architecture, vendors are not concerned about the hardware on which their code will run, because that hardware is developed, customized, and deployed as dedicated equipment for the specific network function. They have complete control over both the hardware and the software running on the device.

That allows the vendors flexibility to design the hardware and its performance factors based on the roles these devices will play in the network. For example, a device designed for the network core will have carrier-class resiliency built into it, while a device designed for the network edge will be kept simpler and will not offer high availability to keep its cost low. In this context, many of the capabilities of these devices are made possible with the tight integration of hardware and software. This changes with NFV.

In the case of virtualized network functions, it is not realistic to make assumptions about the capabilities that hardware has to offer, nor is it possible to very tightly integrate with the bare hardware. NFV decouples the software from hardware, and boasts to offer the ability to use any commercially available hardware to implement the virtualized flavor of very specific network functions.

Virtualization of networks opens up new possibilities in how networks can be deployed and managed. The flexibility, agility, capital and operational cost savings and scalability that is made possible with NFV opens up new innovation, design paradigm and enables new network architectures.

NFV Architectural Framework

The architecture that defines traditional network devices is fairly basic, because both the hardware and software are customized and tightly integrated. In contrast, NFV allows software developed by the vendors to run on generic shared hardware, creating multiple touch points for management.

The NFV architectural framework is developed to ensure that these touch points are standardized and compatible between the implementations of different vendors. This section provides a comprehensive discussion on the framework and the rationale behind its blocks. Understanding the framework enables readers to envision the flexibility and freedom of choice that NFV has to offer.

Need for a Framework

The architecture that defines the traditional network devices is fairly basic since both the hardware and software are customized and tightly integrated. In contrast, NFV allows software developed by the vendors to run on generic shared hardware creating multiple touch points for management. In the NFV jargon the virtual implementation of the network functions is referred to as virtualized network function (VNF). A VNF is meant to perform a certain network function e.g. router, switch, firewall, load-balancer, etc. and a combination of these VNFs may be required to implement the complete network segment that is being virtualized.

> **VNF**
>
> VNF (virtualized network function) replaces a vendor's specialized hardware with systems performing the same function, yet running on a generic hardware.

Different vendors may offer these VNFs, and the service providers can choose a combination of vendors and functions that best suit their needs. This freedom of choice creates the need for a standardized method of communication between the VNFs as well as a way to manage them in the virtual environment. The management of NFV needs to take into account the following considerations:

- multivendor implementations of VNFs
- managing the life cycles and interactions of these functions
- managing the hardware resource allocations
- monitoring the utilization
- configuration of the VNFs
- interconnection of the virtualized functions to implement the service
- interaction with the billing and operational support systems

To implement these management roles and keep the system open and non-proprietary, a framework must be defined for standardization. This standard framework should ensure that the VNF deployed is not tied to specific hardware and does not need to be especially tailored for any environment. It should offer vendors a reference architecture that they can follow for consistency and uniformity in the deployment methodologies of any VNF they implement. Additionally, it needs to ensure that the management of these VNFs and the hardware they run upon does not have a dependency on any vendor. There should be no special tweaking required to implement the network functions in this heterogeneous ecosystem. Essentially, this framework must provide the architectural foundations that allow the VNFs, hardware, and the management systems to work seamlessly within the well defined boundaries.

ETSI Framework for NFV

NFV was first introduced at the SDN OpenFlow World Congress in 2012 by a consortium of key service providers. They referenced the major challenges faced by network operators, especially their dependency on introducing new hardware for enabling innovative services to their customers. The group highlighted the challenges associated with the following concepts:

- design changes around the new equipment
- deployment cost and physical constraints
- need for expertise to manage and operate the new proprietary hardware and software
- dealing with hardware complexity in the new proprietary equipment
- the short lifecycle that makes this equipment become obsolete rapidly
- restarting the cycle before the returns from the capital expenses and investments are fully realized

The group proposed NFV as a way to tackle these challenges and improve efficiency by "leveraging standard IT virtualization technology to consolidate many network equipment types onto industry standard high volume servers, switches and storage, which could be located in Datacentres, Network Nodes and in the end user premises." [3]

To realize this goal and define a set of specifications that would make it possible to move from the traditional vendor and network centric approach to an NFV-based network, seven of these leading telecom operators formed an Internet specification group (ISG)—under an independent standardization organization called the European Telecommunications Standards Institute (ETSI). [1]

This group formally started in early 2013, working towards defining requirements and an architectural framework that can support the virtualized implementation of network functions performed by custom hardware devices from vendors.

This group used three key criteria for coming up with the recommendations:

- **Decoupling:** complete separation of hardware and software
- **Flexibility:** automated and scalable deployment of the network functions
- **Dynamic operations:** control of the operational parameters of the network functions through granular control and monitoring of the state of network

Based on these criteria, a high-level architectural framework was established, defining distinct areas of focus as shown in Figure 1-3.

This architectural framework forms the basis of the standardization and development work and is commonly referred to as the ETSI NFV framework. At a high level, the framework encompasses management of VNFs, relationships and interdependencies, data flow between VNFs, and resource allocation. ETSI ISG categorized these roles into three high-level blocks, namely the infrastructure block, virtualized

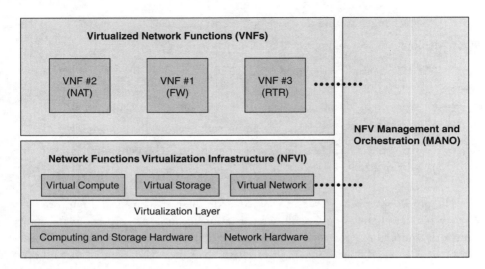

Figure 1-3 *High-Level ETSI NFV Framework*

functions block, and management block. In ETSI's definition, the formal names of these blocks are defined as:

- **Network Functions Virtualization Infrastructure (NFVI) block:** This block forms the foundation of the overall architecture. The hardware to host the virtual machines, the software to make virtualization possible, and the Virtualized resources are grouped into this block.

- **Virtualized Network Function (VNF) block:** The VNF block uses the virtual machines offered by NFVI and builds on top of them by adding the software implementing the virtualized network functions.

- **Management and Orchestration (MANO) block:** MANO is defined as a separate block in the architecture, which interacts with both the NFVI and VNF blocks. The framework delegates to the MANO layer the management of all the resources in the infrastructure layer; in addition, this layer creates and deletes resources and manages their allocation of the VNFs.

Understanding the ETSI Framework

The ETSI framework and the thought process behind its high-level blocks can be better understood if you examine the building process that led to this framework. Let's begin with the fundamental concept of NFV, such as virtualizing the function of a network device. This is achieved through VNFs.

To implement the network service, VNFs may be deployed either as standalone entities or as a combination of multiple VNFs. The protocols associated with the function that is being virtualized within a VNF do not need to be aware of the virtualized implementation. As shown in the Figure 1-4 the VNF implementing the firewall service (FW), NAT device (NAT), and routing (RTR) communicate to each other without the knowledge that they are not physically connected or running on dedicated physical devices.

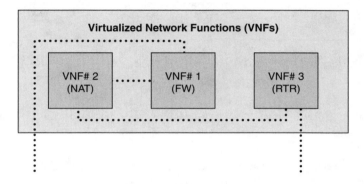

Figure 1-4 *Network Functions Working Together as VNFs*

Since there isn't dedicated or custom hardware designed to run these VNF, a general-purpose hardware device with generic hardware resources such as a processor (CPU), storage, memory, and network interfaces can be used to run these VNFs. This can be made possible by using COTS hardware. It doesn't need to be a single COTS device; it can be an integrated hardware solution providing any combination of the required hardware resources to run the VNFs. Virtualization technologies can be used to share the hardware among multiple VNFs. These technologies, such as hypervisor-based virtualization or container-based virtualization, have been used in data centers for some time and have become fairly mature. These details are covered in Chapter 2, "Virtualization Concepts."

Virtualization of hardware offers an infrastructure for the VNF to run upon. This NFV infrastructure (NFVI) can use COTS hardware as a common pool of resources and carve out subsets of these resources creating "virtualized" compute, storage, and network pools that can be allocated as required by the VNFs, as shown Figure 1-5.

The vendor for the VNF recommends a minimum requirement for the resources that its implementation should have available to it, but the vendor can't control or optimize these hardware parameters. For instance, the vendor can make a recommendation on the CPU cores necessary to execute the code or the storage space and memory the VNF will need—but the vendors no longer get a free hand to design

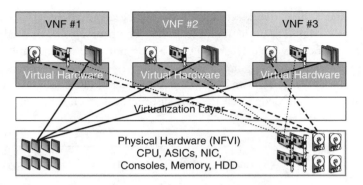

Figure 1-5 *Virtual Computing, Storage, and Networking Resources Provided to VNF*

the hardware around their specific requirements. The virtualization layer using the physical hardware can cater to the VNF resource request. The VNF doesn't have any visibility into this process, nor is that VNF aware of the existences of other VNFs that may be sharing the physical hardware with them.

In this virtualized network's architecture, there are now multiple resources to manage and operate at various levels. In comparison, today's network architecture management is vendor specific and has limited knobs and data points offered by vendors. Any new requirements or enhancements in management capabilities are possible only with vendor support. With NFV it is possible to manage the entities at a more granular and individual level. The NFV architecture, therefore, wouldn't be complete without defining the methodologies to manage, automate, coordinate, and interconnect these layers and functional blocks in an agile, scalable, and automated way.

This requirement leads us to add another functional block to the framework that communicates with and manages both the VNF and NFVI blocks, as shown in Figure 1-6. This block manages the deployment and interconnections of the VNFs on the COTS hardware and allocates the hardware resources to these VNFs.

Since the MANO block is meant to have full visibility of the entities and is responsible for managing them, it is fully aware of the utilization, operational state, and usage statistics of them. That makes MANO the most suitable interface for the operational and billing systems to gather the utilization data.

This completes the step-by-step understanding of the three high-level blocks—NFVI, VNF, and MANO—and captures the reasoning behind defining and positioning these blocks in the ETSI framework.

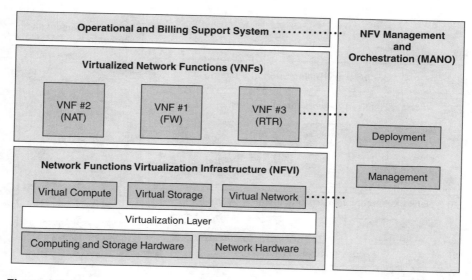

Figure 1-6 *Management and Orchestration Block for NFV*

A Closer Look at ETSI's NFV Framework

The previous section provides a high-level view of the ETSI NFV architecture framework and its basic building blocks. The framework defined by ETSI goes deeper into each of these blocks and defines individual functional blocks with distinct role and responsibility for each of them. The high-level blocks, therefore, comprise multiple functional blocks. For instance, the management block (MANO) is defined as a combination of three functional blocks: the Virtualized Infrastructure Manager (VIM), Virtualized Network Function Manager (VNFM), and NFV Orchestrator (NFVO).

The architecture also defines reference points for the functional blocks to interact, communicate and work with each other. Figure 1-7 shows the detailed view of the framework as defined by ETSI.

This section takes a deeper look into this framework and reviews the suggested functions, the interworking of each of these functional blocks, and their interlinking through the reference points.

For convenience of understanding, these functional blocks are grouped into layers, where each layer deals with a particular aspect of NFV implementation.

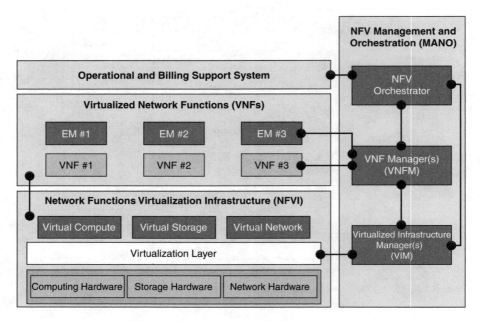

Figure 1-7 *Low Level View of the ETSI NFV Framework*

Infrastructure Layer

The VNFs rely on the availability of virtual hardware, emulated by software resources running on physical hardware. In the ETSI NFV framework, this is made possible by the infrastructure block (NFVI). This infrastructure block comprises physical hardware resources, the virtualization layer, and the virtual resources, as shown in Figure 1-8.

ETSI framework splits the hardware resources into three main categories – computing, storage, and network. The computing hardware includes both the CPU and memory, which may be pooled between hosts using cluster-computing techniques. Storage can be locally attached or distributed with devices such as network-attached storage (NAS) or devices connected using SAN technologies. Networking hardware comprises pools of network interface cards and ports that can be used by the VNFs. None of this hardware is purposely built for any particular network function, but all items are instead generic hardware devices available off the shelf hardware (COTS). These functional blocks can span and scale across multiple devices and interconnected locations, and are not confined to a single physical host, location or point of presence (POP).

It must be mentioned that the networking hardware within the physical location interconnecting the storage and compute devices, or interconnecting multiple locations (such as switches, routers, optical transponders, wireless communication

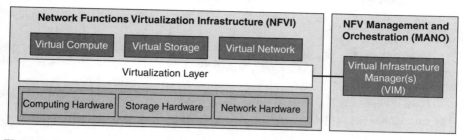

Figure 1-8 *Infrastructure Layer of ETSI NFV Framework*

equipment, etc.) is also considered part of NFVI. However, these network devices are not part of the pool that is allocated as a virtual resource to VNF.

The virtualization layer is another function block that is part of NFVI. It interacts directly with the pool of hardware devices, making them available to VNFs as a virtual machine. The virtual machine offers the virtualized computing, storage, and networking resources to any software that it hosts (VNF in this case) and presents these resources to the VNF as if they were dedicated physical hardware devices.

> **VM**
>
> Virtual machine or VM is a commonly used terminology for the virtualized resource pool, which may be shared hardware resources working independently and isolated from each other.

In summary, it is the virtualization-layer that is decoupling the software for network function (i.e., VNF) from the hardware while provident them isolation from other VNFs and acting as an interface to the physical hardware.

> **Abstraction**
>
> The technique of decoupling hardware and software layers by providing a common independent interface to the software for accessing the hardware resources is referred to as "hardware abstraction", or more simply as "abstraction."

To manage NFVI, ETSI defines a management functional block called the Virtualized Infrastructure Manager (VIM). VIM is part of MANO (Management and Orchestration blocks), and the framework delegates to it the responsibility for managing the computing, storage, and networking hardware, the software that is implementing the virtualization layer, and the virtualized hardware. Because VIM directly manages the hardware resources, it has a full inventory of these resources and visibility into their operational attributes (such as power management, health status, and availability), as well as the capacity to monitor their performance attributes (such as utilization statistics).

VIM also manages the virtualization layer and controls and influences how the virtualization layer uses the hardware. VIM is therefore responsible for the control of NFVI resources and works with other management functional blocks to determine the requirements and then manage the infrastructure resources to fulfill them. VIM's management scope may be with the same NFVI-POP or spread across the entire domain spanned by the infrastructure.

An instance of VIM may not be restricted to a single NFVI layer. It is possible that a single VIM implementation controls multiple NFVI blocks. Conversely, the framework also allows for the possibility that multiple VIMs can function in parallel and control several separate hardware devices. These VIMs can be in a single location or different physical locations.

Virtualized Network Functions (VNF) Layer

The VNF layer is where the virtualization of network function is implemented. It comprises the VNF-block and the functional block that manages it, called VNF-Manager (VNFM). The VNF-block is defined as a combination of VNF and Element Management (EM) blocks as shown in Figure 1-9.

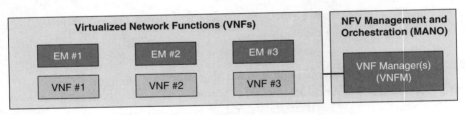

Figure 1-9 *Virtualized Network Function Layer in ETSI NFV Framework*

A virtualized implementation of a network function needs to be developed so it can run on any hardware that has sufficient computing, storage, and network interfaces. However, the details of the virtualized environment are transparent to the VNF, and it is expected to be unaware that the generic hardware it is running on is actually a virtual machine. The behavior and external interface of the VNF is expected to be identical to the physical implementation of the network function and device that it is virtualizing.

The network service being virtualized may be implemented through a single VNF, or it may require multiple VNFs. When a group of VNF are collectively implementing the network service, it is possible that some of the functions have dependencies on others, in which case the VNF needs to process the data in a specific sequence.

When a group of VNFs doesn't have any interdependency, then that group is referred to as a VNF set. An example of this is in a mobile virtual Evolved Packet Core (vEPC), where the Mobile Management Entity (MME) is responsible for authentication of the user and chooses the Service Gateway (SGW). The SGW runs independently of the MME's function and forwards user data packets. These VNFs work collectively to offer part of the functionality of vEPC but are independently implementing their functions.

If, however, the network service requires VNFs to process the data in a specific sequence, then the connectivity between the VNFs needs to be defined and deployed to ensure it. This is referred to as VNF-Forwarding-Graph (VNF-FG) or service chaining. In the previous example of vEPC, if you added another VNF that provides Packet Data Network Gateway (PGW) functionality, that PGW VNF should only process the data after the SGW. As shown in Figure 1-10, this interconnection between SGW, MME, and PGW in this specific order for packet flow makes a VNF-FG. This idea of service chaining is important in the NFV world and requires a more detailed discussion. This topic is covered in depth in Chapter 6, "Stitching It All Together."

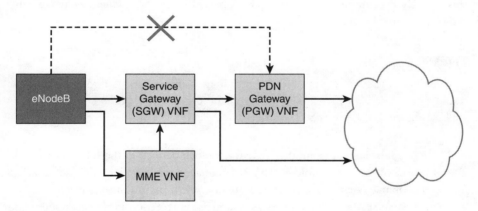

Figure 1-10 *Virtual Evolved Packet Core (vEPC) using VNF-FG*

In the ETSI framework, it is the VNFM's responsibility to bring up the VNF and manage the scaling of its resources. When the VNFM must instantiate a new VNF or add or modify the resources available to a VNF (for example, more CPU or memory) it communicates that requirement to the VIM. In turn, it requests that the virtualization layer modify the resources allocated to the VM that is hosting the VNF. Since the VIM has visibility into the inventory, it can also determine if it is possible for the current hardware to cater to these additional needs. Figure 1-11 shows this flow of events.

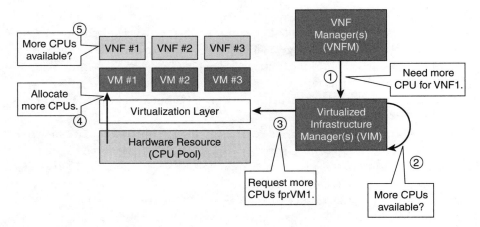

Figure 1-11 *VNFM Scaling Up VNF Resources*

The VNFM also has the responsibility for the FCAPS of the VNFs. It manages this directly by communicating with the VNFs or uses the Element Management (EM) functional block.

FCAPS

FCAPS is a ISO telecommunications management network mode and is an abbreviation for the five main management parameters: fault, configuration, performance, accounting, and security.

Element Management is another functional block defined in the ETSI framework and is meant to assist in implementing the management functions of one or more VNFs. The management scope of EM is analogous to the traditional element management system (EMS), which serves as a layer for interaction between the network management system and the devices performing network functions. EM interacts with the VNFs using proprietary methods while employing open standards to communicate with the VNFM. This provides a proxy to the VNFM for operations and management of the VNFs as shown in Figure 1-12. The FCAPS are still managed by VNFM, but it can take support from the EM to interact with the VNF for this aspect of management.

The framework doesn't restrict the implementation to a single VNFM to manage all the VNFs. It is possible that the vendor that owns the VNF requires its own VNFM to manage that VNF. Therefore, there can be NFV deployments where multiple VNFM are managing multiple VNFs or a single VNFM manages a single VNF, as shown in Figures 1-13 and 1-14.

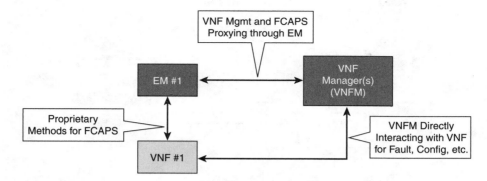

Figure 1-12 *VNFM Managing VNF Directly or through EM*

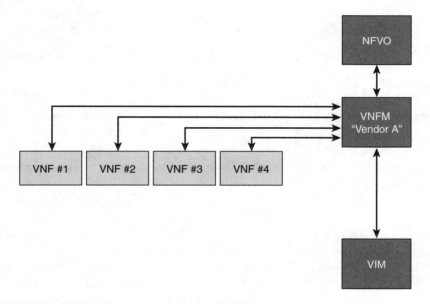

Figure 1-13 *Single VNFM Managing Multiple VNFs*

Operational and Orchestration Layer

When moving from physical to virtual devices, network operators do not want to revamp the management tools and applications that may be deployed for operational and business support systems (OSS/BSS). The framework doesn't require a change in these tools as part of transformation to NFV. It allows them to continue to manage the

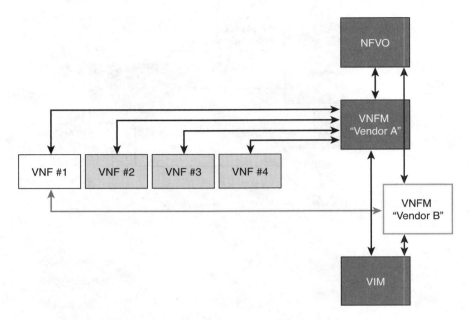

Figure 1-14 *Multiple VNFMs Managing Separate VNFs*

operational and business aspects of the network and work with the devices even though the devices are replaced by VNFs. While this is in line with what is desired, using existing systems has its drawbacks, because it doesn't fully reap the benefits of NFV and is not designed to communicate with NFV's management functional blocks—VNFM and VIM. One path that providers can take is to enhance and evolve the existing tools and systems to use NFV management functional blocks and utilize the NFV benefits (like elasticity, agility, etc.). That's a viable approach for some, but it is not a feasible option for others because these systems are traditionally built in-house or are proprietary implementations that do not allow for managing an open platform like NFV.

The solution that the ETSI framework offers is to use another functional block, NFV Orchestrator (NFVO). It extends the current OSS/BSS and manages the operational aspects and deployment of NFVI and VNF Figure 1-15 shows the two components of the orchestration layer in the framework.

The role of NFVO is not obvious up front and seems like an additional block buffering between current operating tools and VIM and VFNM. NFVO, however, has a critical and important role in the framework by overlooking the end-to-end service deployment, parsing the bigger picture of service virtualization and communicating the needed pieces of information to VIM and VNFM for implementing that service.

NFVO also works with the VIM(s) and has the full view of the resources that they are managing. As indicated previously, there can be multiple VIMs and each one of

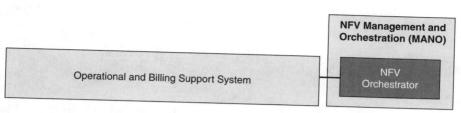

Figure 1-15 *Operational and Orchestration Layer of ETSI NFV Framework*

them has only visibility of the NFVI resources that it is managing. Since NFVO has the collective information from these VIMs, it can coordinate the resource allocation through the VIMs.

Resource orchestration

The process of allocating, deallocating, and managing NFVI resources to the VMs is referred to as resource orchestration.

Similarly, the VNFM is independently managing the VNFs and doesn't have visibility into any connection of the services between the VNFs and how the VNFs combine to form the end to the service path. This knowledge resides in the NFVO, and it's the role of NFVO to work through the VNFM to create the end-to-end service between the VNFs. It is therefore the NFVO that has visibility into the network topology formed by the VNFs for a service instance.

Service Orchestration

The term Service Orchestration refers to defining the service using the VNFs and how these VNFs will interconnect as a topology to implement it.

Despite not being a part of the NFV transformation, the existing OSS/BSS do bring value to management and therefore have a place in the framework. The framework defines the reference points between the existing OSS/BSS and NFVO and defines NFVO as an extension of the OSS/BSS to manage the NFV deployment without attempting to replace any of the roles of OSS/BSS in today's networks.

NFV Reference Points

The ETSI framework defines reference points to identify the communication that must occur between the functional blocks. Identifying and defining these is

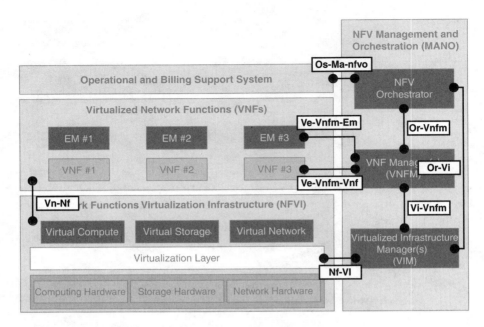

Figure 1-16 *ETSI NFV Framework Reference Points*

important to ensure that the flow of information is consistent across the vendor implementation for functional blocks. It also helps established an open and common way to exchange information between the functional blocks. Figure 1-16 shows the reference points defined by the ETSI NFV framework.

The list that follows describes these reference points in more detail.

- **Os-Ma-nfvo:** This was originally labeled Os-Ma and is meant to define the communication between OSS/BSS and NFVO. This is the only reference point between OSS/BSS and the management block of NFV (MANO).

- **Ve-Vnfm-vnf:** This reference point defines the communication between VNFM and VNF. It is used by VNFM for VNF lifecycle management and to exchange configuration and state information with the VNF.

- **Ve-Vnfm-em:** This was originally defined together with Vn-Vnfm-vnf (jointly labeled Ve-Vnfm) but is now defined separately for communication between the VNFM and EM functional blocks. It supports VNF lifecycle management, fault and configuration management, and other functions, and it is only used if the EM is aware of virtualization.

- **Nf-Vi:** This reference point defines the information exchange between VIM and the functional blocks in NFVI. VIM uses it to allocate, manage, and control the NFVI resources.

- **Or-Vnfm:** Communication between NFVO and VNFM happens through this reference point, such as VNF instantiation and other VNF lifecycle-related information flow.

- **Or-Vi:** The NFV orchestrator (NFVO) is defined to have a direct way of communicating with VIM to influence the management of the infrastructure resources, such as resource reservation for VMs or VNF software addition.

- **Vi-Vnfm:** This reference point is meant to define the standards for information exchange between VIM and VNFM, such as resource update request for VM running a VNF.

- **Vn-Nf:** This is the only reference point that doesn't have a management functional block as one of its boundaries. This reference point is meant to communicate performance and portability needs of the VNF to the infrastructure block.

Table 1-1 summarizes these reference point definitions:

Putting it all Together

Let's see how this model works end to end, taking the example of a simple network service and examining how the functional blocks defined in the ETSI framework collectively interact to implement the service. Figure 1-17 shows a simplified version of the steps involved.

The following steps depict this process:

Step 1. The full view of the end-of-end topology is visible to the NFVO.

Step 2. The NFVO instantiates the required VNFs and communicate this to the VNFM.

Step 3. VNFM determines the number of VMs needed as well as the resources that each of these will need and reverts back to NFVO with this requirement to be able to fulfill the VNF creation.

Step 4. Because NFVO has information about the hardware resources, it validates if there are enough resources available for the VMs to be created. The NFVO now needs to initiate a request to have these VMs created.

Table 1-1 *ETSI NFV Framework Reference-Points*

Reference Point	Boundaries	Use Defined in the Framework
Os-Ma-nfvo	OSS/BSS<->NFVO	• Service description and VNF package management. • Network service lifecycle management (instantiation, query, update, scaling, and termination). • VNF life cycle management. • Policy management (access, authorization, etc.) for network service instances. • Querying network service and VNF instances from OSS/BSS. Forwarding events, usage, and performance of network service instances to OSS/BSS.
Ve-Vnfm-vnf	VNFM<->VNF	• Instantiation, instance query, update, scaling up or down, and termination of the VMs. • Configuration and events regarding VNF, from VNFM to VNF. • Configuration and events from VNF to VNFM.
Ve-Vnmf-em	VNFM<->EM	• Instantiation, instance query, update, scaling up or down, and termination of the VMs. • Configuration and events regarding VNF from VNFM to EM. • Configuration and events from EM to VNFM.
Nf-Vi	NFVI<->VIM	• Allocate, update, migrate, terminate VMs. • Create, configure, remove inter-VM connections. • Failure events, usage records, configuration information to the VIM for NFVI resources (physical, software, virtual).
Or-Vnfm	NFVO<->VNFM	• Instantiation, state query, update, scaling, termination and package query of the VNF. • Forwarding VNF events and state information.
Or-Vi	NFVO<->VIM	• NFVI resource reservation, release, and update. • VNF software image allocation, deallocation, and update. • Configuration, usage, events, and results of NFVI to NFVO.
Vi-Vnfm	VIM<->VNFM	• NFVI resource reservation, allocation, and release information. • Events, usage, measurement results, etc. for a NFVI resource used by a VNF.
Vn-Nf	NFVI<->VNF	• Lifecycle, performance, and portability requirements of VNF.

Step 5. NFVO sends request to VIM to create the VMs and allocate the necessary resources to those VMs.

Step 6. VIM asks the virtualization layer to create these VMs.

Step 7. Once the VMs are successfully created, VIM acknowledges this back to NFVO.

Step 8. NFVO notifies VNFM that the VMs it needs are available to bring up the VNFs.

Step 9. VNF now configures the VNFs with any specific parameters.

Step 10. Upon successful configuration of the VNFs, VNFM communicates to NFVO that the VNFs are ready, configured, and available to use.

Figure 1-17 and the accompanying list depict a simplified flow as an example to help understand the framework. It intentionally doesn't go into many more details associated with this process as well as possible variations. Though these are not being covered in this book, readers can refer to the ETSI document (Section 5, in [2]) for additional details and scenarios.

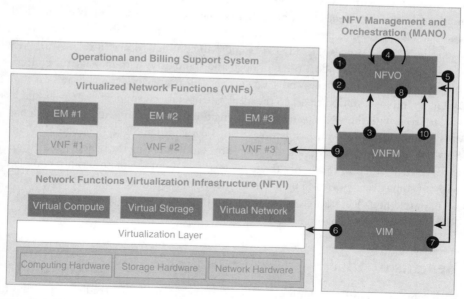

Figure 1-17 *End-to-End Flow in the ETSI NFV Framework*

NFV Framework Summary

The goal of defining the framework and more specifically the individual functional blocks and the reference points is to eliminate (or more realistically, minimize) interoperability challenges and standardize the implementation. The purpose and scope of each of these blocks is well defined in the framework. Similarly, the interdependencies and communications paths are defined through the reference-points and are meant to be open and standard methods.

Vendors can independently develop these functions and deploy them to work smoothly with other functional blocks developed by other vendors. As long as these implementations adhere to the scope and role defined by the framework, communicate with the other blocks using open methods at the reference points, the network can have a heterogeneous deployment of NFV. This means that the service providers will have complete flexibility to choose between vendors for different functional blocks. This is in contrast to the way networks have traditionally been deployed, where service providers were tied to the vendor's hardware (and its limitations) and software (and the challenges to adapt to it for all operational needs), and they had to deal with the interoperability concerns of mixed vendor networks. NFV offers service providers the ability to overcome this limitation and deploy a scalable and agile network using hardware and NFV functional blocks using any combination of vendors.

This doesn't magically eliminate the higher-level protocol interoperability issues that may arise between VNFs implemented by different vendors. For example, a BGP implementation by a vendor of one VNF may have some issue when it is peering with another VNF developed by a different vendor. For these types of interoperability issues, a standardization process already exists and will continue to play a role. Also, NFV doesn't mandate that vendors offer an open and standard way to manage the configuration and monitoring of the VNFs. EM in the NFV framework compensates for that. But in an implementation closer to the ideal, the operations support system should be able to work with the VNFs using standard methods. This is happening through a parallel technology shift towards software-defined networking (SDN). Though NFV and SDN are not interdependent, together they are complementing the benefits and advantages of each other. In this book, the focus is on NFV, but the picture is not complete without some discussion of SDN and how these two complement each other.

Though the NFV framework is well established, the standardization of NFV building blocks is an ongoing effort.

Benefits of NFV

Earlier in this chapter the limitations associated with using the traditional network equipment were listed. Network functions virtualization directly addresses most of these restrictions and brings many additional benefits. It offers a framework to completely transform the way networks are architected, deployed, managed, and operated, while offering many layers of improvement and efficiency across all of these. Figure 1-18 lists a few of the benefits that NFV offers that are discussed in the sections that follow.

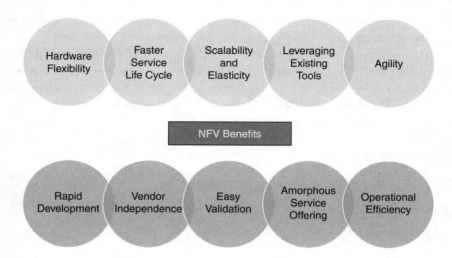

Figure 1-18 *Some Benefits of Network Functions Virtualization*

Hardware Flexibility

Because NFV uses regular COTS hardware, network operators have the freedom to choose and build the hardware in the most efficient way to suit their needs and requirements.

Hardware offered by traditional network vendors has very limited options for its computing, memory, storage, and networking capacities, and any modification leads to a hardware upgrade that costs time and money to the operators. With NFV, providers can now choose between many different vendors and have the flexibility to select the hardware capacities that are optimal for their network architecture and planning. For example, if the Internet gateway being used is running out of capacity to store the full Internet table and needs a memory upgrade, in most current implementations they can achieve this only through a controller upgrade or full device upgrade. In NFV, the provider can allocate more memory to the VM hosting this VNF.

Faster Service Life Cycle

New network services or features can now be deployed more quickly, in an on-demand and on-need basis, providing benefits for end users as well as the network providers.

In contrast to physical hardware, the VNFs can be created and removed on the fly. The lifecycle of VNFs can be much shorter and dynamic compared to physical devices, since these functions can be added when needed, provisioned easily through automated software tools that do not require any on-site activity, and then torn down to free up resources as soon as the need is over. This is in contrast to the deployment effort needed when a new function has to be added to an existing network, which would have required an on-site physical installation, which can be time consuming and costly. The ability to rapidly add new network functions (deployment agility) is one of the biggest advantages of NFV. Services now can also be commissioned or decommissioned with the touch of a button without the need of a delivery truck, drastically reducing deployment times from weeks to minutes.

> **Agility**
>
> The ability to rapidly deploy, terminate, reconfigure or change the topological location of a VNF is commonly referred to as deployment agility.

Scalability and Elasticity

New services and capacity-hungry applications in today's networks keep network operators, especially cloud providers, on their toes to keep up with the fast-increasing demands of consumers. The service providers have been playing catch-up with these requirements, for scaling up the traditional network equipment's capacity takes time, planning, and money. This problem is solved by NFV, which allows capability changes by offering a means to expand and shrink the resources used by the VNFs. For instance, if any of the VNFs requires additional CPU, storage, or bandwidth, it can be requested from the VIM and allocated to the VNF from the hardware pool. In a traditional network device, it would require either a full device replacement or a hardware upgrade to alter any of these parameters. But since VNFs aren't constrained by the limitations of customized physical hardware, they can offer this elasticity. Therefore networks do not need to be substantially overprovisioned to accommodate changes in capacity requirements.

Another way the NFV can implement elasticity is by offloading a VNF's workload and spinning off a new instance to implement the same network function and split the load with an existing VNF. This too is not possible with traditional network equipment.

> **Elasticity**
>
> Elasticity is a word very commonly used in the NFV context to refer to the capability of a VNF to expand and stretch resources or to shirk and scale them down, based on requirements. Also, this term is used to refer to the scenario when we create or remove additional VNFs to share the workload of an existing VNF.

Leveraging Existing Tools

As NFV uses the same infrastructure as data centers, it can reuse and leverage the deployment and management tools already being used in data centers. Using a single centralized pane of glass for management of virtual network and virtual servers gives the advantage of quicker adaption for new deployments without the need for developing new tools and as a result eliminates the cost of deploying, familiarizing, and using new set of tools.

Rapid Development and Vendor Independence

Because NFV provides the means to easily deploy a different vendor's solution without the heavy costs associated with replacing an existing vendor's deployment, it keeps network operators from being locked into a particular vendor. Operators can mix and match vendors and functions, and choose between them based on feature availability, cost of licensing the software, post deployment support model, roadmaps, etc.

New solutions and features can be put into production rapidly, without waiting for the existing deployed vendor to develop and support them. Such rapid deployment is further facilitated by NFV's inherent support for using open source tools and software.

Validation of New Solutions

Service providers often prefer to validate new solutions, services, and functions by deploying them in test setups, prior to introducing them in their production networks. Traditionally, they have had to replicate a subset of their production environment for in-house testing, which increased their operational budget. With NFV, building and managing such a test setups has become much more cost effective. The NFV-based test-setups can be dynamic and thus scaled and changed to meet the test and validation scenarios.

Amorphous Service Offering

An NFV-based deployment is not confined to a one-time design and deployment. It can adapt to market specific needs and offer a targeted set of services to match changing demands. Through a combination of elasticity and deployment agility, it's possible to rapidly shift the location and capacities of network functions and achieve workload mobility. For example, providers can implement a "follow the sun network" by using constantly moving virtual machines based on time of the day, and spinning up or expanding new VNFs to meet the network's requirements for services and capacity as they change during peak and off-peak usage or when major events take place in any geographic region.

Operational Efficiency and Agility

With common hardware hosting different VNFs, tasks associated with running the business, such as inventory management, procurement process, can be centralized. This reduces the operational overhead compared to segregated deployments of different network services using multiple hardware devices.

NFV is inherently automation friendly, and can increase the benefits that can be achieved through use of Machine to Machine (M2M) tools. For instance, its possible for an automation tool monitoring a device to determine the need for more memory in a network function. With NFV that tool can go ahead and request allocation of that memory—without involving any human intervention.

Network maintenance related activates can also significantly benefit from NFV by reducing possible downtimes. NFV allows for spinning up a new VNF, temporarily shift the workload to that VNF, and free up existing VNF for maintenance activities. This makes it possible to achieve In-Service-Software-Upgrade (ISSU), 24/7 self-healing networks, and minimize the operational loss of revenue due to network outages.

> **Note**
>
> Upgrading to new software for introducing new features, scaling changes, bug fixes, etc. while maintaining a high uptime has traditionally been a challenge and sometimes a source of pain for network service providers. This problem becomes more critical in the network edge devices, for they are not generally deployed with physical redundancy. An In-Service Software Upgrade (ISSU) is if the term for one of the solutions offered by network vendors to enhance the upgrade procedure in a way that allows an upgrade to occur without disrupting the device's functionality. ISSU implementations may not always be completely without disruptions, and they could potentially result in a very brief loss of traffic. However, this brief possibility of traffic loss is sometimes acceptable and preferred to the certain loss of service if the device was upgraded without ISSU.

NFV Market Drivers

NFV is more than a transformative technology. Like any new technology that brings major changes and new benefits, NFV has had to go through acceptance and adaption by the market. The market drivers for NFV are very significant, obvious, and promising. These have played a part in making NFV move beyond its infancy in research labs and bringing it into mainstream deployments in a very short span of time.

Access to the Internet and the trend toward digital services across the world are creating a big market for the network service providers. The scale and the bandwidth needs are already straining the existing network infrastructure. Upgrading this traditional network infrastructure requires high levels of time, money, and resources from the providers. This has forced the providers to rethink the network architecture and use new innovations that could keep up with the new cloud and digitalization world. One of the main drivers is the movement to cloud technology coupled with the utilization of the matured technology such as the virtualization and COTS hardware. Network providers are now using the same cloud infrastructure such as the computers (servers) and storage devices and adding the network function to these elements to provide services for new market requirements. By taking this approach, they gain major cost savings, the ability to bring new services to market faster and capacity to adapt quickly to any change in the market landscape.

The NFV market drivers that bring new business opportunities have made network operators eager to transition to NFV. Figure 1-19 lists some of these market drivers, which are described in the sections that follow.

Figure 1-19 *NFV Market Drivers*

Movement to Cloud

With the advent of new smart devices, bandwidth-hungry applications, the new breed of connected devices, and Internet of things (IoT) technologies, the demand for and usage of networks has been increasing exponentially. These recent changes have created market demand for services being provided anytime, anywhere, and on any device. To meet this market shift, providers are looking to build and offer cloud-based services that can satisfy the new requirements.

Research publications forecast that between 2015 and 2020, the NFV market will grow to beyond $9B with a compound annual growth rate (CAGR) of 83.1% [4]. This is a huge market for the traditional providers to miss, and many new providers are now jumping into this market, such as cloud providers, service providers, enterprise, startups, etc.

New Business Services

Consumption-based growth ensures that the network resources grow in close correlation with demand. With the use of traditional network equipment, network growth occurred in jumps, resulting in first overprovisioned and later underprovisioned network capacities, as depicted in Figure 1-20. The use of NFV avoids wastage of time and resource that would have been spent in continuously reprovisioning and decommissioning the network capacity.

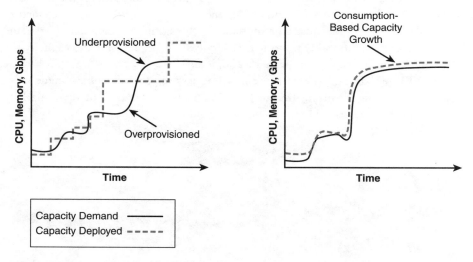

Figure 1-20 *Consumption-Based Capacity Growth*

One of the new business opportunities made possible by NFV is to offer hosting of network and IT services using massive server deployments. This type of service offering has been picking up pace and is proving to be a high-revenue business.

Instead of investing in network and data infrastructure, many enterprises are now opting to lease it as a service through the cloud providers. This is commonly referenced as Infrastructure as a Service (IaaS).

With NFV, providers can offer network services on demand like a shopping-cart experience, allowing consumers to add or delete services and devices through self-managed portals. Since the services will use NFV, these new services can get deployed automatically and become available instantaneously. In this case, if a customer wants to add a new firewall to a branch location, the customer can use such a portal to buy this service with few clicks, and the back-end at the provider will spin off a new virtual machine and deploy the firewall VNF on it as well as connect that VNF to the existing devices for that branch office.

These are just a few examples of NFV's ability to offer new set of business services that can be deployed on-demand and brought up in a short time span. The new breed of services that NFV can make possible are already gaining popularity and creating market enthusiasm. Providers are also offering new business models that utilize consumption-based growth, on-demand deployment, pay-as-you-grow and pay-as-you-use services, and better monetization for the network resources.

Capital Expense Savings

The hardware innovations required in traditional network hardware are costly for vendors to develop and produce. These devices have a small market and are therefore sold in low volume. These two factors are reflected in the cost to the network operators. On top of that, vendors of traditional network equipment have been able to keep the margins high by exploiting the fact that limited alternatives were available to the network operators. NFV revolutionizes this situation by using standard high-volume hardware such as the servers, switches, and storage components.

COTS hardware devices are already mass produced and sold at a reasonable price due to their use in data centers, and the use of off-the-shelf components keeps development costs low and competitive. The low manufacturing cost, combined with economics of scale and efficiency, results in equipment costs that are much less than those of purpose-built hardware.

Operational Expense Savings

With NFV's push for standardized framework, the proprietary aspect of the existing network's vendor-specific hardware and software combination is eliminated or minimized. NFV encourages and supports the use of open standards within its functional blocks as well as their interaction with existing management tools. This makes NFV deploy and operate networks using many existing vendor independent tools from server and data-center space, without new investments.

Virtualized network can share the infrastructure between the network functions as well as applications running on the network, data centers and server farms. The power and space consumed by the infrastructure can therefore be shared and more efficiently used.

Barrier of Entry

With traditional network devices, it's difficult for new vendors or new service providers to enter the market. The development costs for the vendors and the infrastructure costs for the providers present a barrier that is challenging to penetrate. With NFV, which uses open software implementing various network functions and has lower hardware costs, this barrier has been removed. This opens up doors for new vendors and providers to enter the market, bringing innovations and challenging the current vendors by offering lower priced and higher performing implementations of network functions.

Summary

The goal of this chapter is to get the readers acquainted with NFV concepts, standards and benefits. It examines how NFV is transforming the networking industry. It describes how networks evolved from early days of data communication to today's sophisticated networks carrying voice, data, and video traffic. The drawbacks and challenges of traditional network architectures and the ways NFV can help address these issues are discussed. The chapter introduces NFV and examines how it compares with today's networks. It focuses on the importance of understanding the standardization process for NFV. This chapter also provides a detailed study of ETSI's NFV framework. The major advantages of NFV and the market drivers behind it are also covered in this chapter.

References

Please refer to the following for additional information:

[1] http://www.etsi.org/index.php/news-events/news/644-2013-01-isg-nfv-created

[2] http://www.etsi.org/deliver/etsi_gs/NFV-MAN/001_099/001/01.01.01_60/gs_nfv-man001v010101p.pdf

[3] https://portal.etsi.org/NFV/NFV_White_Paper.pdf

[4] http://www.researchandmarkets.com/research/l3cw7s/network_functions

Review Questions

Use the questions here to review what you learned in the chapter. The correct answers are found in Appendix A, "Answers to Review Questions."

1. Which organization is driving the framework for NFV

    a. European Telecommunications Standards Institute (ETSI)

    b. Internet Engineering Task Force (IETF)

    c. International Telecommunication Union (ITU)

    d. Open Network Consortium (ONC)

2. What are the three major blocks of the NFV architecture?

    a. VIM, NFVO, and VNFM

    b. ETSI, MANO, and VNF

    c. NF, NFVI, and MANO

    d. OSS, BSS, and VNF

3. VNFM is responsible for which of the following?

    a. managing the infrastructure hardware and controlling its allocation to the VNFs

    b. managing the lifecycle of the VNF (instantiation, scaling up or down, termination) as well as FCAPS management of the VNF

    c. deploying the end-to-end service in the NFV architecture

    d. gathering the FCAPS information of the physical hardware from VIM and passing them to NFVO so that the resources can be appropriately managed by the upper layers for the ETSI framework

4. Which management functional block facilitates running multiple virtual machines/VNFs on the same hardware?

    a. Virtualized Network Function Manager (VNFM)

    b. Virtualization Infrastructure Manager (VIM)

    c. Element Manager (EM)

    d. Network functions virtualization Orchestrator (NFVO)

5. Communication between different functional blocks such as VIM to VNFM, VNFM to NFVO in the ETSI architecture is called?

    a. communication end points

    b. open network interconnects

    c. FCAPS data points

    d. reference points

6. List three benefits of NFV compared to traditional network devices:

    a. deployment agility

    b. hardware-centric

    c. elasticity

    d. vendor independence

7. The abbreviation "COTS" stands for

    a. custom option to service

    b. commodity-oriented technical solution

    c. commercial off the shelf

    d. commercially offered technical solution

Chapter 2

Virtualization Concepts

Chapter 1, "The Journey to Network Functions Virtualization (NFV) Era," covered the fundamentals of NFV, discussed its building blocks, and described the advantages that NFV brings. This chapter examines one of the key technologies that forms the backbone of NFV and makes it possible—virtualization.

Virtualization technologies form the primary building block for the NFV infrastructure. Therefore, knowledge of virtualization is important in order to achieve an in-depth understanding of NFV deployment and implementation.

This chapter introduces the concepts behind virtualization, focusing on the aspects that are closely related to NFV. The main topics covered in this chapter are:

- Virtualization: history, types and techniques
- Concept of virtual machines
- Virtual environments such as Linux containers and Docker
- Multitenancy considerations in virtualized environment

History and Background of Virtualization

Virtualization is not a new concept. It dates back to the 1960s, when IBM developed the CP-40 Operating System with the goals of implementing time and memory sharing across users and applications. Though CP-40 and its successor, CP-67, didn't gain huge popularity, they laid the foundation for virtualization concepts that exist today.

Virtualization

Virtualization is the technology used to run multiple operating systems (OSs) or applications on top of a single physical infrastructure by providing each of them an abstract view of the hardware. It enables these applications or OSs to run in isolation while sharing the same hardware resources.

Despite its birth in 1960s and some early development in the following decade, the idea of virtualization didn't get much traction. Until the end of the 1970s, mainframe systems were the predominant computing resource available, and it made good sense to share the mainframe's computing horsepower between multiple users and applications—which is essentially what virtualization was promising to offer. However, with the advent of personal computers (PCs), which were relatively inexpensive, it became possible for organizations to set up and manage their own computing infrastructure. The technology was revolutionary enough to see rapid adoption. The efficiency and benefits were quite obvious, while the ability to acquire the hardware, cost of ownership, and operating system were much better compared to the computer technologies that preceded the PC. However, the initial applications and operating systems on these PCs offered single-user environments, and the hardware itself did not have enough computing resources to multitask effectively and run several applications simultaneously. This created the culture of "one application per server"—or single tenant server. Additionally, departments and subteams within the organizations required isolation (for example, sales and marketing wouldn't have wanted to share its data with engineering), and that need for isolated data fueled the idea of isolated and separate computer systems that were running separate applications and used by different teams. This huge shift in the way computing resources were acquired and used kept virtualization from becoming a mainstream concept.

Over the next decade, the 1990s, the Internet revolution created a demand for server farms hosting various applications and databases, performing diverse functions needed to offer the Internet-based services such as Web browsing, email, and file hosting.

Server Farm

The term server farm is used to refer to a collection of many servers that are deployed and managed by an organization for delivering specific computing functions and services that are beyond the capability of individual servers.

Simultaneously, innovations in hardware resulted in much more efficient and powerful central processing units (CPUs), faster memory access, lower prices, high capacity storage, and high-speed networks offering better throughput. These advancements in hardware, use of dedicated servers for applications, and the increasing demand for these applications lead to server farms that were using many separate servers for the applications, but these servers were heavily underutilized. These server farms usually consumed large amount of power and take up large amounts of physical space, because they required running hundreds or thousands of servers. The resulting wastage in space and power, management overhead, and the challenge of maintaining these servers translated into higher operating and procurement costs.

Once again, it made perfect sense to consolidate these applications on shared servers and improve hardware utilization, decrease power consumption, save space, and reduce cabling requirements. Virtualization came out of hibernation. It could meet all the needs for these cost savings without rewriting applications or changing the end-user experience. This time around there were additional requirements, such as a need for stricter isolation and segregation between applications, load balancing based on traffic, resiliency and high availability of applications. Virtualization technology didn't take long to mature and catch up with these new requirements.

The first commercial product to enable virtualization on x86 platforms was released by VMWare in 1999 and called VMWare Workstation. It was soon followed by "VMWare ESX" in 2001 for the server market. Other implementations soon followed, such as Hyper-V (by Microsoft), VirtualBox (by Oracle), and open source virtualization solutions such as Xen and KVM. In 2005, Intel and AMD announced processor capabilities that would offer CPU support for hardware-assisted virtualization. Intel's VT-x and AMD's AMD-V increased adoption of virtualization to a new level. Figure 2-1 summarizes this history behind the

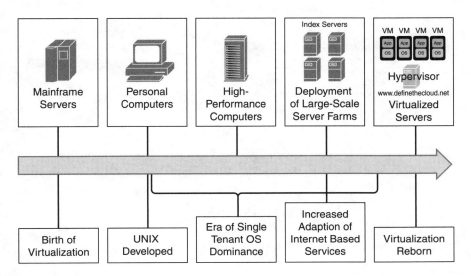

Figure 2-1 *Birth, Hibernation, and Rise of Virtualization*

re-emergence of virtualization technology in the context of demand for and availability of computing resources.

Today, virtualization is the heart of any server farm and datacenter, bringing all its benefits and continuing to offer new ones.

Virtualization Benefits and Goals

The goal behind virtualization is to offer a mechanism to run multiple applications without dependency on or knowledge of each other, while sharing an operating system and hardware resource pool. Each application is made to believe that it owns the hardware resources—but it's not necessarily aware that this hardware is a subset abstracted from a bigger hardware pool. The applications have segregation between their processes, disk and file-system usage, user management and networking.

With virtualization, the number of servers in a data center or server farm was drastically reduced, with a smaller number of servers doing the same job and hosting multiple applications simultaneously. The resulting benefits are obvious: savings of power, space, and operational costs; reduced total cost of ownership; and business resiliency, as illustrated in Figure 2-2.

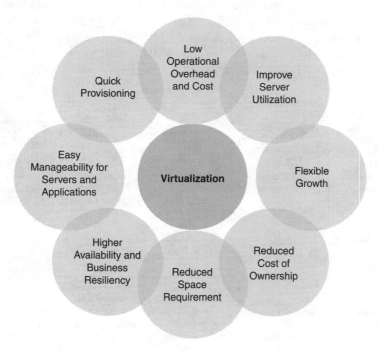

Figure 2-2 *Some Benefits of Virtualization*

Server Virtualization, Network Virtualization, and NFV

The virtualization discussed so far is primarily server virtualization. However, as the concept of virtualization was implemented in places other than servers, like networks and storage devices, it took up different meanings depending on context and use. This section examines three broader areas of virtualization:

- server virtualization
- network virtualization
- network functions virtualization (NFV)

Server Virtualization

Server virtualization was discussed in detail earlier in this chapter. As shown in Figure 2-3, multiple physical servers providing email, database, management and web services can be virtualized into a much smaller number of physical servers. The physical aspect of redundancy still needs to be taken into account, because it wouldn't be a good design and deployment to virtualize the primary and backup database servers on the same physical hardware.

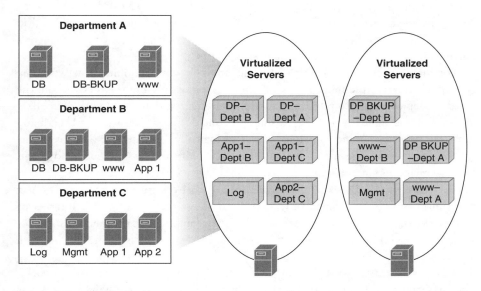

Figure 2-3 *Server Virtualization*

Server virtualization is a fairly mature technology now and has proven to be a very successful and efficient way to consolidate and manage resources. A large number of software tools have been developed with the goal to provide fast and easy deployment of virtualized servers and also to give administrators the ability to manage and monitor their performance and optimize their utilization.

Network Virtualization

Network virtualization is a concept that is often confused with NFV. In reality, it predates NFV and has little relevance to it. It does not have a relationship with the virtualization ideas that have been discussed so far in this chapter. It uses the word "virtual" in a different context than server virtualization. Network virtualization is an approach in which a single physical network is logically split into multiple logical networks. These networks share the underlying infrastructure, but to the end user this sharing is not visible, and the protocols and technologies used make these networks appear to be completely independent and separate networks running on a dedicated infrastructure. The logical networks (or virtual networks as they are often referred to), provide isolation, privacy, and network-level segregation between the networks.

An initial example of network virtualization is perhaps use of virtual LAN (VLAN). As shown in Figure 2-4, this offers a way for a campus or office network to be split into virtual segments that share a portion of the switching and data path with each other.

Some other examples of such virtual networking technologies are IP Layer 3 virtual private network (L3VPN), Virtual Extensible LAN (VXLAN), ATM switch and permanent virtual circuits (SVC/PVC). Notice the use of the word virtual in each of these technologies, because each of them was offering a way to implement a virtual network overlay on a physical network.

For Internet service providers (ISPs) this ability to overlay multiple networks on a shared infrastructure made it possible to offer many different services without the need to deploy separate physical networks for each of them. Network virtualization techniques made it possible to simultaneously run services such as broadband Internet, video streaming, and voice over IP as logically separate networks over same physical network. The major benefits were a significant savings on deployment, management, and maintenance costs of the infrastructure.

For businesses, network virtualization offered cost-effective ways to interconnect their intranet segments, small offices, and remote workers through the Internet or over the virtual private network services that they could receive through ISPs.

A typical ISP today has many separate overlays running on the network infrastructure, as shown in Figure 2-5.

To carry the traffic (predominantly data traffic) for these multiple virtual networks, the physical networks infrastructure has to be provisioned with enough bandwidth as well as designed with measures to prioritize different services in case of congestion or failures. This led to many developments in quality-of-service (QoS) implementations,

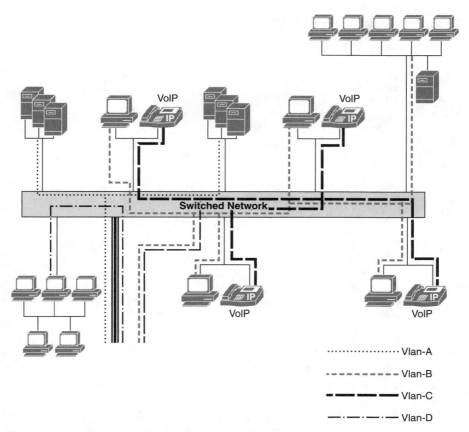

Figure 2-4 *Network Virtualization Using VLAN*

routing protocols, traffic engineering, etc. The details of these are outside the scope this book, but it is important to distinguish between network virtualization and NFV. Network virtualization has heavily influenced network protocols and network growth. NFV too is influencing network protocols and growth—but in a different way.

Network Functions Virtualization

Network functions virtualization (NFV) extends the idea of server virtualization to network devices meant to perform specific functions in the network. It's the success of server virtualization that has attracted network operators to look at NFV, and consequently push the equipment vendors and manufacturers to break away from the "one device, one function on custom hardware" and start allowing their network operating

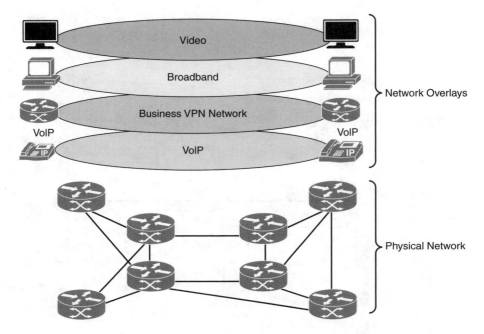

Figure 2-5 *Virtual Network Overlays on Shared Network Infrastructure*

systems to run in virtualized environment. The initial white paper presented on NFV, directly referenced the success that servers virtualization has had and proposed to do the same with network functions with the goal of achieving similar benefits.

The software on network devices has historically been proprietary and custom built, while the hardware anatomy consists of a low-to-medium processing engine, disk storage, and a large number of physical interfaces for data input and output (I/O). These devices also use dedicated CPUs for processing and forwarding network traffic, and specialized memory for address lookup, such as a ternary content-addressable memory (TCAM). These packet processing CPUs are highly customized for implementing network functions such as forwarding, classification, queuing, and access control and are often implemented as Application Specific Integrated Circuit (ASIC) in the traditional networking devices.

Custom off the shelf (COTS) hardware lacks these dedicated packet processing and forwarding CPUs needed for high throughput, the specialized memory for fast lookup, and the special software or operating system that implements the network functions. With NFV, the operating system is virtualized and runs on COTS servers—the amount of computing, storage, and interface resources required for running multiple instances of these operating systems on a single server can easily be accommodated. To make up for the lack of forwarding CPUs and fast-access cache memory, special software techniques have been developed to achieve high performance while using general-purpose CPUs. Some of these techniques such as Intel's Distributed Packet Development Kit (DPDK) and Cisco's Vector Packet Processing (VPP) are discussed in later chapters.

One consequence of massive server farm growth with virtualized servers was the emergence of new architectures designed to be fault tolerant. Because these servers are relativity inexpensive, the applications running on them require 24-hour availability. Software-based management and deployment tools are used to dynamically provision, teardown, or move the virtual servers. The resulting architecture was built to expect and manage failure, and work around those failures (through reprovisioning, moving, or reconnecting the impacted services). In contrast, traditional networks using physical network devices were designed for high availability by trying to ensure uptimes through physical redundancy and overprovisioned or redundant data links. With NFV, the network designs and architecture can adapt the same ways as IT virtualization.

Since virtualization of network functions is following the footsteps of relatively mature server virtualization, it leverages a number of tools developed for that. Some examples of server virtualization tools being adapted for NFV deployments are Openstack, VMWare's vSphere, and Kubernetes.

Virtualization Techniques

In the initial years when virtualization was evolving, support for it was primarily in software. Running multiple operating systems in parallel (where each of them representing an application or a set of applications that would have run on an standalone system) required either collaboration between those operating systems or introduction of a mediator (virtualization layer) to allow hardware sharing. Otherwise, when those operating systems, or the applications running on top of them, wanted to access the hardware simultaneously, it would have caused disorder. Virtualization provided a solution to make this possible by bringing in separation between hardware and operating system and adding *virtualization layer* as a bridge between them. There were different techniques and methodologies that were used for this implementation. A few of those techniques are discussed in this section.

To understand these methods, let's take a high level look at the classic x86 architecture. In this architecture, there are four privilege levels defined for interaction to the hardware (CPU and memory). Lower privilege levels have a higher priority and run closer to the hardware. In the classic standalone usage, applications run with privilege level 3, while device drivers run using privilege levels 1 and 2. The operating system needs to be in privilege level 0, so that it can interact directly with the hardware, as shown in Figure 2-6.

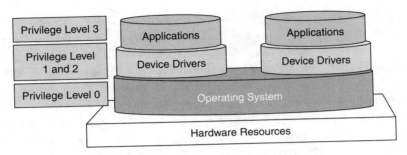

Figure 2-6 *Applications and OS on x86 Hardware*

Full Virtualization

In the full virtualization technique, the operating system (OS) is moved to the higher layer, and the virtualization layer now occupies Layer 0, interacting with the hardware as shown in Figure 2-7. So the instructions from the OS to the hardware are now translated by the virtualization layer and in-turn sent to the hardware. With this method, there is no need to develop or change the code in the guest operating system and all the existing applications and guest operating systems can run on this virtualization layer without any modifications. Full virtualization therefore decouples the Hardware and the OS. Some examples of this technique for virtualization are VMware's ESXi, Linux KVM/Qemu, etc.

Guest Operating System

Operating systems normally run on dedicated servers. In a virtualized environment, the virtualization layer abstracts the hardware and allows it to be shared between multiple OSs running in isolation. In virtualization jargon, the instance of the OS that is running on the abstracted hardware offered to it by the virtualization layer is referred to as a guest operating system.

Paravirtualization

Full virtualization brings independence, but there is a cost associated with the translation of the data from the OS to the virtualization layer and then to the hardware. For some applications, this delay can be critical and results in inefficiency. In other cases, it may be required for application to communicate directly with hardware. To mitigate these situations, the operating system can be allowed to interact directly with the hardware for some functional calls, using a technique called hypervcalls, while continuing to work through the virtualization layer for other needs. This virtualization technique is called paravirtualization.

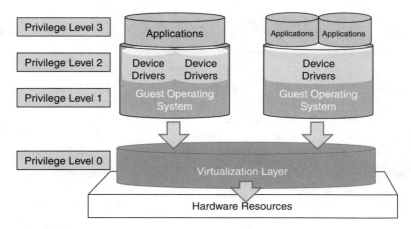

Figure 2-7 *Full Virtualization*

Para is a Greek word that means "beside." In this technique, the virtualization layer works along the guest operating systems at the same privilege level (layer 0), as shown in Figure 2-8, providing the operating system access to the hardware to execute time-critical functions.

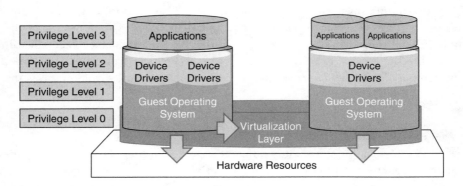

Figure 2-8 *Paravirtualization*

With paravirtualization, all the guest OSs running on the hardware need to be aware of each other to be able to share the resource. Due to this requirement of the interaction with other guest OS as well as the virtualization layer, there is development effort needed on the guest operating system side to work in this environment. An example of this technique for virtualization is Xenserver.

Hardware-Assisted Virtualization

As mentioned in the previous section, x86 hardware is catching up with virtualization and adding the capability to virtualize into the hardware itself, making it possible to provide high performance and throughput. Hardware-assisted virtualization is the technique that utilizes this built-in hardware support. The OS and the virtualization layer can leverage the hardware-assisted function calls to provide the virtualization, as shown in Figure 2-9.

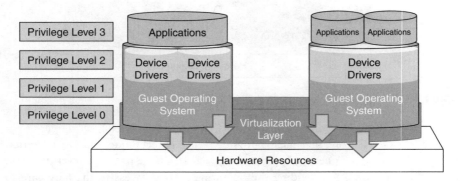

Figure 2-9 *Hardware-Assisted Virtualization*

Many of the operating systems and virtualization vendors are utilizing this feature to provide increased performance and capabilities. The drawback in the full-virtualization technique, where the operating system was unable to access hardware directly, is now resolved with hardware-assisted virtualization. Therefore, the combination of hardware-assisted virtualization with full virtualization is the preferred deployment technique.

OS-Level Virtualization

OS-level virtualization is a slightly different approach. In this case, instead of running the separate guest OS with their applications running on the same hardware, these applications can run directly on the single common OS using OS-level virtualization. In this technique, the OS is modified to give these applications their own working space and resources. It ensures separation between the application's resource usage, making it look like they are still running on independent standalone servers. Figure 2-10 shows a representation of OS-level virtualization. Examples of this virtualization technique are Linux containers and Docker, which are discussed in depth later in this chapter.

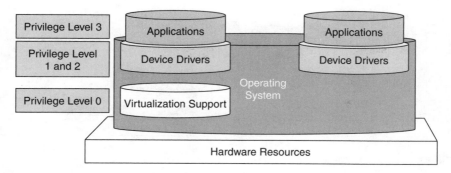

Figure 2-10 *OS-Level Virtualization*

Virtualization versus Emulation

Emulation and virtualization are sometimes used interchangeably, but there is a significant yet subtle difference between these two.

In emulation, special software (the emulator) acts as a translator to any application running on top of it and simulates the presence of hardware to that application. The hardware that the emulator can simulate (CPU, memory, disk, I/O) is not restricted to what was allocated to it by the underlying OS. An emulator is commonly used to enable an application built for one type of OS (or CPU) to run on a different type of OS (or CPU). It doesn't require the emulated OS to be run in it, but rather takes the function calls from the application and translates them to the ones available on the OS that is running it. The translation back and forth has an associated cost on performance, as well as being limited by the instruction sets defined in the emulator code. Additionally, since the emulator runs as an application on the base OS, it relies on that OS's resource sharing and allocation capabilities. It doesn't provide any additional mechanism for guaranteeing availability or separation for resources like storage or I/O.

In contrast, virtualization has isolation and segregation included in its base ingredients. Irrespective of the technique used to virtualize, the applications or guest OSs are able to work independently and share the hardware without impacting each other.

Emulation is often used for the purpose of running an application developed for one OS or platform on a newer or different OS or platform. For example, an emulator can be used to run an old application compiled for MS-DOS on a Linux operating system. Virtualization has a very different goal defined for it: it is meant to share the hardware resources between different applications or different OS. Figure 2-11 compares these two side by side to highlight the difference between them.

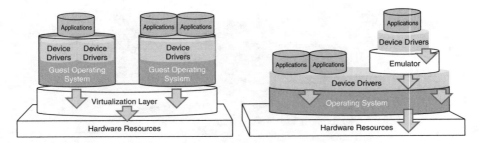

Figure 2-11 *Virtualization versus Emulation*

Virtual Machines

As defined previously, virtualization provides an isolated virtual hardware environment for an operating system or application to run upon. The resulting environment is usually referred to as a virtual machine. Sometimes it is loosely referred to as a virtual container, virtual-environment, or simply container (since it offers a self-contained environment). In a stricter definition of these terms, there is a subtle difference between virtual machines and containers. Both provide virtualized environments. But the way they are implemented needs to be differentiated, for it has an impact on the level of isolation and performance that is achieved.

Components of a Virtual Machine

Virtual machines have three main components:

- host operating system
- virtual machine manager (VMM, or hypervisor)
- guest Operating System

Host Operating System

The host operating system (host OS) is the operating system that is running directly on the hardware. The host OS must have support for virtualization and the right set of applications installed.

The host OS has the visibility of the full set of hardware resources that are available to be allocated to the virtual machines. The host OS's capabilities (such as addressable memory range, or I/O devices it can support) can restrict or limit the capabilities of the virtual machine, because the virtual machines are created inside the host OS.

Hypervisor

Originally the term virtual machine manager (VMM) was used to describe this function, but in the early 1970s the term hypervisor was coined by IBM engineers since this software was running on top of the operating system that IBM nomenclature termed as supervisor. Essentially the job of hypervisor is what is described as virtualization layer in NFV architecture. A hypervisor enables the creation of the virtual machine, allocating the resources to that virtual machine, modifying the virtual machine's parameters, and deleting the virtual machine.

Hypervisors are categorized into two types. The type names do not give much information about the differences between them, and are simply called type-1 and type-2

Type-2 Hypervisor

This type of hypervisor runs as a regular software application on top of a host OS. The host OS can be any traditional operating system with virtualization capabilities. The hypervisor runs as an application on this OS, along with other applications and processes, and has specific hardware resources allocated to it.

In a type-2 virtualized environment, the host's role is very minimal and meant to provide a platform for the hypervisor to run. Additionally, the host provides the interface to communicate with the devices, memory, disks, and other peripherals. Generally the host OS is not meant to run any resource-heavy applications. The host OS should be a quite thin and lightweight layer, fulfilling its basic function and conserving most of the resources for the guests (virtual machines) to utilize.

Type-1 Hypervisor

This type of hypervisor leverages the fact that the host has a very lightweight and basic role to play. A type-1 hypervisor absorbs those host OS roles into the hypervisor code. The hypervisor runs directly on the hardware without the need for an underlying OS. This type of hypervisor has an expanded role as it needs to communicate and manage the physical devices and incorporate the needed device drivers into the hypervisor code. The resulting increase in complexity of the hypervisor code and the higher time to develop this type of hypervisor is balanced by the reduced communication overhead that was present in type-2 hypervisors.

Since it runs directly on the hardware, this implementation is also called a bare-metal implementation.

Comparison of Type-1 and Type-2 Hypervisors

Figure 2-12 describes the two hypervisor types side by side and provides examples of some of the commercially available hypervisors for each of the types. Type-1 hypervisors are self-contained, and because of their direct interaction with the hardware

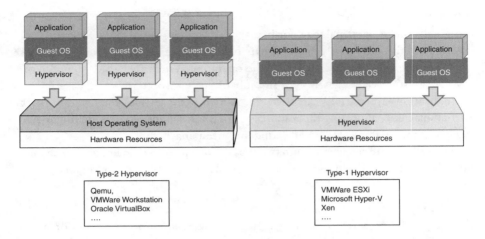

Figure 2-12 *Type-2 and Type-1 Hypervisors*

they have more flexibility and are considered to be more secure. Additionally, they can be optimized better since their code is developed purely for hypervisor functionality. The performance of this type of hypervisor is generally higher than that type-2 versions because the overhead and dependency on communicating with the hardware via the host OS are removed.

On the other hand, type-2 hypervisors are easier and quicker to develop and are more flexible because they do not have to be developed or tested against specific hardware. For this is the reason, type-2 hypervisors were the first ones that became available for the x86 architecture, while type-1 hypervisors (which were originally conceived on mainframes) took longer to be developed and brought to the market for x86-based platforms. Type-2 hypervisors can support a wider variety of hardware, again because there is no hardware dependency. All the dealings with the hardware devices are left out to the host OS. As long as the host OS is compatible and validated to work with the hypervisor code, the underlying hardware type or drivers to work with that hardware are not a concern for the hypervisor.

Guest Operating System

When the hypervisor hosts a virtual machine, that virtual machine doesn't inherit any software components from the host OS. The bare-bones virtual machine that is created is very much like a regular server. Like any other server, it needs an operating system to boot up, manage the devices, and run applications on it.

The OS that runs on this virtual server is called the guest operating System (guest OS). This OS can be of be any type, but it needs to be compatible with the hardware resources offered by the hypervisor. For example, an OS based on Reduced Instruction Set Computer (RISC) architecture cannot natively run on an hypervisor that is offering an Intel x86 architecture using Complex Instruction Set Computer (CISC) CPU resources.

The guest OS doesn't need any modifications for it to run in the virtual machine and views the virtual machine as if it was running on is a real hardware system. Therefore it has no visibility into the true hardware resources or awareness of any other virtual machine that may be present by another instance of the hypervisor.

The user within the guest OS can run any number of applications that are supported by that OS. When the application (or the guest OS itself) wants to access the disk, memory, or CPU resources, the hypervisor acts as an intermediary and maps that request to the resources managed by the host OS. The response to these requests is passed back by the hypervisor by the host OS, and then to the requesting guest OS, creating an impression that the guest OS was talking directly to those hardware entities.

Resource Allocation to the Virtual Machine

The goal behind using virtualization is to optimally share the hardware resources, such as memory, CPU, interfaces, and disk space. The hypervisor is meant to share these resources with minimal impact or penalty. The sharing mechanisms have drastically improved over the recent years. The following section examines some of the methods used for sharing the host resources.

CPU and Memory Allocation

When a virtual machine is created, the hypervisor allocates a defined amount of memory and CPU to it. The CPUs allocated to the virtual machine, are viewed by guest OS as physical dedicated CPUs. Since some guests may have limitations on the number of CPU sockets they can support, the newer versions of hypervisor allow to offer CPU resources at the granularity of number of CPU sockets and cores per socket. The amount of CPU horsepower that can be allocated is based on the CPU resources available at the host OS's level. For example, if the host server is using Intel's Xeon E5-2680v2 CPU that has 10 cores/socket and is dual threaded, up to 20 virtual CPUs may be available for the hypervisor to offer to the virtual machine. This allocation doesn't bind any CPU (or CPU core) to the virtual machine; rather the hypervisor allows a proportional amount of CPU cycles to the VM. The CPU requests from virtual machines are intercepted by the hypervisor, which then schedules this request on a CPU core that is available and passes the response back to the guest OS. The Hardware-assisted virtualization technique that was described earlier in this chapter plays a key role in the sharing of CPU resources across the virtual machines.

Memory allocation to the VM also uses sharing techniques. The memory allocated by the hypervisor using these techniques appears as physical memory to the guest OS. Techniques such as memory paging and disk swap space are used to present the virtual machine's OS a view where it sees the full amount of allocated memory available for its exclusive use.

Input/Output Device Allocation

Serial and other I/O devices are shared between the virtual machines by allocating them to one virtual machine at a time. They allow the hypervisor to switch this allocation based on specific trigger. For example in ESXi, if the keyboard is allocated to a virtual machine's console interface and the key combination (Ctrl+Alt) gets intercepted by ESXi, and it causes the keyboard to be detached from that console and made available to be reattached to any other virtual machine.

Disk Space Allocation

When the virtual machine is first created, the hypervisor is told the size of disk space to allocate to the guest OS. Depending on the type of provisioning method used, a file or a set of files is created on the host OS. There are two popular disk space-provisioning methods used: thick provisioning and thin provisioning.

Thick Provisioning

In thick provisioning for a virtual machine's disk space, the entire amount of disk space that is allocated to the guest is preallocated and reserved on the host OS. This is done by creating a file of that size (or multiple linked files with that combined size). The disadvantage of this approach is that if the guest is not fully utilizing the disk space allocated to it, from the host OS's viewpoint that space is used and no longer available for other purposes. The advantage is obviously that the guest will always have the exact amount of disk that it was provisioned with.

When thick provisioning is used, it can either wipe out the information in the space that is pre-allocated to the virtual machine (called *eager-zeroed thick provisioning*), or it may choose to leave data there until the time the space is actually needed to store something by the guest (called *lazy-zeroed thick provisioning*). The eager-zeroed thick provisioning can require more time when the disk is initially allocated to the virtual machine, since it has to wipe out the entire allocated space. On the other hand, the lazy-zeroed thick provisioning has better odds of data recovery of the original disk contents if such a need arises.

Thin Provisioning

This method of provisioning saves disk space and prevents wastage by only pre-allocating the amount that is needed by the guest OS. It spoofs the full capacity that was provisioned to the guest OS while the actual file created and reserved on the host OS is relatively much smaller in size. As the guest starts to fill up the pre-allocated space, the hypervisor expands the allocation on the host and lets it grow up to the size that was actually provisioned.

This more optimal use of disk space comes with a slight risk that if the disk space to the guest OS is over allocated, and all of those guest OS try to grow at the same time, then the host OS is not able to accommodate to this situation and runs out of space.

The files that are created as a result of the provisioning of virtual machine are packaged in one of the supported formats and contain the entire file system of the guest OS within them. The guest is once again unaware of this disk virtualization, and is led to believe that it has a standalone disk available to it self. Some of the most commonly used file formats employed for packaging the virtual machine's disk space are as follows:

- **Virtual machine disk (VMDK):** This is one of the most popular formats to package the virtual machine disk space. The format was original developed by VMWare, but it is an open format now.

- **Virtual Disk Image (VDI):** This format is used primarily by Oracle's Virtual-Box hypervisor.

- **Virtual hard disk (VHD):** This format is originally developed for use by Microsoft's Hyper-V (rather its predecessor, Connectix Virtual-PC). The format is open, though, and any vendor can choose to support it if they like.

- **QEMU Copy-On-Write Version 2 (QCOW2):** This format is natively supported and used by the QEMU/KVM hypervisor. It is an open source disk image format. QCOW2 uses the copy-on-write (COW) method, where the delta of any base image being used can be written to a separate space without modifying the original.

Network Communication

The virtual machines are isolated environments and therefore need a mechanism for network connectivity to be able to transport data to the external world (outside of the physical server they are hosted on) or for data communication between virtual machines hosted on the same server.

The physical machine's network interface cards (NICs) can be used for this purpose. As with other resources like CPU and memory that are shared between the virtual machines, it may be required to share the physical NICs to achieve better utilization and optimal use. Various techniques are used to make this sharing possible. One of the techniques used is that the hypervisor creates virtual NIC (vNIC) instances and presents those as NICs to the guest OS. In this implementation, however, the hypervisor (in case of Type 1) or the host OS (in case of Type 2) needs to map those multiple vNICs to the physical NIC or NICs. This is the same role that a hardware switching device performs in a regular network. In the virtualization world, a virtual-switch (vSwitch) is used to achieve this vNIC to physical NIC connectivity.

On Linux-based hypervisors, the Linux bridge application can serve this purpose if the virtual machines reside on a single host and redundancy between virtual machines is not needed. For each of these bridges its possible to define the vNICs and physical NICs connected to the vBridge. Example 2-1 shows the Linux command output where vlan100 and vlan200, belonging to VM1 and VM2 respectively, are able to send data to each other and to an external facing interface (via eth2) This is accomplished by making all of these members of a virtual bridge named `sample_bridge` as shown in Figure 2-13.

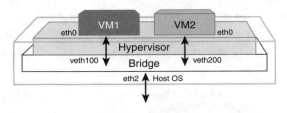

Figure 2-13 *Linux Virtual Bridge*

Example 2-1 *Linux Virtual Bridge with Virtual and Physical Ethernet Members*

```
linux-host:~$ brctl show sample_bridge
bridge name    bridge id              STP enabled      interfaces
sample_bridge  8000.72466e3815f3      no                     eth2
                                                         veth100
                                                         veth200

linux-host:~$
```

Similarly, ESXi, which is a type-1 hypervisor, has a vSwitch built in with the hypervisor. It can be used in a similar manner by mapping the virtually created NICs belonging to the virtual machines to the physical port for external connectivity, as shown in Figure 2-14.

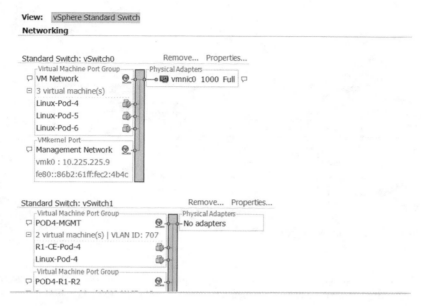

Figure 2-14 *ESXi vSwitch*

For a separate set of vNIC to physical-NIC mappings, an additional virtual bridge or vSwitch can be defined.

The basic Linux bridge can be used for a small number of virtual machines on single hosts, but to support multiserver virtualization deployments (which is often the case) or scenarios where virtual machine redundancy is needed, a more sophisticated switch is needed. When a virtual machine is moved from one physical host to another (or within the host) for reasons such as load balancing, redundancy, or physical proximity purposes, the new virtual port and switch it connects to may need to replicate the configuration of the original virtual port such as VLAN, QoS, and other features. Additionally, to ensure consistency and ease of management, a multi-server environment may require a centralized controller to manage the switch's policies and configurations. These needs result in the development of Open vSwitch (OVS) for Linux environments. OVS was developed as an open source switch and offers many capabilities, such as support for migrating a virtual machine across hosts, OpenFlow support for centralized management by a software-defined networking (SDN) controller, and optimized switching performance.

For ESXi-based hypervisors, these requirements are fulfilled by a variant of ESXi standard vSwitch, called Distributed vSwitch (DVS). It offers centralized configuration management, troubleshooting, and monitoring of all the virtual machines that are deployed across the distributed physical hosts as shown in Figure 2-15.

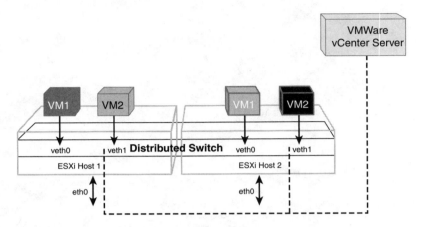

Figure 2-15 *vCenter Managing ESXi and DVS*

Other network vendors have also developed some vSwitch solutions to address these requirements for various hypervisors, such as Cisco Nexus 1000v, HP 5900v, and NEC PF1000. Table 2-1 lists some of the vSwitch supported for popular hypervisors. This is not a comprehensive or complete list but presented here to give a view of the available options. A more detailed list of virtual switches can be found in the references [1].

For completeness, it should be mentioned that it's also possible to dedicate the physical interface to a virtual machine. In that case, the vSwitch l performs a 1:1 mapping or in the case of some hypervisors (like KVM) the physical switch can be directly passed to the virtual machine, referred to as Ethernet pass-through. Figure 2-16 shows how this compares against the shared vSwitch option. Employing pass-through is not the most optimal use of the physical resource since sharing isn't possible. However, in certain situations where a dedicated and guaranteed bandwidth is required or throughput performance is critical (for example, an interface carrying data path traffic), this methodology can be used.

Ethernet pass-through

When a host's physical interface is directly mapped and dedicated to a virtual machine running on that host, and thus the virtual machine has a direct unshared access to that networking interface, its referred to as Ethernet pass-through.

Packaging a Virtual Machine

The disk image formats discussed earlier are meant to store the deployed virtual machine's files and represent the running system's disk space. However, sometimes

Table 2-1 *Some Virtual Switch Options Available for Popular Hypervisors*

Hypervisor	Native Virtual Switch	Third Party vSwitch Options
Linux Kernel-based Virtual Machine (KVM)	Linux bridge	Cisco Nexus 1000v
		OVS
VMware ESXi vSphere	Standard vSwitch Distributed vSwitch	Cisco Nexus 1000v
		Cisco Application-Centric Virtual Switch (AVS)
		IBM DVS 5000v
		HP Virtual Switch 5900v
Microsoft Hyper-V	Native Hyper-v Switch	Cisco Nexus 1000v
		NEC FP1000
Xen	OVS	OVS

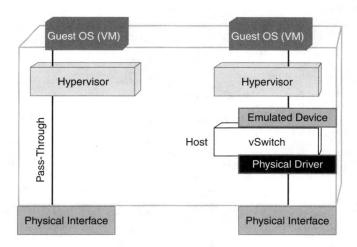

Figure 2-16 *Network Connectivity Using Pass-Through versus Using vSwitch*

these are also used to package the virtual machine for transporting across hosts since these files contain the entire file system of the guest OS and all the applications running inside it. There are many available tools that can convert the virtual machine disk files from one format to another. So when the new host is using a different hypervisor, it is usually possible to convert to the format that the hypervisor supports.

An alternative to distributing virtual machines is to package the virtual machine's source image in the International Organization for Standardization (ISO) file format.

The ISO file system format has been in use for many years and was originally created for optical disks. An ISO file contains the entire optical disk's image, and many tools exist on all popular operating systems that allow mounting the ISO file as a virtual disk, emulating the presence of a real optical disk. This idea is also commonly used to package and transport a virtual machine's image. In this case, the ISO image contains the full operating system (for the guest OS) and is created as a bootable media. If the contents of the ISO file are viewed, as shown in Figure 2-17, it contains basic boot information and file structure to represent the disk whose image it's carrying. Since it's a single file, this ISO can be ported from one host to another and mounted. It is common practice to allow a newly created blank VM disk (perhaps created as a VMDK file) to mount and boot from an ISO image that acts as a bootable install drive and create the needed file structures on the virtual machine's disk image (such as a vmdk file). The virtual image file is used for all future purposes, while the ISO file provides a porting mechanism.

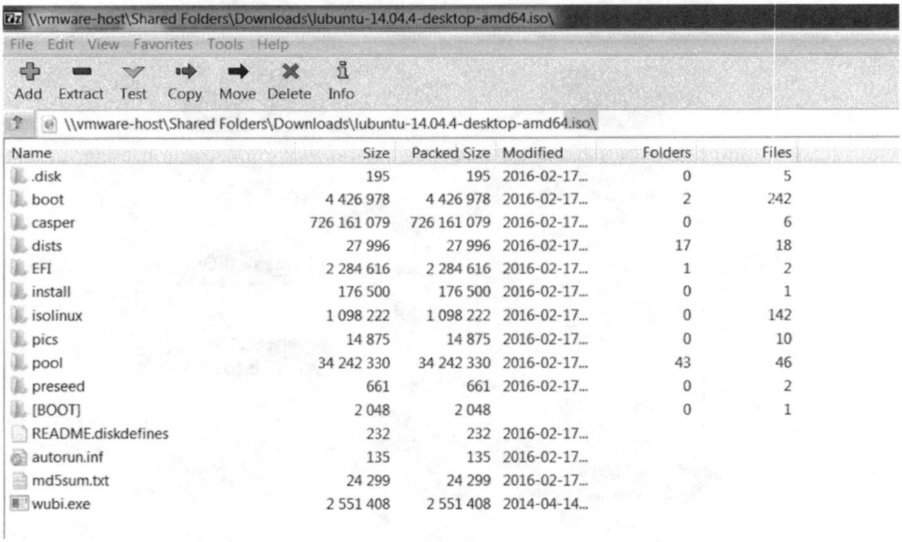
\\vmware-host\Shared Folders\Downloads\lubuntu-14.04.4-desktop-amd64.iso\
File Edit View Favorites Tools Help
Add Extract Test Copy Move Delete Info
\\vmware-host\Shared Folders\Downloads\lubuntu-14.04.4-desktop-amd64.iso\
Name Size Packed Size Modified Folders Files
.disk 195 195 2016-02-17... 0 5
boot 4 426 978 4 426 978 2016-02-17... 2 242
casper 726 161 079 726 161 079 2016-02-17... 0 6
dists 27 996 27 996 2016-02-17... 17 18
EFI 2 284 616 2 284 616 2016-02-17... 1 2
install 176 500 176 500 2016-02-17... 0 1
isolinux 1 098 222 1 098 222 2016-02-17... 0 142
pics 14 875 14 875 2016-02-17... 0 10
pool 34 242 330 34 242 330 2016-02-17... 43 46
preseed 661 661 2016-02-17... 0 2
[BOOT] 2 048 2 048 0 1
README.diskdefines 232 232 2016-02-17...
autorun.inf 135 135 2016-02-17...
md5sum.txt 24 299 24 299 2016-02-17...
wubi.exe 2 551 408 2 551 408 2014-04-14...

Figure 2-17 *ISO File Contents*

Despite the ease of being able to port these images from one to another host, these formats are not the most suitable ones for porting virtual machines. This is because the formats do not carry information about the type of resources that need to be allocated to the virtual machine at a new location. When formats such as VMDK are used to replicate, share, or transfer the guest OS, information about resources that the virtual machine needs and expects to be deployed has to be communicated separately. The ISO format has the same deficiency, so when ISO files are used to package the source files for creating a virtual machine, the file doesn't contain any data about the resources that the resulting virtual machine may need to have available. That information needs to be communicated through other means.

For the transporting and sharing of virtual machines, a more appropriate packaging method is to package the entire environment and resource requirement details along with the virtual machine's image. These formats still use the ones described earlier, but add the additional information and re-package the contents. Some of the more popular options are described here.

Open Virtualization Format (OVF)

This is an open format specifically meant for packaging of virtual machine images and is not tied to any particular hypervisor. OVF complements the runtime formats like VMDK, VHD, and QCOW2. Unlike those formats, OVF contains information about the resource parameters, which the virtual machine expects to be allocated to it. Usually it's a collection of files, where the .OVF file contains the deployment information and a separate file represents the image. OVF also usually contains a manifest file (.MF) that has the MD5 keys of all the files. When the OVF files are packaged together (as a tar file), it's referred to as an Open Virtualization Appliance (OVA). Example 2-2 shows a simple way to view the contents of an OVA file using the Linux tar command.

Example 2-2 *OVAfFile Contents*

```
linux-host:~$ tar -tvf ubuntu32.ova
-rw------- someone/someone 13532 2014-11-12 09:54
Ubuntu-32bit-VM01.ovf
-rw------- someone/someone 1687790080 2014-11-12 10:01
Ubuntu-32bit-VM01-disk1.vmdk
-rw------- someone/someone  45909504 2014-11-12 10:05
Ubuntu-32bit-VM01-disk2.vmdk
-rw------- someone/someone     227 2014-11-12 10:05
Ubuntu-32bit-VM01.mf
```

Vagrant

Vagrant is a recent way to set up and port an environment for virtual machines based on a standard template. Vagrant uses a vagrant box that contains the virtual machine as a VMDK file, along with a configuration file that indicates how the virtual machine should be set up. The vagrant wrapper can use this box file and its contents to instantly create the virtual machine and set it up for use in a different environment. A vagrant box can easily be ported from one host to another and uses a simple set of commands to add, delete, or bring up a new vagrant environment.

Commonly Used Hypervisors

A detailed discussion and comparison of hypervisors is better suited for a book on virtualization and is beyond the scope of this book. However, a brief review of the commonly used hypervisors is helpful to deploy any virtual machine, including VNFs. This section covers the basics of some of the popularly used hypervisors today:

KVM/Qemu

KVM and Qemu are commonly used and perhaps the most popular hypervisors in the Linux world. Because they are open source and free, they are often the default choice when the virtual machines are on a Linux-based host. Qemu is short for Quick Emulator and was intended as an open source machine emulator. It can be used as a hypervisor as well, using it in combination with a Kernel-based Virtual Machine (KVM). KVM contains the virtualization extensions to a Linux kernel that enables Qemu to use hardware-assisted virtualization techniques. Using KVM/Qemu gives the guest OS direct access to the virtualized hardware and achieves almost the same performance if that guest OS was run natively on a physical machine [2][3].

ESXi

ESXi (rumored to be an acronym of Elastic Sky X-integrated) is VMware's flagship hypervisor. It a type-1 hypervisor and runs directly on bare metal. At the time of this writing, ESXi is the predominant and most widely deployed hypervisor. ESXi is a commercial product, and VMWare has built many support and usability tools around the ESXi architecture, such as VMotion and VCenter, that have contributed to its success and popularity.

ESXi uses a small kernel, called vmkernel, which has the support required for managing virtual machines as well as interaction with the hardware. VMware's management tools such as vSphere or vCenter are used deploy, monitor, and manage the virtual machines on ESXi.

Hyper-V

Hyper-V is offered by Microsoft Corporation as its virtualization solution using Windows Server. Hyper-V uses the term partitions instead of virtual machines for its isolated environments, and employs a parent or root partition to manage the others partitions (called child partitions). Though Hyper-V is an installable component in Windows Server, the hypervisor itself runs directly on the bare metal, and therefore it is categorized as a type-1 hypervisor. Figure 2-18 shows the Hyper-V architecture.

XEN

XEN is an open source virtualization software and offers a type-1 hypervisor. It uses a concept similar to Hyper-V's parent partition. In case of XEN, it employs a virtual machine called Domain 0 (Dom0), which has the special role to manage the other virtual machines on the system, referred as Domain U (DomU).

XEN uses a paravirtualization technique, where the guest virtual machines request the hardware resource to be sent to Dom0 on an as-needed basis. With this additional requirement for the guest OS to interact with Dom0, special device drivers are needed on the guest OS.

In XEN, Dom0 has direct access to the hardware and manages the device drivers on the hardware, in addition to running an application that is being virtualized. Figure 2-19 shows the XEN architecture.

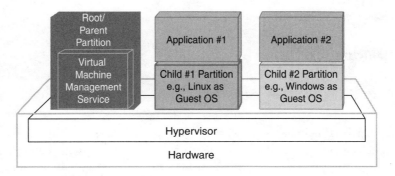

Figure 2-18 *Hyper-V Architecture*

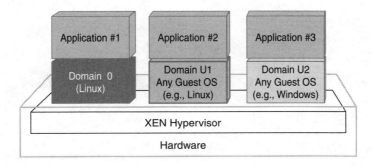

Figure 2-19 *XEN Architecture*

Linux Containers and Docker

The virtual machines described in the previous section provide a very isolated and self-contained environment. With hardware-assisted virtualization and full virtualization techniques, the virtual machine implementation is very efficient. But there is still a performance and resource cost that is associated with them due to the overhead required to emulate the virtual hardware. In some cases, however, the virtual machine's level of isolation is not really needed and a compromise with a lighter level of isolation may be acceptable to regain some of the performance degradation in hypervisor-based virtualization. This can be achieved by using a simpler virtualization technique called container-based virtualization.

This type of virtualization uses an OS-level virtualization technique and provides a closed, restricted and segregated environment to the applications within the operating system. This environment is called a container, and the applications can run independently within it.

Containerization

To differentiate container-based virtualization from virtual-machine virtualization, sometimes the term containerization is used to refer to it, instead of virtualization.

The virtualization implemented through containers has some differences compared to virtual machines, Unlike virtual machines, containers can run standalone application without any guest OS. The two approaches are compared a bit later in this section.

Container-based virtualization has its roots in the evolution of UNIX/Linux kernels. The capability to implement this virtualization is a direct result of the efforts made to provide kernel level support for isolation between applications. Because of this close relationship, sometimes containers are called Linux containers (LXC) even though not all containers are LXC.

LXC

LXC, which is abbreviated form of Linux containers, is a set of functions and protocols for programs to interface with the application (also referred to as Application Programmable Interfaces or API). LXC APIs provide an interface to the container features offered by the Linux kernel. The abbreviation is often used beyond its primary meaning and used to reference any containers implemented in Linux. Sometimes it's used very loosely to refer to container-based virtualization when differentiating it from hypervisor-based virtual machines virtualization (LXC versus virtual machine).

Just like the dictionary meaning of the word container, LXC containers provide the isolated environment. However, they fall short of fulfilling the other aspect of the word container, that is, portability. That's where Docker comes in. Simply put, Docker is a technology developed to enable portability and packaging of containers. Docker is discussed in detail later in this section. Before examining Docker, let's first understand container-based Virtualization, the technology behind it, and how it compares to virtual machine virtualization.

Understanding Containers

Containers offer lightweight virtualization through the OS virtualization technique. To achieve this, they use capabilities built into the Linux kernel like chroot, apparmor, and others. Two of these capabilities, namespace isolation and control-group, contribute more significantly than the others—to the extent that some people view containers or LXC as simply a combination of these two kernel capabilities.

Namespace Isolation

Namespace isolation, or simply namespace, was implemented in Linux kernels to limit the visibility of certain resources used by a process, and not allow processes using separate namespaces to see each other's resources. For example, an application (which would be running as a process under the Linux kernel) and using its own process namespace could spawn many processes within its namespace. These processes and process IDs would not be visible to other applications which are not using the same process namespace. Similarly, network namespace (commonly referred to as **netns**) can be created and assigned to an application, making it possible for that process to maintain its own copy of the routing and network stack. An interface or route created in an application using a specific network namespace wouldn't be visible to other applications on the same host if those other applications are not sharing that network namespace.

Namespace isolation is implemented for few of the kernel resources. Though many more type of namespace isolation has been proposed, there are currently six that are implemented in the Linux kernel.

A very brief description of these namespaces is listed in Table 2-2. To readers who are not familiar with UNIX/Linux jargon, some of these descriptions may sound like gibberish, but the sole intent of listing them is to give a very high-level view of the type of segregation that is possible through this namespace capability. A more detailed understanding of these is not needed for deploying NFV.

Control Group

The idea behind using namespace was to create a different view of the system resources for different processes. While this provides some amount of isolation—one

Table 2-2 *Linux Namespace*

Type of Namespace	Purpose
User Namespace	User namespace provides a way to create separate set of user and group IDs for a process
UNIX Time-Sharing (UTS) Namespace	This namespace creates a separate view for hostname and domain name for the application. Any changes to these by the application using a separate UTS namespace are not reflected to other processes.
IPC Namespace	Inter-process communications (IPC) such as pipes and message queues are used for processes to communicate with each other. It's possible for a process to create its own namespace for IPC (perhaps shared with some other processes that it wants to restrict communications with) by using a separate IPC namespace.
Mount Namespace	For a process to have its own view of the mounted file system, it can use its own mount namespace. A mount namespace inherits all the mount points existing previously (when the namespace was created) but any mounts and unmounts within this namespace are not visible to the rest of the applications running on the same host (and hence kept private to the process that owns that namespace).
PID Namespace	Process ID (PID) can be isolated from rest of the applications on the host by using PID namespace; for example, an application using a separate PID namespace can spawn child processes, which will use PIDs that may be same as existing PIDs on the host but wouldn't conflict with it due to namespace isolation. Other processes using a different PID namespace wouldn't see these PIDs at all.
Network Namespace	Just like the other namespace categories mentioned earlier, the network namespace provides a means to create a separate view for network interfaces, routing table, etc., which is visible only to processes that are using that namespace.

of the prerequisites for virtualization—it doesn't restrict the use of the resources. For example, the **mount** namespace can't limit the maximum amount of disk space, which a process may be able to consume. This aspect or resource allocation is addressed by control-group functionality. Control-group (**cgroup**) was a project that started in 2006 to provide a way for resource management and accounting by the Linux kernel. Starting with release 2.6.24 of Linux (released in early 2008), cgroup became part of the kernel. The cgroup functionality controls resources like CPU, memory, disk I/O, etc. It can prioritize resources or limit use of these resources; for example, it can allocate higher levels of CPU (or restrict CPU usage) for certain processes or limit the amount of system memory that a process can use. Additionally, cgroup can also measure the resources certain processes are using.

Cgroup and Namespace

The cgroup feature and namespace complement each other. An analogy of their roles is that of a campground, where all campers have the freedom to choose their own tent color, make their own campfire (or not), and make changes to their own surrounding area. The camper is sharing the campground, but to the campers the area around them shows their own view of nature. There isn't, however, anything restricting the campers from the amount of water they can use from the shared showers, or how big a bonfire any camper can make. Without these limits, the freedom of one camper can step over and infringe upon other campers—affecting the whole campground. A solution would be to put limits in place and define boundaries by regulating the use of camp resources. By doing that, you have a more cooperative use of resources. Although all campers are now sharing the resources, they still maintain the freedom to keep a personal view of nature within those limits. That's what cgroup does in a Linux kernel; that is, cgroup enforces the restrictions on the amount of resources that can be used by processes. On the other hand, namespace allows independence and separate private views of system resources to the process. LXC uses the combination of these two (as well as some other features) to implement virtualization.

Container versus Virtual Machines

The level of virtualization by use of container isn't the same as a virtual machine. Containerization doesn't create a new (virtual) machine within the host OS by emulating presence of real hardware. Instead, containers provide means to apartheid the use of system resources, and define restrictions around their usage. For this reason, containers are often referred to as a virtual environment to differentiate them from virtual machines.

Note that the terms virtual environment, virtual machine, and containers are quite often used interchangeably and the context about the level of virtualization puts them in the correct meaning.

Some of the important differences between the two methodologies are:

* shared kernel versus use of hypervisor
* resources saving in containers compared to virtual machines
* restricted options in applications compared to virtual machines
* higher performance in containers
* less security compared to virtual machines

Shared Kernel versus Use of Hypervisor

In the case of a container the host OS's kernel is shared by all the containers, and virtualization occurs at the process level by using kernel features mentioned earlier (like namespace, cgroup). There isn't any need for a hypervisor, instead APIs to access the needed kernel features are used, like LXC. This API layer can be viewed as container's flavor of hypervisor, but unlike a virtual machine hypervisor, the APIs are very lightweight and directly interface with the kernel.

Resources Saving in Containers Compared to Virtual Machines

Since a container uses the host operating system, it doesn't need to run a new operating system within it. That allows containers to run applications directly within them, in contrast to a virtual machine, where an operating system is needed before an application could be run in the virtual machine. This saves resources when the applications that are to be virtualized can use the same kernel, binaries, and libraries as the host OS.

Limited Application Choices Compared to Virtual Machines

The sharing of the host OS kernel, binaries, and libraries saves resources, but it has some drawbacks compared to a virtual machine implementation. An application that needs a different operating system can't be put into a container on this host. In comparison, a virtual machine is much more flexible on what it can run. Virtual machines can run any type of application and on any guest OS that requires the same hardware architecture as the host. Also, due to sharing of kernel between the containers, there is a possibly vulnerability where one container's behavior can affect the others.

Higher Performance in Containers

There is a performance impact from the use of a hypervisor (which is essentially an application) to interface between the application (or guest OS) and the virtualization capabilities in the host/hardware in a virtual machine. The lightweight virtualization environment that containers create doesn't have the overhead that is associated with virtual machines since hypervisors are not used. Therefore, when compared to virtual machines, containers offer higher throughput for read/write operations or better CPU utilization [4]. In most cases, containers are able to achieve near-native performance of the host system.

Less Security Compared to Virtual Machines

The shared kernel and shared libraries reduces the level of isolation as well, therefore containers offer a relatively less secure virtualization compared to virtual machines. Also, the isolation between the host OS and the container's application is not too thick. For example, the host OS can see the processes being run in the Container.

There are restrictions in place (like those implemented via cgroup) to offer security and isolation. For instance one container can't monopolize the entire host's CPU resources. However, there are still possibilities where behavior of one container can potentially impact others. For example if a container's application causes a kernel to crash, then this also impacts other containers running on this host.

Table 2-3 summarizes these differences side-by-side between virtual machine–based virtualization compared to container-based virtualization, and the architectural implementation comparison between these two is depicted in Figure 2-20.

Table 2-3 *Virtual Machines vs Container*

Virtual Machines	Containers
Allocate chunks of hardware resources to create a virtual machine	Process-level virtualization doesn't allocate hardware, but restricts usage and provides isolated view of hardware.
Needs an operating system with in the virtual machine	Can run standalone application (using the host OS as its operating system) or a different operating system (guest OS)
Can run any operating system (guest OS) on top of another (host OS)	The guest OS or application can only be something that is capable to run on the same kernel version that the host OS is running

(Continued)

Table 2-3 *Continued*

Virtual Machines	Containers
Provides high level of isolation and security. Very unlikely for an application in the virtual machine to affect the other virtual machines or Host.	Doesn't provide pure isolation, as lots of components (including the kernel itself) are shared. Possible for one container's application to affect the entire host or other containers
Performance impact—usually slower since hardware emulation has to take place through the Hypervisor	Near native performance since there is no middle layer (virtualization layer, or Hypervisor)
Resource overhead—if the guest OS is running the same kernel as the host OS, then resources (disk space, memory, etc.) used by this guest are wasted.	No resource overhead, since the kernel's built-in capabilities are used.

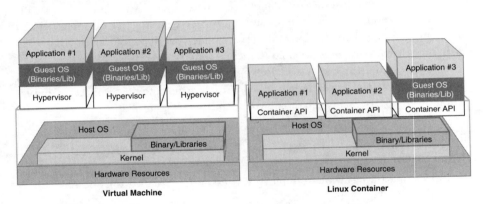

Figure 2-20 *Virtual Machines versus Linux Container*

Application Container and OS Container

Applications running in a container can be either standalone applications or another operating system running as a guest OS. Based on the application, containers can be split into two categories:

- OS container
- application container

OS Container

When the application in the container is an operating system, then that container is referred to as an OS container. Just like in case of virtual machines, the operating system running in the virtualized space is called guest OS. This guest OS can then run applications within it.

Why would someone run a guest OS inside the container instead of running the application directly? That is because the applications in the container use the kernel, libraries and binaries of the host OS and it is possible that an application may require more independence, needing a different set of libraries or system binaries while using the same kernel. In OS containers, the application running within the guest OS uses the libraries and system binaries from that guest OS. This removes the dependency on host OS libraries and binaries; however the kernel is still shared between the guest an host OS. Another reason to use an OS container is to achieve better isolation, security, and independence for the containerized application.

OS containers look a bit similar to virtual machines, but instead of the hypervisor, it uses container APIs. This type of container takes a slight hit on performance and resources because of the additional operating system (guest OS) and its libraries/binaries. Also, since the kernel is shared between the host OS and the guest OS, the guest OS needs to be compatible with the host's kernel—for example a Windows operating system can't run on a Linux kernel.

Application Container

Application containers (app containers) are simply containers that run the application directly. The application uses the system binaries and libraries from the host OS and the same kernel, but has its own namespace for networking and disk mount point. Application containers are designed to run a single service at a time.

Because containers are very lightweight, the use of application containers makes it possible to isolate the various services running in the host OS, and containerize all of them, thus creating a group of application containers, each offering a service. This approach to the software architecture has gained a lot of popularity in recent years, and is referred to as microservices.

In a simpler Linux deployment, these services run as processes in the host (such as the Apache daemon, the secure shell or ssh daemon, or database server) and share CPU, memory, and namespace with each other. By putting them as containerized microservices, the applications perform the same tasks but their resource use is now controlled and they have isolation from each other by using their own namespace.

Figure 2-21 compares these two types of containers side by side.

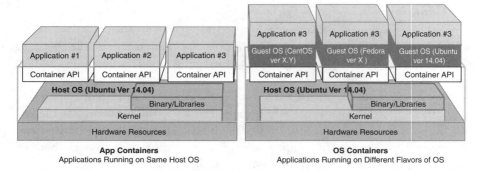

Figure 2-21 *OS Container versus App Container*

MicroServices

The term microservices represents a software architecture in which applications are running isolated based on the service they provide. Each service runs independently, can grow and scale separately, can have its own resources at disposal, can be altered or upgraded without impacting other services, and yet still is able to communicate with each other using APIs. This is a more modular approach compared to the monolithic architecture, where the services are bundled together in one software. Microservices can achieve better isolation, scalability, and resiliency. The use of lightweight container technology makes it easily possible to create Microservices architecture.

Enter Docker

Since containers provide a virtualized environment to applications as well as sharing files with the host OS, replicating and porting a container from one host to another may require special considerations. A container may be composed of the following:

- configuration files by defining its environment
- a set of files on the disk that represent its mount namespace
- executable files and libraries belonging to the application

Additionally, it assumes that certain host system libraries and binaries are present. Therefore, porting a container is not as simple as moving just the configuration file and application binary. LXC doesn't offer a way to package container files and environment together as a group.

This is where Docker comes in. Docker started with the name dot-cloud in early 2013, and was meant to provide a method to package containers for portability, replication, and version control. It would run as a single process, called Docker Engine, and work with Docker Image files. As shown in Figure 2-22 Docker image files package together the application, all the needed binaries an dependencies, and put those together as a single image which can be ported and replicated.

Docker

Docker is an application that provides container capabilities by talking directly to the operating system, and offering a way to create containers that can be packaged, replicated, ported, backed up etc. In Docker community's own words: "Docker is a platform to build, ship, and run distributed applications" [5].

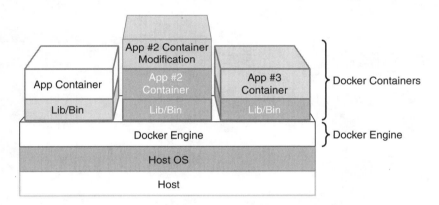

Figure 2-22 *Docker Architecture and Image File*

Docker Image

The Docker logo shows a stack of containers being transported by a whale; that literally reflects Docker's ability to transport containers as stack of deltas between them instead of one huge container for each modification. When a container is created by a Docker client it can be published to the Docker repository, called Docker Hub [6]. From the repository, the container can be downloaded and used by any other Docker client running on a different host because Docker packages the dependencies, environment, libraries and binaries needed along with the application itself. If this subsequent Docker client makes changes to the Docker Container, it can push these changes back to the repository. Docker uses copy-on-write (COW, just like QCOW is used by Qemu) to keep track of the changes and only this delta of changes (diffs) is pushed back to the repository. All subsequent changes made and pushed back by other clients are stored in the repository as new container carrying the diffs and keeping the link to previous set of diffs. For any client to replicate the final container environment, it can download the base container as well as all the diff containers. Figure 2-23 shows an example of how this works.

As shown in Figure 2-23, a container may be built with a customized Apache server and pushed to the repository as a base container with all needed dependencies. This container can then be downloaded and modified by another host which (say) added MySQL to it. This host (Host#1) pushes the delta of these changes back. Another host (Host#2) may make more changes to it by adding Python libraries and publish the changes to the repository. A new host (Host#3) can download the entire stack and get the replica of the final flavor of this container, or it can choose to download only a partial set of diffs (say, Apache+MySQL only) and modify or use it.

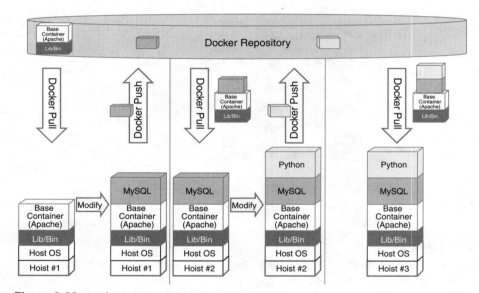

Figure 2-23 *Docker Image Stacking and Repository*

Docker versus LXC

Earlier versions of Docker were built on top of LXC, using the LXC API calls and only adding portability and packaging capability. However, in later versions (starting with version 0.9) the Docker team removed that dependency on LXC and rewrote the kernel interface APIs. These APIs were responsible for the creation, modification, and deletion of a Docker container. They were called libcontainer, to contrast with the libvirt kernel toolkit that LXC uses. With time, libcontainer transitioned to what is now called runC.

LXC and Docker both use containers for virtualization, but they are different enough so that the term LXC or Docker is often added to clarify the type of container being referred.

Docker has a many tools and applications developed around it, which makes it a powerful alternative to using LXC containers. Some of the differences that are mentionable are:

- portability and easy sharing
- targeted for app containerization
- version control capability
- reusability

Portability and Easy Sharing

The file format defined by Docker packages contains all the needed application files, configuration (like networking, storage), dependencies (Linux distribution, libraries, host binaries), and other information into a single Docker package. This package can very easily be ported to a new host and run using the Docker client on that host.

This capability to abstract all details needed for porting a container was the main motivation behind Docker from the very start.

Targeted for App Containerization

LXC containers are more suited for multiple applications running in the container, like OS containers. On the other hand, Docker is designed with the idea that single application can run within the Docker container.

This is not a restriction, since LXC can run as an App container, and Docker containers can have a guest OS. However, since Docker packages the libraries and host binaries in the Docker container (which was the primary motivation for running a guest OS in the container), Docker containers are more optimized to be App Containers.

Version Control Capability

With the use of copy-on-write and keeping track of diffs from one version of the container to the next, version-control capability is implicitly possible in Docker containers. All the changes made to Base containers, and subsequent containers, are kept stacked together, and at any time the current view can be rolled back to a previous state of this stack. Additionally, Docker offers tools to compare the Diffs between two versions, history tracking of a container, updating to the most recent version of a container.

Reusability

This comes with portability and the ability to take any container (which may be modified from its original base container) and use it as a new base container for further modifications. A previous example is shown in Figure 2-23. Apache+MySQL+Python Docker container can become the base container for a new host, which may re-use this stack and add some additional tools and tweaks to it for its use.

Container Packaging—Beyond Docker

Docker is the most popular way to package and port containers today. However, some other standards are emerging and still in their infancies at the time of this writing. They will be mentioned here for sake of completeness.

Rocket

Rocket (or Rkt as it is usually abbreviated as) provides a mechanism to run an app container in Linux. It was originally put forward by CoreOS team after it separated its path with Docker due to differences on implementation of security, openness, and modularity in the Docker environment. CoreOS proposed the use of an open specification for container packaging, which it calls App Container, abbreviated as appc (this term shouldn't be confused with container type running application, which is also called App Container). Appc defines an image format to package containers, which it calls App-Container-Image (ACI). ACI uses a tarball to package all the required files and information, just like Docker does it for its image format [7]. Rocket supports the appc specification.

Open Container Initiative

This is a very new forum introducing an open and common standard for container technology, including a common image format [8]. Open Container Initiative (OCI) is supported heavily by Docker and CoreOS as well as many others, and is still in its early stages at the time of this writing. It is yet to be seen if OCI format replaces both Docker and *appc* formats, and comes up with a universally acceptable format that all container tools can use and adapt.

Single and Multitenant Environment

Virtualization capabilities lead to two type of customer deployment architecture with respect to ownership sharing of the server—single-tenant and multitenant architecture. In the standalone scenarios without virtualization, only one tenant has ownership and control of the entire server. That tenant has the flexibility to modify the hardware and the software that runs on this server, since they are the sole owner. Any changes that this tenant makes wouldn't impact any other user of a different server. This is referred to as single tenancy.

> ### Tenant
>
> A tenant, by its dictionary definition, is someone who is a user of an infrastructure for a limited amount of time. In the context of server deployment architecture, the word tenant is used to reference the customer who is using the hardware/software resources on the server.

With virtualization, it's possible to share the server between many tenants. These tenants share the resources of hardware and software on the server. Changes made to these shared resources by one tenant do have impact on others. Therefore one tenant doesn't have the freedom to modify the system without consent of the others. This is called multitenancy.

As an analogy, a single tenant system is just like the tenant of a single-family home, where any action by the tenant of this home doesn't impact its neighbors and the tenant is free to do any changes within the home. In contrast, a multitenant situation is analogous to tenants in a multistory shared apartment, where one tenant's action can impact neighbors who are sharing the apartment's infrastructure and resources. Figure 2-24 shows a pictorial comparison between these two tenancy models.

Multitenancy inherits the benefits of virtualization, but it reduces the level of isolation between the tenants. Therefore it lowers the level of security and increases vulnerability compared to single-tenant architecture. This disadvantage-vs-benefit is a decision factor to adapt virtualization. The industry trend has heavily favored multitenancy and virtualization due to the major benefits that were discussed previously. Sometimes the disadvantages become a critical factor (often due to regulatory requirements) and dominate the choice between the single tenant and multitenant deployments. Improvements in virtualization are constantly being done to reduce or eliminate the disadvantages.

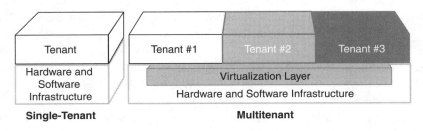

Figure 2-24 *Single versus Multitenant Environments*

Virtualization and NFV

NFV is the result of adaption of server virtualization to networking. A considerable amount of focus was given here to go through the fundamentals of virtualization, as this forms the core of the NFV architecture. Looking back to the ESTI architecture, the NFVI block has the virtualization layer, which is implemented via a hypervisor (if using VNF as virtual machines), or LXC/Docker (when using containers for VNF). The concept learned in this chapter is applicable to this virtualization layer of NFVI Block.

The evolution in server virtualization has a direct influence on the way VNF are deployed and implemented. For example micro-services with containers is being explored as an option to further optimize NFV deployment efficiency, since container reload and deletion times are much shorter. In the long run, this option may justify a trend towards use of containers in NFV rather than a virtual machine.

Similarly, some enhancements are being pushed into virtualization due to its use by NFV. For example the VNF interconnectivity uses the same tools that Virtualization uses to interconnect the virtual machines or Containers. This has pushed for development of more efficient virtual switches, as well as optimized packet-processing techniques at the kernel level and network interface card (NIC) level, such as Intel's Data Plane Development Kit (DPDK).

Summary

This chapter focused heavily on virtualization technologies, types, and methodologies. The level of information is relevant for understanding the implementation of NFV. Some of these technologies are still in very early stages (for example, OCI) and their future development will also play a role in NFV deployments.

Some time was spent going through the history of virtualization, and why it has become a de-facto way of deployment server in recent years. The techniques and advantages of virtualization were discussed and compared. The two main methods of achieving virtualization, virtual machines and container-based virtualization, were covered in some depth. The advantages and disadvantages as well as various tools to implement each of these were compared.

The topic of virtualization is worthy of a book itself. But the goal of this chapter was to introduce it just enough for the fundamentals of NFV to be solidly laid down, and discuss the higher layer concepts of NFV in subsequent chapters.

References

Please refer to the following for additional information:

[1] https://www.sdxcentral.com/comprehensive-list-virtual-switching-routing/

[2] http://www.linux-kvm.org/page/Main_Page

[3] http://wiki.qemu.org/KVM

[4] http://domino.research.ibm.com/library/cyberdig.nsf/papers/0929052195D-D819C85257D2300681E7B/$File/rc25482.pdf

[5] https://blog.docker.com/2015/06/runc/

[6] Docker repository/hub: https://hub.docker.com/

[7] https://github.com/coreos/rkt/blob/master/Documentation/app-container.md

[8] https://www.opencontainers.org/

Review Questions

Use the questions here to review what you learned in the chapter. The correct answers are found in Appendix A, "Answers to Review Questions."

1. What is a server farm?

   a. The term server farm is used to refer to a collection of many servers that are deployed and managed by an organization for delivering specific computing functions and services that are beyond the capability of individual servers.

   b. The term server farm is used to refer to a collection of many servers that are deployed on a space that was previously used for farming.

   c. The term server farm is used to refer to a collection of many hardware that are owned by multiple organizations and reside in a single physical location.

   d. The term server farm is used to refer to a collection of many datacenters that may carry user information distributed across many storage servers.

2. What are at least four benefits of virtualization?

   a. hardware and software integration

   b. lower operational cost

    c. improved utilization of disk space

    d. quick provisioning,

    e. bare metal throughput,

    f. high availability,

    g. reduced space requirements

3. What is the difference between type 1 and type 2 hypervisors?

    a. Type 1 hypervisors require a host OS; the hypervisors run as an application on the host OS.

    With type 2 hypervisors, The hypervisor runs on bare metal and doesn't required a host OS.

    b. Type 1 hypervisors don't require a host OS; the hypervisor runs on bare metal.

    Type 2 hypervisors use host OS running on bare metal, and the hypervisors run as an application in the host OS.

    c. Type 1 hypervisors use Linux containers instead for virtualization.

    Type 2 hypervisors use KVM for virtualization on top of the host OS.

    d. Type 1 hypervisors don't require a guest OS, and the hypervisor runs on group of servers.

    Type 2 hypervisors use a host OS which also acts as a guest OS running on bare metal, and hypervisors run as an application in the host OS.

4. List three advantages of container-based virtualization compared to virtual machines:

    a. resource savings,

    b. high level of isolation

    c. ability to run Windows container on Linux

    c. better performance,

    d. Application independent

    e. Faster failure recovery

5. List two advantages of virtual machines compared to containers:

    a. high level of isolation

    b. more secure

    c. ability to run Windows container on Linux OS

    d. faster failure recovery

    e. better performance

6. Which is the most commonly used tool for packaging Container images?

    a. ISO

    b. VMDK

    c. Docker

    d. LXC

7. What is the difference between an app container and a OS container?

    a. OS-containers run the applications directly in the container, thus using the binaries, libraries, etc. from the host OS. They are meant for single-service use.

    App containers run a guest operating system, which may host multiple applications. These are more suitable for multiservice use, or for applications that can't run using the host OS's libraries.

    b. App containers run the applications directly on the hypervisor without using the host's binaries.

    OS containers runs a guest operating System on the hypervisor which uses the host OS's binaries.

    c. OS containers run the applications directly on the hypervisor without using the host's binaries.

    App containers runs a guest operating system on the hypervisor which uses the host OS's binaries.

    d. App containers run the applications directly in the container, thus using the binaries, libraries, etc. from the host OS. They are meant for single-service use.

    OS containers run a guest operating system, which may host multiple applications. These are more suitable for multiservice use, or for applications that can't run using the host OS's libraries.

8. Which functional block in ETSI Framework does virtualization play a role?

    a. Virtualized Infrastructure Manager (VIM) block

    b. Virtualized Network Function Manager (VNFM) block

    c. NFV Infrastructure Block, or more specifically at the virtualization layer

    d. hypervisor and container block

Chapter 3

Virtualization of Network Functions

Chapter 1, "The Journey to the Network Functions Virtualization (NFV) Era," and Chapter 2, "Virtualization Concepts," covered two important areas of NFV fundamentals and virtualization basics. These two topics are key to understand the function and implementation of virtualization and infrastructure blocks in the European Telecommunications Standards Institute (ETSI) framework. These blocks form the foundation for running the virtualized network functions (VNFs). With this foundation properly laid out, this chapter builds on top of it and focuses on VNFs and the considerations involved for the design and deployment of networks using these VNFs.

This chapter provides some examples and use cases of the type of network functions that are being virtualized today. It revisits the advantages of NFV and shows how these benefits are achieved using VNF for different types of network services.

The main topics covered in the chapter are:

- Design, deployment, and transformation to NFV networks

- Challenges and considerations when implementing NFV networks

- Examples of virtualization of various network functions and the influence it has on bringing new and innovative network services.

Designing NFV Networks

IP-based Networks originated as means to transport data traffic. However, over the years many other applications and services such as voice, video, and mobile began to utilize these networks. Each of these services had traditionally been using an independent network, but in the recent years these networks have been converging towards a single network and migrating their traffic to this common (IP-based) network.

The primary motivations for this convergence have been the ability to offer new services and reduce deployment and operational costs. However, consolidating networks in pursuit of this goal has resulted in networks getting more complex and stringent as each of these services brought an additional set of constraints for the network design. For instance, voice over IP (VoIP) traffic requires that jitter stays under 50ms while the end-to-end delay should be below 150ms. These create new quality-of-service requirements for the IP network, though neither of these requirements would have existed for networks carrying only web traffic. As these networks grew, were rebuilt, and evolved in a piecemeal fashion over time to accommodate the new requirements, the resulting networks of today are more of a patchwork to achieve short-term results. The subsequent networks did not achieve the desired operational simplicity and cost reduction. Nor have these networks done very well for scalability, migration, and interoperability issues. This spaghetti of networks is still leaps away from an optimized cost-effective network and lacks the agility needed for today's fast-shifting market requirements.

NFV was conceived as a fresh approach to address these challenges. It offers promising solutions to simplify, optimize, and transform the network to a cost effective and flexible network. To fully implement the solution that NFV brings and realize the advantages and benefits, the network's design methodologies have to evolve and change compared to the way networks have been designed using legacy hardware-based networking equipment. The transformation of a network to NFV is more than just a transition from physical to virtual. It needs a paradigm shift in the way networks are built. The principles of traditional network design have to be augmented with the design principles for NFV, such as placement of the Virtualized Network Function (VNF) and infrastructure design.

The following sections expand on the design goals and considerations that have been factored in for a network built using NFV. The subsequent section that follows the design discussion will highlight new challenges brought up with the shift in design principles.

NFV Design Considerations

Traditional network designs have been hardware centric, and the requirements limit the scope of the design to a limited range of devices. If the hardware that is available from vendors doesn't meet the design requirements (lack of features, scale, or capacity) then the designs need to be adjusted to work with the limited options available. The resulting network design is tightly wrapped around the hardware devices and their capabilities. This network is rigid and cannot easily adapt to any future changes that may be required for introducing new services. Even when changes are made, it requires physical access and human labor. NFV-based design is meant to remove this restriction and provide flexibility that is not restricted by networking hardware. Additionally an NFV design could meet changing network requirements by incorporating elasticity, scalability, and software-centric approach. With NFV's ability to offer speedy transition and agility, the resulting network can avoid longer lead times which has been plaguing new service adoption in the traditional networks.

To utilize the capacities of NFV and reap its full benefits a different approach is required for the design and deployment for NFV networks. As emphasized earlier, the network functions are decoupled from the hardware, so the choice of VNF types and vendors doesn't have a correlation with the design of the physical infrastructure. Similarly, the physical infrastructure can be designed without influence from the VNFs it will host and run. Another design dimension is added by the considerations for management and deployment of the network functions. Each of these blocks can be designed individually and fairly independently since they are influenced by different factors and involve a different thought process. Figure 3-1 reflects these three dimensions of NFV design. The subsequent sections provide the details of these design categories.

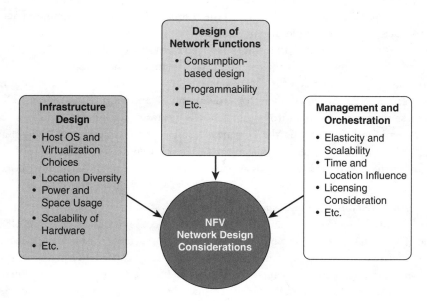

Figure 3-1 *NFV Network Design Considerations*

Despite the independence in the design of multiple blocks in NFV, the goal behind each layer's design should still have a common definition of the capabilities and performance that the resulting NFV network shall have. Any inefficiency or deviation from this goal at any one of the layers can create a bottleneck and lead to performance degradation for the entire network. Similarly, if one of the blocks is designed around higher performance network goals, that performance will not translate to the resulting network performance.

Designing NFV Infrastructure

The infrastructure for the NFV is not designed to meet the needs of a specific network and services. The infrastructure is meant to be generic and should ensure that it can allow for scalability and elasticity of the VNFs. It's also possible that this infrastructure is shared with server and data-center applications and not dedicated to NFV. The criteria for implementing a flexible and open platform for VNFs are discussed in the following subsections.

Scalable Hardware Resources

The infrastructure hardware should have flexibility to scale up and down if needed. Since the infrastructure is designed fairly independently of the overlying networking layer, it's not always possible to predict the hardware resource requirements that may arise. The primary approach to design around this is to pad the deployment resources as much as possible, as well as to design the resource pool so it can be shared across infrastructures. For example, use of shared disk pools instead of using servers that have built-in storage disks will result in reduced chances of wastage.

Even though operators want the initial deployment to have abundant hardware resources to avoid the need for future updates, it is still possible that the deployed hardware might prove insufficient for growing needs and require upgrades. To handle these situations, the operator should choose hardware equipment that can be easily scaled without impacting the current virtualized applications and VNFs that it may be hosting. This could mean that the servers chosen need to be capable of scaling up the hardware resources such as network interface cards (NIC) and memory.

Hardware Cost and Capital Expenses

The cost of the hardware is always an important selection criterion. Custom off the shelf (COTS) hardware is perceived to be the best way to achieve the optimal price point for hardware, but vendors like Cisco, HP, IBM, and Dell have been offering server products and pricing them competitively against COTS. Operators may be inclined to choose these commercially available servers, since the vendor built hardware would have been tested for any compatibility issues between components, and the servers are backed by the support contract from the vendor. Essentially this choice is not much different from the choice an end user has to make between a custom-built personal computer using individual components, or a commercially built one from a vendor such as Dell, Lenevo, or HP. Whether the design results in choosing individual components separately, opting for COTS, or going with the vendor-built system, the choice impacts the overall capital expense for the deployment. This choice is also influenced by the expected reliability of the network and support available to resolve possible issues.

Choice of Host Operating System and Virtualization Layer

The host operating system (OS) and hypervisor must be compatible and integrate smoothly with the deployed hardware. Together they should offer a stable base to build the rest of the structure. When using COTS or a commercially available server, there is a wide range of choices for a host OS, hypervisor, and even orchestration tools. To narrow down these choices, consider the following:

- type of technical support available for these software pieces
- licensing costs
- procurement costs
- the roadmap for future support
- upgradability support
- stability
- ability to interact with open source and commercially available tools

Finding the right balance between all of these factors is a design decision. Some operators may prefer fully bundled software solutions from companies like VMware, RedHat, or Canonical. Others may find confidence in choosing from the other side of the spectrum for an open source, freely available OS like Ubuntu or CentOS running open source hypervisors such as a Kernel-based Virtual Machine (KVM). In the former case, the operator will incur licensing costs but will be comforted by the fact that the product has a proven track record, technical support structure, and has a secure future with a clear roadmap and upgrade path. In the latter case, however, they can eliminate the licensing costs and rely on in-house, third-party, or community-based support structures for future growth and issue resolution.

Efficiency in Power and Space Usage

Power and space requirements for the infrastructure hardware are reflected in the long-term operating expense of the network. This becomes much more critical in parts of the world where real estate is hard to acquire and power tariffs are high. To get a perspective on how critical the space and power efficiency issues are, compare the deployment scale of the data centers being built today to host virtualized servers. These data centers are spread over many acres of land (or multiple floors of high-rises in densely populated locations) and consume hundreds of megawatts of power. Any improvements in the amount of space and power consumption for the individual servers can have a big impact in the operational cost of the NFV point of presence (PoP). It must be mentioned that the optimization in power consumption is not a direct result of virtualizing the network functions, but rather a result of utilizing the elasticity of the VNFs to scale on demand.

Common and Repetitive Footprint

The infrastructure can be designed in a way that the variability across different locations is minimal. Deployments can be simplified by designing for a common hardware and software footprint, which can be repeated across the NFV PoP. Achieving this simplification and the possibility of design replication requires that the power requirements, space needed, installation and commissioning expertise, provisioning tools, and methodologies stay unchanged. The common hardware infrastructure reduces the amount of redundant spare parts required to deal with possible replacement of failed hardware. On the other hand, creating a repetitive footprint might require some extra planning and care during the design phases.

Location Diversity

It is important to consider the choice of locations when designing the NFV infrastructure. Ideally the infrastructure deployment should be geographically diverse and more heavily deployed in possibly critical locations for traffic such as downtown areas. A metropolitan environment has more concentrated networking requirements compared to the suburbs.

One reason for diverse locations is to have redundancy against localized faults or disasters. However, another very important reason to diversify the locations is to ensure that the VNF has flexibility to be spun up where and when needed, without running into resource constraints. Later sections discuss the reasons behind requiring VNF placement based on geographical locations and the importance of availability of the infrastructure to make that flexibility possible when deploying VNFs. It is possible that a VNF may need to exist closer to the customer edge or that a particular location is expected to have an increased demand for VNFs during certain times or days.

Redundancy and High Availability

The design to mitigate failures in traditional networks is based on the assumption that one of the network functions can be lost if the device performing that function goes down, possibly due to even a single component failure. The redundancy in those traditional networks must be ensured at the device level to protect against possible network outages resulting perhaps from a single component failure. For instance if a single hard drive fails on a router, then it can affect the entire functionality of that router causing an network outage or traffic glitch. Depending on the level of importance of this device, a redundant device (or devices) or a backup traffic path is pre-provisioned and ready to carry traffic if needed.

In contrast, in NFV the high availability and redundancy is implemented per component; therefore the chances of loss of a network function due to a single component failure are highly minimized. For example, if a router is deployed as a VNF on a server using a Redundant Array of Independent Disks (RAID) technology, then the failure of one of the disks doesn't have any impact. Since an NFV infrastructure is shared, building redundancy in the infrastructure is cost effective, as multiple VNF are benefiting from this simultaneously.

In addition to the server hardware level redundancy, the infrastructure hardware design should also be able to offer redundancy to the virtual machines or container. Between the infrastructure switches, Spanning Tree Protocol and its variants like Rapid STP (RSTP), Per-VLAN STP (PVST), and Multiple STP (MSTP) have been used for a long time. More recent protocols that offer such redundancy are Transparent Interconnect of Lot of Links (TRILL) [1], Link Aggregation Control Protocol (LACP) [2], Multi-Chassis Link Aggregation (MC-LAG), and Ethernet VPN (EVPN). These and other similar protocols offer a number of choices and methods to provide redundancy for NFV Infrastructure hardware.

Redundancy and VM Mobility design and support offered by the virtualization layer should also be considered for a robust design. Some examples of this are VMware's VMotion and Openstack's Live-migration.

Infrastructure Life Cycle

The hardware devices used to form the infrastructure must be refreshed over a period of time. As shown in Figure 3-2, the life cycle starts with planning and procurement, and the hardware is discarded after their estimated life has passed. This life cycle duration of the hardware is based on the average amount of time the pieces of hardware are expected to operate without failures, as well as the duration of support contract and repair component availability.

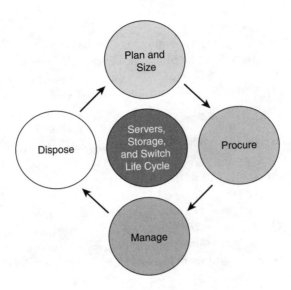

Figure 3-2 *NFV Infrastructure Life Cycle*

NFV Infrastructure (NFVI) design considerations should include the life cycle of the servers, storage, and switches used in the infrastructure. The servers and storage devices used in typical datacenter generally have a useful life cycle of three to five years [3]. Switches are considered to have a slightly longer shelf life spanning approximately six years. In this time frame, these devices have paid off the investment made on procuring them. To keep the odds of failure to a minimum, these devices are swapped out with newer ones once this life span has passed. The same time estimates and practice are applicable to NFVI as well. Additionally, the host OS, hypervisor, and VNF have their own life spans after which they will need to be upgraded, either for enhancements, support renewal, or bug fixes.

The design should therefore consider the coordination of these multiple factors to avoid possible pitfalls. For example, the software support and release cycle for the VNF may be one year, the hypervisor may have a suggested refresh time of two years, and switches and servers may have a six and three years life span respectively. The life span in this example do not align well with each other, and if proper design and planning is not done to handle this in the most optimal way, it can result in a constant network churn with upgrades. The design goal should be to minimize the impact due to upgrades, as well as to plan ahead to mitigate the possibilities of post-upgrade issues. These issues can be minimized through proper preintegration production testing.

Designing Networks using Network Functions

Once the NFV infrastructure is in place, the network and its functional blocks such as VNF can be viewed as an overlay on top of this infrastructure, as depicted in Figure 3-3. The design of the network is therefore independent, flexible, and free from constraints of the physical hardware. The network design could be focused purely on the services offered by the VNF that need to be implemented, and any needed computing, storage, or networking resources can be assumed to meet the design requirements.

A key differentiator with NFV is that the design and deployment takes a software-centric approach so the core functionality of the network is implemented in software.

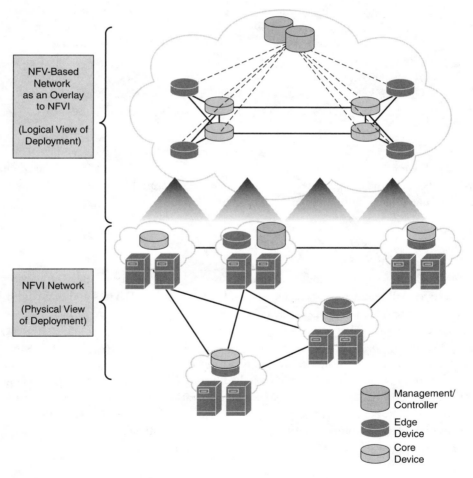

Figure 3-3 *Network Overlay on Top of Physical Infrastructure*

Therefore the network functions (VNF) can be added, scaled up and down, removed, and relocated purely in software. The VNFs are also expected to support open APIs, which allows any third-party orchestration and management tools to control the placement and life cycles of the VNFs. The orchestration tool instructs the virtualization layer to interconnect the VNF in any desired order, and new VNFs can be instantiated and added to the data or control traffic's path on the fly. Programmability of the VNF via the open API leads to software-defined networking (SDN), which is touched upon in a later part of this book.

> **Open API**
>
> Open API support in the software provides a documented and publicly available way for any third-party software to access and retrieve data from the application or pass programming/configuration parameters to it. *Open API* support by VNFs implies that in addition to the proprietary way of configuration and management (typically using a text-based command line interface or CLI), the VNF supports and documents APIs that provide a way for configuration, monitoring, and management needs.

Since the design elements in NFV involve both the VNFs and their management, the following sections in this chapter cover them as a single element. Some common ingredients in the design criteria are the reduction of capital investment and operational costs, along with optimal utilization of the resources.

Capital Expense and Operation Expense Reduction through
Resource Optimization

When the efficiency of today's networks is analyzed, the transport and device resources will be found to be running at subpar-utilization. Devices and bandwidth are overprovisioned to meet capacity requirements based on future growth predictions or demand spikes at certain time of the day, week, month, or year. To protect against failure of hardware device, network connectivity, or networking software, additional redundant resources are also provisioned. The resulting network is underutilized for most of its life, and this severely dilutes the investment gains by increasing the capital cost to deploy the network and the operational cost to manage and run it.

In contrast, NFV benefits from virtualization that allows the VNF to request and own only of the resources that they need, and dynamically allocate more resources or release unneeded resources based on changes in requirements, thus maximizing the utilization.

Therefore, the network designer doesn't need to extensively overprovision computing power, memory, throughput capacity, and other such resources for the VNF, as these parameters can adapt in NFV network. Additionally, the design has the flexibility to eliminate or have minimal function redundancy since VNFs can be recreated on the fly if and when needed.

Consumption-Based Design

NFV-based networks can be scaled up and expanded on-demand. Hence it is possible to design using a true consumption- and demand-based growth model. For example, if a mobile providers is using NFV and wants to add a new type of service (like the ability to use voice over WiFi), or explore a new vendor for a network function (such as a new type of media caching server), then the provider can introduce this in some segments of the market and evaluate the user experience, feedback, investigate possible glitches, and analyze the potential gains and cost benefits. Based on the feedback from this trial run, the provider can easily make alterations to the design of the virtual devices or VNFs that are implementing this new service. Once the provider is ready to expand the service and has achieved a comfort level and revenue justification, the provider can go ahead and expand this service gradually to other market segments or regions.

For network designers looking to introduce a new type of service or altering any existing service, the change doesn't need to be designed and generalized for mass deployment from the very start. These services can be created and initially kept simple to start as a pilot solution for tapping the target market. Then it can be refined and perfected as the deployment grows and expands in scope. Additionally, if the market demands wind down for the service, the VNF can be removed and the same physical hardware can be repurposed to provide a new service by initiating a different VNF on this physical infrastructure.

Leverage Infrastructure Redundancy

For traditional network designs to ensure the redundancy needed for traffic path and bandwidth, the device and transport need to be factored in the requirements. In the case of NFV, redundancy for network functions does not need to be preemptively provisioned.

The redundancy to protect against hardware failure is already taken care of in the infrastructure layer's design, as described earlier in this chapter. The hardware redundancy implemented at the component level ensures that a failure of one component (CPU or memory module) may not propagate to the VNF, and it may continue to work without any impact. If, however, the hardware failure is catastrophic, such as a failure of multiple disks or multiple top of rack (ToR) connection failures, then the orchestration layer could take care of instantiating the affected VNFs at a new hardware with minimal impact to the network.

In this context, the design considerations in NFV redefine disaster recovery and failure mitigation. Measures for protection against failure are offered in multiple layers as shown in Figure 3-4. The infrastructure architecture shown in the figure has been proven to be resilient in the data center and server virtualization deployments, and NFVI designs can leverage this time-tested architecture to create a highly available infrastructure for NFV. Similarly, management and orchestration technologies dealing with VNFs can inherit the methods and tools used for server virtualization such as vMotion. With these mechanisms in place, the VNF design can be kept simple and doesn't need to implement another layer of redundancy to achieve high availability for the network services.

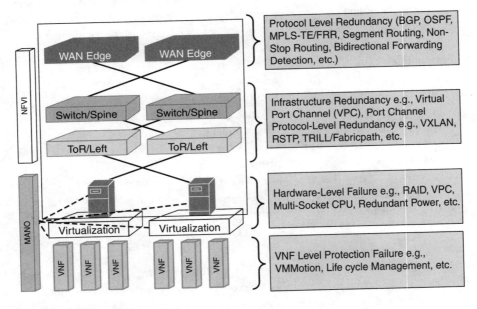

Figure 3-4 *Redundancy in NFV*

Agility through Modularity

With NFV, it's possible to deaggregate the network functions into separate VNFs (or a group of VNFs) without any cost or resource penalty. The network design should therefore take a modular approach, designing around functions and not devices.

As shown in Figure 3-5, a legacy router could possibly have multiple functions bundled into one device, such as firewall (FW), Network Address Translation (NAT), and routing at the same time. Any upgrade needed in any of these functionalities will, in most cases, require changing the entire software package or possibly even the hardware. In NFV, design modularity brings flexibility and agility. Any design changes based on pilot and production network's feedback is easily incorporated into the design. This change can be surgical and tightly focused to a specific function, making it easily possible to redesign, validate, and deploy the new feature in a short span of time. Being flexible, the design has a wide range of choices for the different implementations of the network functions. It can mix and match the VNFs offered from multiple vendors to create a customized solution. The VNFs for NAT, firewall , and other network functions such as routing protocols can be from different vendors, and selected based on the best match for the provider's requirements of the individual functions.

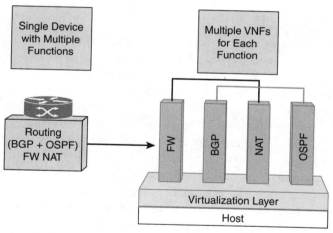

Figure 3-5 *Modular Design*

Elasticity and Scalability

In an NFV network's design, capacity planning is performed very differently than traditional designs. With the software-centric approach and automation support, the VNF resources can be expanded or shrunk on the fly without impacting the network. This capability, called elasticity as previously noted, also enables offloading of a VNF's workload by spinning up new VNF instances for that same function and distributing the load between them. In a previous example, if the number of BGP peers for a VNF is exceeding the capabilities of the CPU that is allocated to it, VNF elasticity can be used to add more CPUs or to instantiate a new VNF that starts acting as a alternative BGP peering node, as shown in Figure 3-6.

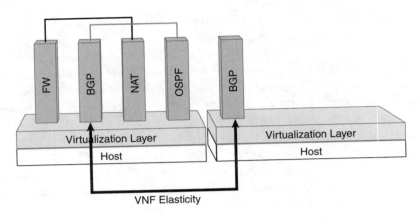

Figure 3-6 *VNF Elasticity*

The design of the network could also take into account the business needs. If a service offering guarantees a specific level of service, then the design can ensure this by using the elasticity of VNFs. For elasticity to accommodate the business and technical requirements, the orchestrator should be designed to analyze the VNF monitoring data, determine any constraint or limitation that needs to be addressed, and circumvent it by instructing the NFVI and/or VNF layers to take the appropriate action. The logic and rules that determine the changes needed and decide when they are needed are designed into the orchestration layer.

Though the examples previously mentioned show situations where the design had to accommodate the need for expanding resources, it should also be kept in mind that logic and rules could also exist to scale down resources. This too is part of the elasticity of NFV design. Taking the earlier example of BGP VNF, if the number of peers get reduced to a value that can be handled by only one of the VNFs, then the other one can be brought down by the orchestration layer, freeing up NFVI resources for others to use.

Predeployment Design Validation

Any design must go through some level of validation. The validation process is not only time consuming but also adds a significant amount of cost and resources. In a typical Internet service provider (ISP) deployment using legacy devices, the test and validation process can take a few months and possibly even a year. Therefore, the design has to be perfected as much as possible before investing the effort into its validation, especially since a design flaw could potentially void the entire effort.

NFV eases this requirement in multiple ways. It reduces the validation period by shrinking the amount of time needed to set the system up. The test network consists of virtual functions that are elastic and can be rearranged and reconnected easily using the software knobs. The design can be perfected while its being tested and majority of these steps can be automated to provide the flexibility or quick validation to any design changes. The test and validation cycle can be incorporated using a basic pilot deployment in a production network. Based on the experience through the initial setup, the possible production issues can be vetted out and the resulting feedback can be used to improve the design.

Dynamic Design for Demand-Based New Services

With the ability to instantiate VNFs anytime, anywhere, and to insert and connect them to an existing network, a new dimension of service offerings has become possible. NFV-based designs should consider the network as fluid and dynamic, with the option to offer a range of choices for the end user or customer. The provider can offer these enhancements and choices to the service package that customers have subscribed to and let them add, remove, or change these whenever they desire, As an example, if the provider is offering a cloud-based Digital Video Recorder (DVR) functionality for a residential service, the customers can be provided with the choice to increase the video storage space on the fly. Another example is a business service designed to allow customers to add load balancers or a firewall to their private Internet service or to increase the route limit they are allowed to send towards their service provider. These options translate to increased revenue opportunities for the provider, as well as improved customer experience by offering flexibility and choice.

Though these possible services do not need to be deployed from the start, they have to be preconceived at the time of the network design. The network designer therefore has to ensure that these are factored-in during planning of the infrastructure.

Reduced Downtime for Planned Events

Redundancy and disaster recovery design approach were discussed earlier to address any unplanned failure event. However, planned events (such as upgrades and migration) that can result in downtime also need to be recognized as part of the design. The design should consider probability of planned upgrades in three categories:

- VNF upgrade or planned downtime
- hypervisor Upgrade
- host upgrade

Modern hypervisors are able to update resources like CPU and memory to a running VNF, and ideally the VNF should be able to accept this change without any impact to its function. However, it's possible that the VNF being used doesn't have this capability (this deficiency could be one of the factors to consider when selecting the VNF during the design process), and therefore a resource change to it may impact the VNF's function. This type of planned downtime requires taking precautionary measures. One possible approach is to instantiate a new VNF with the needed capabilities and then hand-off the function to it gracefully, followed by removing the original one, as shown in Figure 3-7.

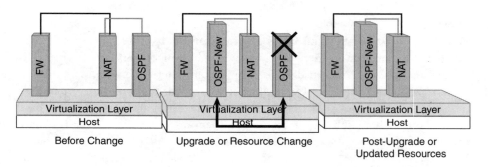

Figure 3-7 *VNF Upgrade*

It must be noted that in a complete and proper VNF implementation, the need for such actions shouldn't arise, as these VNFs should be designed to accommodate this physical resource change automatically without impact on service or uptime. Exceptions and nonideal implementations are possible by vendors. Sometimes a VNF may still be deployed due to other good characteristics even if it doesn't provide support for this flexibility.

Upgrades for the hypervisor, host OS, and hardware also need to be considered in the design. These upgrades can potentially impact multiple VNFs. One possible way to minimize this downtime is to shift the VNFs to a different host in the shared infrastructure before scheduling the hypervisor or host OS upgrade.

In all these cases, the design should consider the need for accommodating the challenges of possible VNF downtime due to planned events such as migrations and upgrades for any of the functional blocks.

Location-Based and Time-Based Deployment

Since NFV network functions are not tied to a specific piece of hardware or location and can have a variable and short life cycle, the designs for these networks could include considerations for location of the VNF and the amount of time the VNF is active.

Properly exploiting the location independence of the VNFs and strategically placing them can lead to a simplified and optimized network. For example, in a traditional design of Mobile Packet Core, the Packet Data Network Gateway (PGW) would be placed in centralized locations to minimize costs. However, since all the traffic (including device to device traffic) needs to be forwarded to the PGW, it makes this implementation very inefficient by increasing congestion, adding delays, and wasting bandwidth. Spreading out the PGWs by creating multiple VNFs and pushing them out towards the edge closer to the eNodeB can result in a much more efficient design. This wouldn't be feasible in traditional networks for reasons such as the cost of deploying high number of PGW devices. In NFV-based networks, however, it is a viable option and the design should factor this in. Similar examples from data networking are the use of distributed denial-of-service (DDoS) detection and scrubbing engines on each entry point of a provider's core, as shown in Figure 3-8. It is not cost effective to do that in traditional network implementations, but NFV makes it possible without a significant added cost or design change.

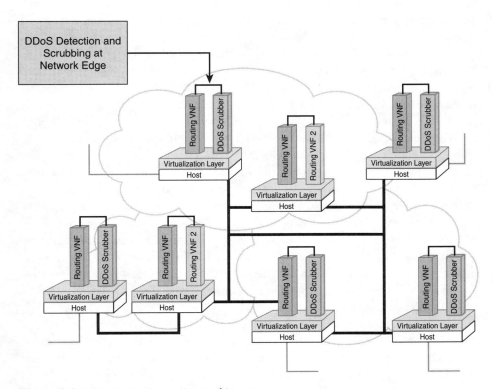

Figure 3-8 *VNF Positioning to Optimal Location*

Through optimal design it is possible to place the VNFs at the right locations, providing a network with efficient utilization of the infrastructure's bandwidth, and the reduction in delay and jitter avoids possible congestion in the network.

In the legacy networks, traffic is often steered towards a certain path based on demand, usage, and cost factors. Multiprotocol Label Switching Traffic Engineering (MPLS-TE) tunnels are a good example of how providers try to balance the resource usage across their network due to high network demand or traffic in one location. This traffic heat map can be distributed by shifting some of the traffic towards other parts of the network that are experiencing lower utilization. Though this degrades the performance (by adding delay and latency) and adds complexity (mesh of such tunnels can get complicated to troubleshoot and manage), in today's networks these downsides are justified by the operational and deployment cost savings that can be achieved. With NFV, however, the network can be designed to shift the functions based on time, demand, and utilization. For example, if the traffic is always higher at specific locations during specific hours of the day, then the network functions can be brought up and brought down to follow that demand. This approach, shown in Figure 3-9, is referred to as following the sun. The approach makes a very efficient use of the network while avoiding the disadvantages that were associated with the traditional fixed networks.

As the network traffic grows exponentially with the advent of Internet of Things (IoT)-based data, use of smart devices, ultra-high-definition (UHD) video streaming and such, the importance of location-based network becomes much more significant. Data from IoT nodes is predicted to reach 400 zetabytes (1 zetabyte equals 1 billion terabytes) [4]. In this data-driven economy, analyzing this data from IoT sources goes a long way. Using computer services that are remotely located through cloud computing and cloud networking isn't most effective for this. The most optimal location to process, consume, analyze, and react to this data is one closest to the data sources. This gives birth to the use of fog computing and fog networking (also called fogging), which advocates location proximity between the sources of data and the network functions and computing elements to absorb this data. Most of the data is from sources that are mobile, such as smart devices, smart cars, and automated trains, which requires the fog networking resources to be able to move between locations based on time, demand, and circumstances. This affects NFV design factors in both cloud and fog networking requirements for location and time of network deployments.

As a side note, the term cloud computing is used to describe the use of distributed computing resources for storing, managing, processing, and accessing data. These computing resources are generally connected using the Internet and can share the applications and databases. Cloud computing makes it possible to access data from anywhere and therefore removes the need to keep local storage

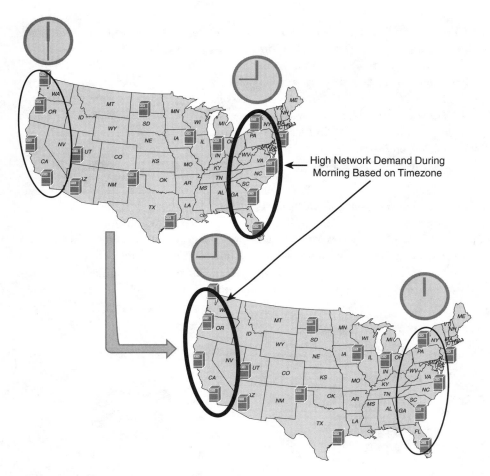

High Network Demand During Morning Based on Timezone

Figure 3-9 *VNF Relocating Based on Time of Day Demand Shift*

servers. It is also viewed as diminishing the need to build private compute and networking infrastructure. Instead, the infrastructure and networking services hosted though cloud-based resources can be used. All that is needed locally is the ability to access these resources through the Internet. Consumer-based services such as Google Drive allow users to store photos and collaborate on documents. Services such as Amazon Web Services (AWS) offer processing and networking resources on top of storage, which allows corporations to offload their entire IT infrastructure. Cloud computing has proven to decrease operating costs, improve collaboration, and increase availability.

FYI: *The drawback with cloud-based computing and networking is that the processing engine and storage are often far away from the source of the data. With big data, the amount of information generated and collected has become very high. Instead of sending this large amount of data to remote cloud-based services, it is often more desirable to process it closer to the data source or client. This saves bandwidth and decreases latency to achieve run time analysis. The idea to bring cloud resources and technologies closer to the sources, and away from the main cloud, resulted in use of the term fog and the coining of the terms fog computing and fog networking.*

Life Cycle Management and Licensing Costs

It is important to consider the life cycle of the VNF for multiple reasons. The phases of the life cycle consist of instantiation, monitoring, scaling, updates, and termination, as shown in Figure 3-10. Anytime a VNF is not needed (perhaps due to its location and time-based deployments, as discussed earlier) the hardware resources that the VNF is using can either be completely released or scaled

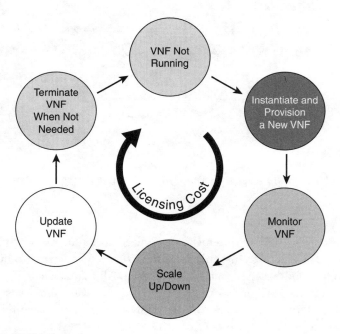

Figure 3-10 *VNF Life Cycle*

down. This allows the resources to become available to other VNFs that might need them.

The other reason to design for optimal life cycle management is the cost of licensing when running a VNF. Network equipment vendors have traditionally positioned hardware as the focal point of their revenue generation. But with NFV, this focus has shifted towards software. That has resulted in vendors using licensing and other usage-based charges for revenue. These charges are usually structured around features, number of instances, and capacity.

The network design should factor in the optimal number of VNF instances needed as well as the capacity and features required for the actual VNFs. Looking back at an earlier example of a follow-the-sun time-based network, the total number of VNF instances across the two coasts could remain the same. The licensing cost could be kept low by designing in such a way that the orchestrator terminates VNFs in the low-demand zone and brings them up in the locations that need them.

Multi-Tenancy

Multi-tenancy is already used heavily in server virtualization. An NFV design can also benefit from this capability by catering to multiple customers grouped together based on relevance of services needed. For instance, customers requiring Layer 2 Virtual Private Network (L2VPN) and Layer 3 VPN (L3VPN) services can be put into two groups of tenants. Similarly, various customers that require the same functions can be tenants on the same infrastructure.

Another aspect of multi-tenancy is the ability to offer a varying level of service to customers, depending on the SLA, features, and isolation requirements. VNF placement is based on factors to meet the expected resource needs, For example some VNFs require a dedicated CPU core or NIC to achieve the required performance. The NFV design could therefore utilize a shared infrastructure and implement multiple simultaneous VNFs meeting a varying set of tenant requirements for scale and SLA.

Automation and Programmability

Most of the advantages offered by NFV cannot be tapped unless the system is designed with built-in automation support. Automated tools and scripts are implicitly required to implement many of the design aspects that have been mentioned earlier. These automation engines require predefined work-flows and policies that determine the action that needs to be taken based on certain criteria. The design of NFV network should create the logic to be used on this policy-driven network in order to implement capabilities for automatic remediation of known issues, handle failures at various levels, and provide a flexible mechanism to set the criteria for design goals such as location/time-based services and elasticity.

Automation should also be able to tweak or reconfigure the parameters within the VNF. However, in a typical NFV deployment, the VNFs could be a heterogonous mix across multiple vendors. To enable the automation to interface with these functions, the VNF should offer a common programmable interface. The lack of this support can flatten some of the gains that NFV is meant to bring in.

DevOps Support

DevOps is an abbreviation that represents the merging and collaboration of efforts for development and operations of a product. The DevOps approach breaks away from the traditional model, in which development and operational roles work in siloes, and it encourages these groups to openly communicate and execute their tasks side by side instead of in tandem.

The NFV revolution runs in paralleled with and is supported by two major game changers in the software development world: the use of the DevOps approach and the trend of open software development, which replaces older approach of proprietary software development that was seen as hampering innovation. NFV design is able to benefit from compliance with the DevOps and open software development model to be able to adapt to new changes and incorporate them quickly in the design and deployment phases.

Summarizing NFV Network Design Constraints

The previous sections list some of the important design characteristics when planning and deploying the network whether it is a transition from an existing hardware centric network, or a green field NFV deployment. NFV design criteria are quite flexible, and instead of a one-size-fits-all approach, it allows the network design to be tailored to business needs and requirements. By using any or all of these design factors, the resulting network could exhibit the following:

- improved efficiency while reducing cost
- optimization
- new dimension of services
- faster innovation and solutions
- improved customer experience

NFV Transformation Challenges

The advantages of NFV come with a set of challenges. The design discussion is not complete without considering the limits, boundaries, and possible blind spots. It is important to work around these issues and completely avoid or minimize any impact they can have. These challenges are new and different compared to those faced by traditional networks, so they need to be studied in detail. The following subsections examine some of the crucial challenges

VNF Throughput and Latency Performance

In regard to networks, the importance of data throughput and the capability of VNFs to deliver desired rates are quite critical. In traditional hardware, high throughput is achieved by implementing dedicated application-specific integrated circuits (ASIC) and processors that are customized to process packets at a high packet-per-second (pps) rate. Additionally, these customized ASICs are closely paired with the physical interfaces, without involving any intermediate processor to facilitate the transmission of the data packets. These platforms try to ensure that most, if not all, of the data packets are handled by the ASIC's code and not processed by the software. This is because the software processing path is much slower compared to the throughput that is achieved by processing the packets in hardware. For any exceptional cases that the hardware can't handle, the software-based packet process is engaged at the cost of degraded performance for those data packets.

In contrast, NFV is software-centric and therefore at a relative disadvantage because it does not have specialized hardware processing engines. The data packets are processed inherently in software, and the code that processes the packets implemented in VNF software run on general-purpose CPU resources on the server hardware. To make up for the lack of specialized hardware processing, special techniques are used to enhance and heighten the performance of the packet-processing algorithms built into the VNF as well as the device drivers it uses to interact with the NICs. Nevertheless, it must be emphasized that even though the gap is narrowed with these techniques, the packet processing rate achievable with software-based packet forwarding still lags behind hardware-based processing techniques. Jitter and latency are the other aspects of performance of the data path that need to be highlighted. These may be very important for time-sensitive traffic such as voice and video, or for time-sensitive applications such as a Session Border Controller (SBC) in a mobile packet core. If the virtual CPU available to the VNF for handling the packets is not dedicated, then despite all the optimization in the algorithms for packet destination lookup and applying data path features, the latency may still be unpredictable. This could result in jitter and high latency in the data traffic. Chapter 6, "Stitching It All Together," examines the various knobs that can be used to alleviate this situation as well as techniques that can reduce the gap between software-based and customized hardware packet throughput performance.

Virtualization adds another layer of overhead and imposes a tax on the achievable throughput. The use of shared resources, as well its role as an intermediate interface between the real and virtual hardware, adds an overhead that can degrade the packet rate. When the VNFs are communicating through the hypervisor, they do not need drivers to work with the physical NICs (pNIC); instead they use virtual interface drivers. The virtual drivers then communicate with the pNIC, but this process increases the hypervisor tax. An alternative is to use paravirtualization techniques and include the pNIC device drivers into the VNF. This approach, called passthrough, helps reduce the virtualization overhead but comes at the cost of requiring the VNF to support physical interface devices.

Figure 3-11 summarizes all of these performance impacts in a VNF compared to purpose-built hardware.

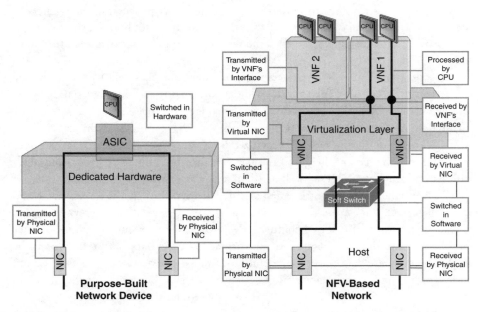

Figure 3-11 *Packet Processing in VNF versus Purpose-Built (Traditional) Network Device*

VNF Instantiation Time

The time to bring up a VNF can generally be expected to be faster than the boot time for a purpose-built device. That's because the stages and processes for hardware booting are skipped and only the software portion has to be brought into service. However, the time it might take a virtual machine to be completely up and running cannot always be ignored. The initial boot time or reboot time of the VNF application (within the virtual environment) can vary, based on a number of factors. The influence of some of these choices can be predictable; for example the type of virtualization, containers or virtual machines, can make a difference. Containers are lighter weight and therefore the boot, reboot, and decommission times for containers can be shorter compared to those for virtual machines. Other factors that influence the instantiation and deletion times may not be known in advance, such as CPU load on the host or heavy use of the disk resource that could slow down the VNF initiation or deletion times. Other factors that may add to this issue are the response times of the management and orchestration systems. These systems are susceptible to the same resource constraints and may not be able to act in real time to start or configure a VNF.

All of these factors combined can make the VNF creation, configuration, and deletion times significant enough to be considered a potential issue for the design. Many of the design principles, such as high availability and time of day deployment, rely on almost instantaneous creation or deletion of VNFs, and the few extra seconds or milliseconds that required could have major impact on the design.

Reliability of the Infrastructure

The flexibility of multiple vendors is a plus, but it also brings along the challenge that each vendor may have performed validation only on their component and under conditions best suited for their product. When products implementing various layers are integrated together, the resulting reliability may not be the same as evaluated by the individual component owners. Any reliability issues on the weakest component can impact the entire infrastructure. The earlier discussion of the design criteria for infrastructure indicated that the low price-point offered by COTS hardware may have an associated cost on reliability. Stability was also one of the design criteria when choosing the software for the infrastructure. However, stable and robust software and a reliable hardware platform don't necessarily translate to stability for the combined infrastructure. Achieving that stability may require integration testing and validation for the infrastructure that has been put together using building blocks from a diverse set of vendors.

Aside from in-house testing, another possible solution to mitigate this risk is to choose prevalidated offerings from vendors. Some vendors offer packaged options that bundle scalable hardware along with a complete host OS and hypervisor. These bundles have the advantage of pretested for compatibility issues, backed up with a support contract with the vendor and offer a long-term road map. For the vendors, this is an opportunity to capture the huge NFVI market, while from the operator's perspective it is an option for faster NFV deployment. Some examples of these are PowerEdge FX (by Dell) and Cloud Services Platform (CSP, offered by Cisco).

Taking another step further and looking at the networking gear associated with NFVI (top-of-rack switches, devices to interconnect PoP, aggregation routers) the same reliability problem resurfaces once more. The solutions stay the same; perform in-house validation, or opt for the pre-packaged and validated solutions are offered by vendors. Some examples of such solutions which offer a fully integrated NFVI system, including the virtualization server, storage, and networking, that are being offered today are FlexPOD (by NetApp) and Vblock (offered by VCE).

> **FYI:** *Both Vblock and FlexPOD use a combination of Cisco's Unified Computing System (UCS) servers, Cisco's switches, EMC's or NetApp's Storage devices, and VMware's hypervisor. The vendors test and validate this integrated solution and advertise it a as a pretested solution for operators, providers, and customers.*

High Availability and Stability

In the traditional network, high availability from hardware and software is much more confined to a single vendor. Most of the failure and high availability scenarios are validated by the vendor. This changes in the NFV networks, as now there are possibilities of multiple vendors and each may have a different high availability mechanism. The service provider may still want to provide the five 9 (99.999 percent) reliability as the existing carrier class hardware offers, but while using NFV the provider needs to look at software resilience and a different architecture to achieve this.

> **FYI:** *Carrier class hardware and services boast to offer high availability, fault tolerance, and low impact for failures. It guarantees that the system is designed in a way that redundancy is put in place to achieve resiliency, and if any impact does happen due to failure, then it will be addressed within 50ms of traffic loss.*
>
> *This high availability is gauged by the percentage of time the system is up and fully available. For example, 99.999 percent (called five-nines) means that the system doesn't experience more than 5.256 minutes (out of 8760 hours) of unexpected downtime in the whole year. Four nines (99.99%) would mean 52 minutes of cumulative downtime in the whole year.*

With multiple layers of NFV, challenges arise as the operators need to collect data from the diverse systems, correlate all of the information, and identify the problem in the system. If any change occurs in any one component, such as the hypervisor or host OS, then this correlation needs to be updated to reflect the new vendor change. The stability of the NFV systems may also need to factor-in many more variable components from the server hardware, hypervisor, host OS, and the VNF. NFV system stability brings in additional challenges with the elasticity and relocation of a VNF to a different system that needs to be validated to make sure the stability goals are achieved.

Cost of Licensing

As hinted earlier, the adoption of NFV in the networking industry is making the network equipment vendors change their pricing structure and shift towards charging for software use rights through licensing. In addition to the VNF license, other software components may have their own licensing requirements. As a result, multiple licenses come into play for the NFV network, such as the host OS, hypervisor, VNF, configuration management applications, and the orchestration system.

The licenses are usually multitier and multidimensional, as shown in Table 3-1. Some possible licensing choices are also listed here as an example. For each category, there is the choice of going with a cost-free option, but that may not be a preferred choice since it lacks a support model and clear roadmap. The choices typically made by the providers are highlighted in bold. For these choices, as the table shows, there may be associated costs based on various factors. VNF vendors, for example, can choose to charge licensing costs based on multiple options such as throughput the VNF is handling, the features that are enabled on it, the duration of use, and the network role this VNF is deployed for.

Free Software License

Free software licenses imply that the users have the freedom to run, copy, distribute, study, change, and improve the software. Open source licenses, such as GNU's General Public License (GPL) and Massachusetts Institute of Technology (MIT). license are examples of various free software licenses available today [5].

The total ownership and running cost after considering all of the licenses and the hardware could outweigh the cost of a traditional networking device or single-vendor solution. That makes the licensing cost an important consideration when it comes to choosing these individual components.

Multiple Layers of License Management

As mentioned, various tiers and dimensions of licensing may exist in an NFV network. Aside from the cost factor associated with them, the management aspect of these

Table 3-1 *Cost of Licensing*

	Examples of Possible Licensing Choices	CPU	Memory	Throughput	Duration	Features
Hardware	COTS (Vendor built)	✓	✓		✓	
Host OS	Free Software Licenes (FSL), **FSL with support model**, Proprietary software					✓
Hypervisor	FSL, **FSL with support**, Proprietary	✓				✓
VNF	FSL, **Proprietary**			✓	✓	✓
Orchestrator	FSL, FSL with support, **In-House built, Vendor built**				✓	✓

licenses can bring a different kind of challenge. To implement and enforce these licenses, vendors may use proprietary license models. License management may be built-in to the software itself, or it may require an external management server. The location of this server (within the management network for this infrastructure or hosted externally by the vendor) can add one more layer of complexity. For example, as depicted in Figure 3-12, the hypervisor may have implemented a license using an in-house license server, one of the VNF vendors may have implemented its license in the cloud (hosted by the vendor), while the other VNF vendor may have designed their licensing in a way that requires license servers to be hosted within the intranet. The design and operations should factor in the support and implementation requirements of these variations in the license management methodologies.

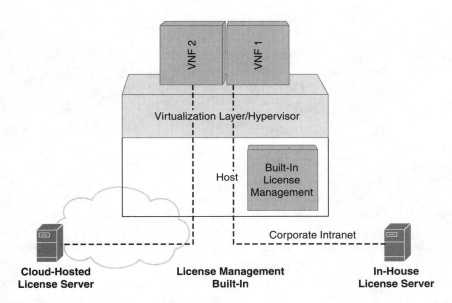

Figure 3-12 *Licensing Server Options*

Evolving Standardization

Standardization for interfacing between the NFV functional blocks is still maturing, and the communication protocols used between the management tools, VNFs, and operating systems are still evolving. Most implementations by vendors today are customized to their environment and may experience compatibility challenges in a mixed vendor situation or may not be fully complaint with the NFV Management and Orchestration (MANO) block of ETSI's NFV framework. This limits the scope of the freedom and selection choice that NFV promises.

The network operator migrating to NFV today has to face the challenge of continuing to adapt to changes due to this evolution. The standards of current tools may be temporary and get replaced with other options, chosen over time through market adoption. One example of such transition is the shift away from use of Extensible Markup Language (XML) configuration models (which was viewed as a replacement for CLI-based configuration) and is now getting replaced by the push to use Netconf/YANG and OpenConfig for managing network functions. Use of Netconf for southbound communication (that is, communication from the management system to the VNF) and Restconf for northbound communication (that is, communication from the management system towards operational and business support systems (OSS/BSS)) while using open APIs is the direction most vendors are leaning towards.

YANG

YANG stands for Yet Another Next Generation, and uses a standardized syntax to model device parameters and configuration. Netconf is the protocol generally used to carry YANG data between VNFs and orchestration and management tools.

Security

NFV can improve the implementation of network security by helping to create granular security zones and making it possible to place security VNFs such as firewalls, intrusion detection systems (IDS), and DDoS scrubbers close to sources of traffic that needs monitoring or scrubbing. However, NFV also brings a challenge of implementing and ensuring security of the network at multiple levels against possible vulnerability. With the multiple independent layers of operational and management entities, like hardware, hypervisors, containers, and VNFs, security parameters have to be considered for each of them. It may be required to maintain user authorizations and credentials for each of the layers. A weak spot in any one of the layers can result in a breach that could impact all others. Each layer must be secured, free of vulnerabilities, grant access to the right set of users and authorize to execute commands accordingly.

To secure NFV network from intrusions and block off unwanted access and traffic, separate firewalls may be needed at multiple levels. The first layer is for the individual VNFs, which need to be protected, just like traditional appliances. Virtual firewalls (running in a separate VNF perhaps) can be used for this purpose. The second layer uses firewall in the hypervisor, protecting the path that the data takes to reach each VM. This type of firewall, called an introspective firewall, protects the virtual machines within the host against access that can exploit open ports accessible via the hypervisor irrespective of its operational state. A third layer of protection might be to implement a firewall to protect the host OS itself. Protection of the infrastructure components and ensuring that unwanted traffic is blocked from and towards them might require yet another layer of firewalls. The firewalls protecting host OS and infrastructure may be part of the NFVI itself and would likely be provisioned and maintained to work independently to the intro-spective firewalls and VNF firewalls.

Figure 3-13 depicts the various aspects that should be considered for security eval-uation and implementation in NFV.

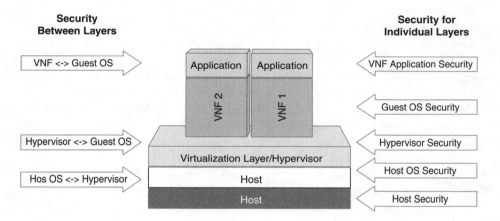

Figure 3-13 *NFV Security Considerations*

The few breach points to consider are as follows:

- The individual direct attack to the component-level security for each of the layer. Managing the authentication, command authorization, logging and monitoring, and protection from threats for each of these layers can be challenging.

- There could be security concerns for the flow of information/packets between the components. For example, there could be concerns whether the VNF appli-cation is able to access the guest OS, and whether the hypervisor allows for one VNF to communicate with another VNF or completely isolate them.

- Depending on level of isolation between the VNFs, a security breach in neigh-boring VNFs can potentially be a concern for other VNFs sharing the NFVI.

- There is a security challenge to mitigate issues with service chaining and to ensure that the VNF forwarding graph doesn't have rogue or unwanted blocks in the path.

One more challenge to mention for NFV security implementation comes from the use of multivendor software in the NFV network and especially the VNFs. Since the VNF, as well as all other layers, can be composed of implementations from many different vendors, each one of them may need to be separately evaluated and validated to ensure that it is secure and robust. A re-evaluation may be required if the VNF is switched from one vendor to another, therefore creating additional overhead for the VNF selection process.

Migration Challenges

NFV transformation can be revolutionary or evolutionary. In both cases, it faces challenges related to migration—not only from a technology perspective, but also from operational process changes and change in the business model. In an evolutionary migration, the transformation to NFV may happen in stages and require that legacy technology coexists in parallel with NFV for some time. This overlap can be technically challenging. In addition to new design criteria, the design also has to absorb and implement the current set of services offered by legacy equipment without creating a hurdle for the new NFV-based services. The evolution has to be planned, built, managed, and operated in a way that doesn't dilute NFV's advantages during the phased migration.

It was earlier established that NFV is much more than just virtualization of existing networking code running on today's hardware. Therefore, the replacement of one piece of legacy hardware could occur through the use of multiple modular VNFs from multiple vendors at multiple locations. From an operational perspective, managing and monitoring applications must go through changes to manage the VNFs. These adjustments could require adding a new set of tools that work in parallel with the current ones, or enhancements to an existing set of tools that enable them to work with both NFV implementation as well as with the legacy systems simultaneously. The operational teams also need to be able to tackle issues that occur from the legacy equipment as well as new ones. This could be challenging in terms of skill sets and expertise that may be required. Most importantly, with a network in a transitional state during its migration to NFV, the interoperability challenges of old (physical) and new (mix of virtual and physical) implementations of functions and services must be taken into consideration for day to day operations.

The other migration approach to NFV is to replace a network instead of converting an existing one. This revolutionary migration would imply that the NFV deployment can assume a green field, which frees it up from constraints possibly imposed by the current network it was meant to replace. In this case, the business development and planning must adapt a fresh approach and develop services that make the best use of the new design and deployment possibility the network inherits through NFV.

This type of rapid transition by switching to NFV without overlap means that new tools, operational techniques and troubleshooting skills must be adapted at the same pace. There could also be the possibility that some requirements aren't yet implementable due to lack of available support from VNF vendors.

Challenges in Management Systems

NFV network's management is very different from classical networks. The management system has to deal with various layers and with multiple vendors—host, virtualization engine, VNFs, and hardware. If the transformation to NFV in a network is not immediate, the management system still has to deal with legacy equipment. The challenges of interoperability become dominant in such a network. Another challenge that NFV brings to the current management system is the need for agile and dynamic network management. The management system is expected to monitor the network in real time and take the actions required to deal with problems. Programmability and automation have to be an integral part of these systems. The management tools also need to be enhanced to effectively implement NFV features and design advantages like elasticity, hardware allocation/de-allocation in real time, reconfiguring network connectivity (between VNF), and provisioning new service on-demand. In fact, the concept of orchestration, which is closely linked with monitoring and management, is quite new concept in the networking world.

As the NFV network grows, scales up, moves, evolves, and updates at a pace that wasn't possible before, keeping track of it and avoiding a sprawled network can be another challenge to consider. To avoid these situations, the design templates and connectivity details for the services need to be more strictly enforced than ever before. Anything short of a systematic, well-planned approach could result in a mesh that could void the efficiency gains made by implementing NFV in the first place. Management applications that vendors are offering today are still quite short of addressing all of these challenges. Most of the tools are still fairly tailored to the vendor's own NFV solutions, and are still evolving to find the perfect ways to manage and monitor NFV-based networks. In the case of providers, which have been using in-house management tools, this transition to the new style and way of management is even a bigger problem. The need for adapting to the management changes is not limited to only tools and software, but a parallel evolution is needed by the network operations team. They have to be trained to use the techniques to manage an NFV network.

The operation of an NFV system involves management and monitoring at multiple levels. The infrastructure may require different tools and a team than those responsible for the hypervisor, host OS, or VNF. This is one of the reasons that the ETSI framework defines multiple sub-blocks in the MANO functional block such as Virtualized Network Functions Manager (VNFM), NFV Orchestrator (NFVO), and Virtual Infrastructure

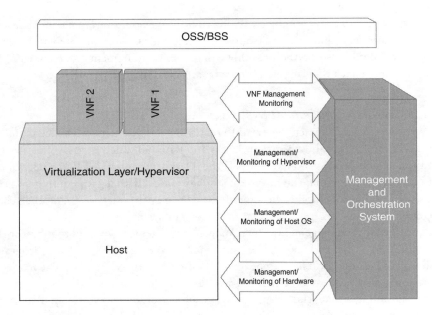

Figure 3-14 *NFV Management and Monitoring*

Manager (VIM). As shown in Figure 3-14, these multiple layers of management may work independently of each other; but have to coordinate and communicate between each other for implementing the management of the entire NFV deployment.

Resource Constraint

Virtualization provides sharing and isolation, but the boundaries it creates may still prove insufficient in some cases. It's possible that one misbehaving VM can causes a resource hog, affecting all its neighboring VMs on that host. This situation is referred to as the noisy neighbor effect [6] and poses a potential disadvantage compared to a bare metal approach. In the case of a virtual environment using containers, where the isolation is relatively less compared to a virtual machine, this may become more of a problem. This can be resolved through better containment of resources, efficient sharing and high availability mechanisms offered by the virtualization layer.

Troubleshooting Challenges

Fault detection and troubleshooting in an NFV network could become challenging if not planned ahead of time. Any troubleshooting performed may require debugging at multiple levels. A problem at one level can trickle to other levels; for instance if a host CPU has a high workload or the system is experiencing a noisy neighbor syndrome, it might impact the VNF's performance. Debugging at the VNF alone will not be enough to figure out the root cause of the problem. Similarly, when a failure or fault occurs at a lower level, it might generate multiple faults at higher levels. For instance if a hypervisor crashes, the monitoring system will see failures of all VNFs as well. Without looking at the complete picture, troubleshooting to investigate the VNF's cause of failure will be in vain. The real root cause of all these failures can only be found once the hypervisor's crash is investigated.

Because the hardware and software are decoupled in NFV, monitoring and troubleshooting the hardware must be performed mostly through the host OS. This differs completely from hardware troubleshooting in legacy networks, which was an integrated function in the operating system running on it. As the network functions from those operating systems are moved to VNF, the hardware troubleshooting functions move towards the host OS, for it runs closest to the hardware. Some aspects, such as monitoring virtual CPU and memory, may still be part of the VNF, but those can help in limited capacity and for hardware troubleshooting the host OS has the best visibility.

The software troubleshooting for the networking functions can add a dimension of complexity because of the multivendor approach and dynamic nature of VNFs. The networking industry has been pushing towards a common set of APIs and models to manage the VNFs, but the support for these are still not fully available in most VNFs. The information that can be pulled off using these APIs aids in basic troubleshooting exercises, but even when you have a standardized way to manage the network, that doesn't imply that debugging is possible using common APIs. For example, some basic level of troubleshooting may involve checking if a route is being learned or if the routing protocol is up. But to troubleshoot the reasons why routing hasn't come up, you may need to use VNF-level debug statements. These debug statements are typically very closely tied to the vendor's implementation. While vendor independence and ability to dynamically and quickly switch between one vendor's VNF to another is an advantage of NFV, this could pose a challenge for troubleshooting if the operations team is not equipped with the required debugging skills. Most monitoring systems today rely on alarms and syslog alerts that are generated by the devices to detect a problem. These logs and alarms can vary in format and content based on the implementation by the vendor. Once again, the fact that VNFs can be dynamic and multivendor can mean that the operational tools need to interpret and understand the messages from each type of devices, as well as be aware of device's life cycle state. Standards-based monitoring techniques, such as the Simple Network Monitoring Protocol (SNMP), can be used to slightly solve this situation, but that is fairly limited in its scope and use.

Virtualization of Network Infrastructure and Services

The first-waves of VNFs that vendors implemented were focused around enabling their current network software to run under a virtualized atmosphere. The VNFs were replicating the classical devices functions and not designed to take advantage of NFV benefits. As implementations matured, the VNFs being offered now are more focused on the functions that they intend to virtualize and are optimized for virtualized deployment and management; they are being developed with NFV knobs and requirements in mind. The sections that follow examine the use of such VNFs and the associated use cases that are being implemented today are beginning to surface. These example case studies focus on three main network technology tracks, and view the transformation in these areas brought by NFV adoption and the motivations behind it.

NFV for Routing Infrastructure

When virtualization of routing is discussed, the view often projected shows that servers running VNFs will replace every device function. In reality, however, NFV cannot bring benefit for the network device whose primary function is high-rate packet switching. As shown in Figure 3-15, the routing and networking functions that involve utilization of CPU processing or memory usage are the ones that are the

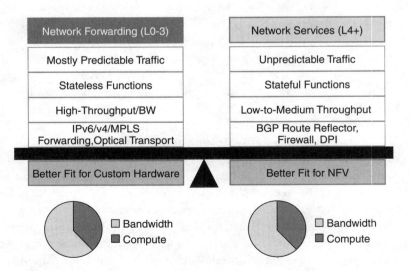

Figure 3-15 *Network Functions That Benefit from Virtualization*

best candidates for NFV transformation of the infrastructure. The underlying infrastructure—such as top of the rack (ToR) switches, spine switches, peering routers between providers, and devices to interconnect NFVI PoPs—are examples of routing and switching devices whose primary function is packet forwarding and aggregation. They are not tapped as candidates for NFV in the initial phase. On the other hand, devices such as BGP route reflectors, provider and customer edge routers, and gateways for voice and video are devices that can benefit from location flexibility and can be optimized through processing power or memory variations. The following sections explain some examples from this category of devices and functions and show how NFV benefits them.

Virtualizing the BGP Routing Plane

In a BGP network, the route reflector (RR) holds a pivotal position and helps manage the large route scale without overloading the edge devices. For example, in networks that are geographically spread out, as is the case for a network across North America, multiple RRs are used (such as East, West, North, South, and Central POP) to offer better location proximity to the edge routers. The RRs hold the routes per region based on their locations. As the network services grow with L3VPN, L2VPN, and IPv6 peering, it might become inefficient for one BGP device to perform the RR functionality for each service and store all the routes—that has led to per-service BGP RR implementations. Additionally, given the critical role of RR in the network, use of redundant BGP RR is always a good design practice, but it obviously means that the number of route reflector devices will double. Whenever a resource, such as memory or CPU performance, is becoming a bottleneck, the only choice is to replace the network device.

In addition, BGP RR is a control plane functionality, where the resource utilization is the CPU and memory, so that makes a BGP route reflector a good choice for NFV-based implementation. What made it even easier for providers to offer this implementation right away was the fact that the RR's role was purely at the control plane and it also had the ability to use memory to scale up the routing table stored. By virtualizing the route-reflectors used for each service, and creating virtual route reflectors (vRR), VNFs now have the following benefits:

- can be placed in one or different hosts
- can be dynamically or permanently relocated to areas closer to the group of edge devices they serve to
- can still have a redundant copy (perhaps on a physically and geographically separate host)

Figure 3-16 shows this view, and as the figure depicts, using NFVs to perform BGP RR functionality offers a much simpler and cleaner solution without compromising performance, independence of operation between the RRs, and high availability while also gaining flexibility and scalability. Any time scale requirements increase, VNF elasticity can be used to cope with it (in contrast to changing the hardware or platform, which would have been the case if legacy equipment was being used). If a new set of services require new BGP RRs to be installed, they can be easily brought up without any effort, and once again the use of NFV helps in a big way by saving time and truck-rolls and allowing for agility of services. Using the VNF redundancy mechanism, upgrade and migration to new code can be done without impact to the network control or data traffic.

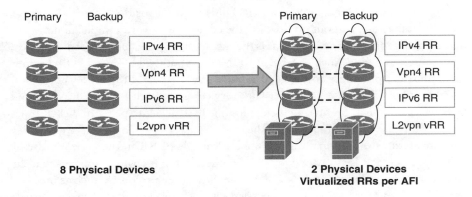

Figure 3-16 *VNF-Based BGP Route-Reflectors*

Virtualizing the Provider Edge (vPE)

Service Provider Edge Equipment (PE) is generally configured with multiple services, feature rich, and serve many customers. They are all bundled on same physical appliance normally called Multiservice Edge. This was implemented to save the operational and capital expenses of multiple routers per service. There are many downsides to this approach, since the scaling capabilities of the device get stretched in multiple dimensions and the increase in scale requirements for one feature or one customer may require a decrease in the scale of some other feature. For the same reason, new features and services can't be added easily, because a change might impact the existing scale and performance. Additionally, from a high availability perspective, unless the customers are dual-homed, the impact of any glitch on the PE can simultaneously impact multiple customers and services.

All of these challenges can be addressed with NFV. In the NFV model, the PE doesn't need to be shared across customers or services. Individual VNFs can serve for implementing a service, a customer, or a combination of both. For example, as shown in Figure 3-17, the L2VPN, L3VPN, and Internet (INET) services for three customers could be deployed as separate independent VNFs. These VNFs can be scaled and managed independently and may or may not be co-located with other services being offered for same customer. If one of the customers (say Customer C) now wants to add L2VPN as a new service, those VNFs can be added at the desired locations without any disturbance to or constraints from the existing VNFs in that location. In addition to the base PE functionalities such as label imposition and disposition, these VNF-based vPE services can be individually scaled, enhanced, tuned, managed, and upgraded.

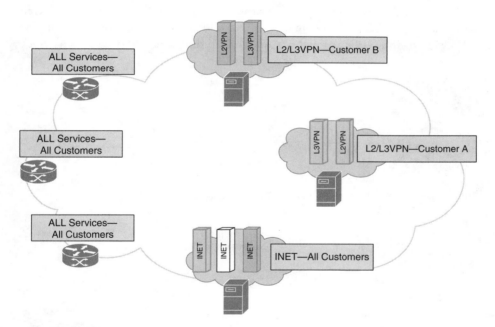

Figure 3-17 *VNF-Based Provider Edge (vPE)*

It should be noted that unlike vRR—which is only a control plane function—in the case of vPE the packet processing performance, latency, and jitter are important, for it needs to handle both data and control traffic. Therefore the vPE selection should consider this aspect of the VNF in addition to the quality-of-service (QoS) capabilities, routing features, and PE functions that the VNF vendor offers to support.

The issue of impacting multiple services and customers with single point of failure is also mitigated by an NFV solution. Failure of one VNF is transparent to the other customers or other services that are running there, and virtualization takes care of isolating the issue. It could also be used to resolve the situation quickly by instantiating a new VNF to restore service.

Virtualization of Customer Premises Equipment

In today's classical enterprise network, the branch office connects to the head office for all communication, and branch-to-branch connectivity needs to traverse via the head office. The customer premises equipment (CPE) appliance at the branch and head office are physical appliances, performing all the functions for this connectivity to work, such as routing , NAT, and QoS. These CPE appliances are managed by the service provider, as shown in Figure 3-18, and are also referred to as managed CPE. If a customer desires to add additional functionality, such as a firewall, or if a service provider wants to introduce a new service such as video

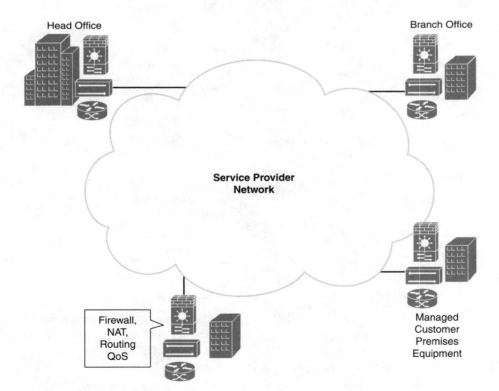

Figure 3-18 *Traditional Enterprise Customer Deployment*

conferencing capabilities to their CPE, then in the majority of cases the service provider may need to replace or upgrade the existing appliance at all the locations, This makes the addition of new service costly and slow to implement, which results in lost time and revenue.

If a virtual CPE (vCPE) device is used instead of the physical one, the enhancements to routing and other features and functionalities are now offloaded to the service provider network, and a simple L2 or L3 device can be deployed at the branch location, as shown in Figure 3-19.

With functionality for this feature now in the service provider data center, the provider has more flexibility and control; this gives the provider the ability to add, delete, or modify functions with agility. Now it is easy to add new services such as a firewall, because CPE is now a VNF and new services can be added to it on the fly. The switch to use an NFV-based vCPE enables business continuity to the end customer and expansion, for the provider now has a cost-effective and faster way to deploy and enable new services. This provides a better customer experience and additional revenue to the provider.

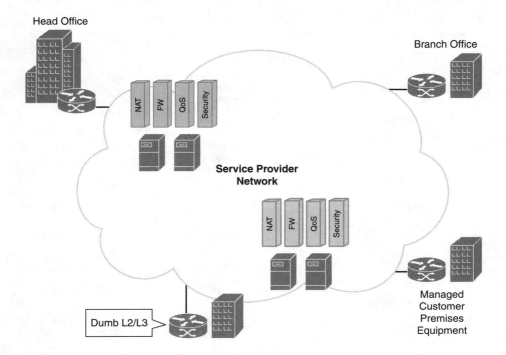

Figure 3-19 *Virtual CPE in Enterprise Network*

Virtual Load Balancers

If the application hosting a website or source of data is sitting on a single server handling client requests, it can start to get overwhelmed by the number of requests as the clients increase or start to query more frequently. Not only can the server's own resources (CPU/Memory) become the limitation, but also the bandwidth available for its uplink can start to choke the traffic, resulting in slow or no response to clients. To overcome these issues and avoid the single point of failure (server and its connectivity), such services are typically offered through multiple sets of servers (or virtualized servers) that are connected through load balancers. Load balancers become important to manage and distribute the traffic load in this client-server data exchange. By utilizing load balancers, the traffic to the application is now distributed across these multiple servers, reducing the load on the single server/application, improving the responsiveness and mitigating the single point of failure as shown in Figure 3-20. The load balancer can further be tuned based on applications that the servers are running and server resource utilization data.

With server virtualization, the servers are typically virtual machine based. They can utilize elasticity to cope with the rise and fall in demand load but can't cross the physical server's boundaries and use the server pool unless load balancers are used. The load balancers can be VNF based and therefore added and configured on demand. This enables the virtualized servers to gain the full efficiency out of the

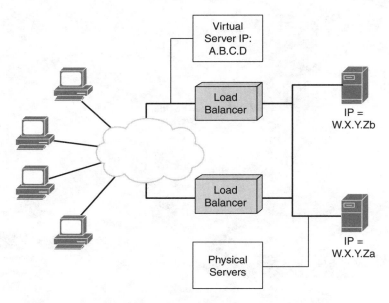

Figure 3-20 *Use of Load Balancers*

deployed servers. The virtualized load balancers can now allow the application's virtual machines to create a replica on any server that is within the reach of the VNF and divert traffic away to it. These load balancers do not have to be in proximity to the physical servers and can provide active hooks for the application to manage the flow of traffic based on user demand. Figure 3-21 shows what the network looks like with the use of virtualized load balancers.

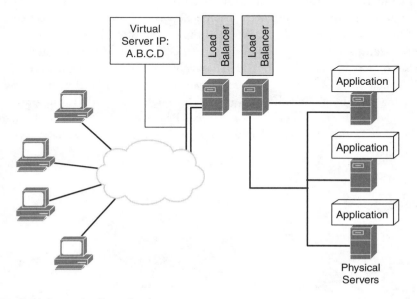

Figure 3-21 *Virtualized Load Balancers*

Virtualization of Triple Play Services

Services provided to residential subscribers, such as triple play services (Internet access, voice over IP, and video) can benefit from NFV adoption. In these deployments, the customer owns (or leases) the CPE device. This device may be serving as the residential gateway (RGW) for Internet data as well as the voice gateway for VoIP, and it provides hooks for video traffic and replaces the traditional set-top box (STB).

CPE devices are limited in their capabilities and features. When the availability of hardware improvements, fixes, and vendor changes result in new varieties of devices, the service provider needs to validate them before offering them to subscribers. Even after the provider switches new subscribers to the new hardware, it may still have to deal with the large subscriber base that may still be using older versions. Replacing those older CPEs is a significant overhead cost. But at the same time, maintaining service consistency and generating new sources of revenue from existing subscribers isn't always possible if they continue to use older CPEs. In some cases, the older devices may not be able to match the capabilities to run the software for new service. These multiple reasons hamper the growth aspects that a provider could potentially offer.

Using NFV can remove these road blocks. The CPE can be generic hardware and not tied to a vendor for its features and functionalities. The CPE needs to host the VNF that would provide the basic consumer services. Most of the services can then be offloaded to servers in a data center at the central office locations. As shown in Figure 3-22, the VNF on central office servers could be used to implement the current set of services as well as provide an easy and scalable way for the providers to provide new services. The consumer can benefit from this model by accessing and managing their home network and gateway through the cloud. To the provider, it opens up doors for many new services that can be marketed and produced at a quick pace—services such as a home firewall management, personal media storage, and cloud video recording.

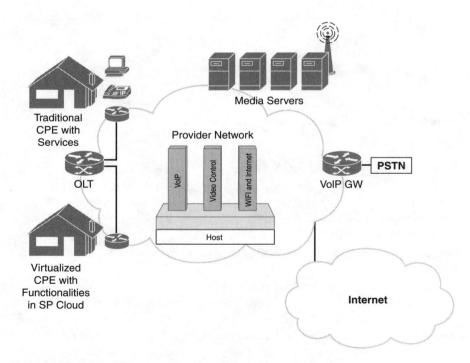

Figure 3-22 *Virtualized Triple Play Services*

Virtualization of Content Delivery Network Devices

Delivery of bandwidth-heavy video content is one of the biggest strains on most networks today. The numbers of viewing devices such as tablets, smartphones, laptops, and TVs, have dramatically increased over the last few years. The choices of content and improved viewing features (such as record, pause, rewind, and picture in picture) have caused video traffic to increase dramatically. The strain on networks due to this traffic has also multiplied many times with the demand for high picture quality (HD720p at first, then UHD 4K, and Beyond 4K Ultra HD). For example, Ultra-High-Definition (UHD) consumes almost nine times the bandwidth of standard definition video. One easy way to minimize the strain on the network infrastructure is to position the media servers and caching devices much closer to the subscribers. Akamai, Google/YouTube, and Netflix which are some of the major sources of video traffic, try to place their caching servers or content delivery servers on such strategic locations inside the provider's networks. Netflix's OpenConnect and Akamai's Aura projects are good examples. Not only does this placement reduce the amount of traffic for the service provider, but also it offloads these content providers' servers. Determining the strategic and most optimal location for these caching services can be a complicated process because demands can change in volume and location—especially since mobile video is a big piece of the media traffic. Therefore the operator ends up deploying various caching servers from different content providers, and these caching servers are designed for maximum capacity. The result of this is complexity and waste of resources.

This is where NFV can help. NFV makes the caching servers fluid and elastic. These servers can be placed closest to the user, can vary their caching and capacity, and be multiplied in number if it makes sense to deploy many of these servers to spread over a region. For a live event, or special occasions the virtualized caching servers is allowed to expand their resources, and during off peak times the resources could be used elsewhere.

Virtualization of Network Security

Network security functions such as firewalls, intrusion detection systems (IDS), DDoS detection and scrubbing functions, and deep packet inspection (DPI) may have a lot of added value if they are virtualized. VNFs for these functions can be placed at diverse and strategic locations and by utilizing the benefits of NFV these functions offer a level of flexibility and on-demand scalability that wasn't previously possible.

Virtualization of Network Infrastructure Protection

Protecting the network infrastructure against attacks, especially distributed denial of service attacks, is an important aspect of network security and availability. DDoS attacks can involve sending high aggregate volume (called volumetric attacks) or targeting exploitation of a protocol vulnerability (called application attacks). These attacks need to be detected, and then the suspicious traffic needs to be diverted to scrubbing centers to be filtered. Depending on the type of DDoS attack, detection and scrubbing should take place as close to the network boundary as possible or close to the network asset, server, or application that is being protected. However, placing a detection and scrubbing network device at a wide range of diverse locations creates a cost challenge and forces the designers to be selective about the placement. Virtualization of these functions eases off the constraints and allows for positioning the DDoS detection and scrubbing VNFs at network peering points, transit points, and network devices (including firewalls, routers, and servers). These VNFs can also easily relocated and added to the traffic path by altering the service chaining without disrupting an existing design on a need basis.

Virtualization of Network Firewall

The traditional firewall appliance in an enterprise or service provider customer is targeted to be deployed at the edge of the network to protect the internal infrastructure. The role of the firewall appliance is to protect against undesired access to the internal infrastructure. These traditional firewalls are usually deployed at the network perimeter to optimize the number of devices, but with all of the traffic passing through them, the firewalls can become a bottleneck. The capacity, capability, and location of firewall function can benefit from NFV implementation. With virtualized firewall functionality, it is possible to place the firewall closer to the hosts or at the edge of the network. The capacity of these virtual firewalls can be scaled up if traffic surges. The providers are also free to choose a firewall from any vendor who offers it as a standalone VNF without bundling it together with other device functions.

Virtualization of Intrusion Protection

Intrusion detection systems (IDS) and intrusion prevention systems (IPS) are needed to monitor the traffic path or be in the path itself to block off unwanted content or detect suspicious and out of policy activities. These devices need to stay ahead of the curve and be updated to provide the best protection. Yet the challenges of the physical network get in the way of the quest for fast adoption. NFV is a natural transition path for these types of applications and helps in more than one way. For example, because IPS is in the traffic path, it may be required to offer higher capacity at certain times. NFV provides a simple solution through elasticity. Another example is easy upgrades to the speeds that the network demands. For such upgrades, in addition to pushing out new signatures and rule updates, the whole software can be upgraded more frequently by creating a new VNF and connecting that to the network with no disruption to the network traffic. This enables an always updated intrusion protection system and offers better security to the network infrastructure. Some products that currently offer this are Cisco's Next Generation IPS (NGIPSv) and IBM's Security Network IPS (VNF flavor of XGS).

Virtualization of Mobile Communication Networks

The demand for mobile-based services has increased exponentially, creating the requirement for faster and better mobile networks. These requirements have forced mobile technologies to evolve and improve their networks and keep moving to new standards that support the new services. The innovations, such as 5th generation (5G) mobile technology, that enable this network evolution require building new network architectures and creating new services. Mobile providers have been trying to build networks and infrastructures that are flexible and can evolve without heavy re-investment and upgrades. This makes mobile communication networks likely to be tapped as the first adopters of NFV, for they need its features. Figure 3-23 shows a high-level view of long-term evolution (LTE) architecture, and as the figure shows, there are number of functional blocks involved in the mobile network. Three main areas in this

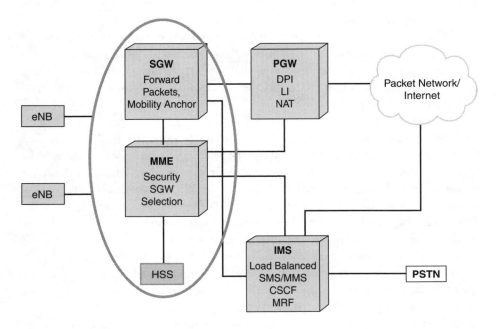

Figure 3-23 *LTE Network Architecture and Functional Blocks*

architecture of mobile networks can benefit by transitioning to NFV-based implementation of their functions:

- virtualization of Evolved Packet Core
- virtualizing IP multimedia subsystems
- virtualizing C-RAN

Virtualization of Evolved Packet Core

Evolved packet core (EPC) has the blocks such as Mobile Management Entity (MME), Serving Gateway (SGW), and PGW. These blocks have multiple functions that are grouped together. In traditional deployments these functional groups are offered by a single device. For example, one hardware device deployed as PGW will perform NAT, IP allocation, lawful intercept, firewall, and packet inspection functionalities.

All of these individual functions and services do not have to be correlated. The requirement to upgrade one of them shouldn't force the mobile service provider to upgrade the entire set that is being offered through the single physical device.

This reasoning alone justifies the case for using NFV. The functions that are part of SGW, PGW, and MME can each be implemented as a VNF, which can enable it to be scaled, upgraded, and updated independently. This also opens up the opportunity for the mobile provider to choose the most suitable version offered by any vendor. It can also combine these into a multi-vendor implementation of what was a single vendor device in its legacy hardware network. The virtualization flavor of these blocks is referred to as virtualized EPC or vEPC. Figure 3-24 shows how the LTE architecture looks with vEPC.

The vEPC can now be designed to benefit from other NFV values, especially high availability, elasticity, modularity, and localization. For example, the PGW is looked upon a single centralized entity for data-plane functionalities. All the traffic must be forwarded through it, even traffic between two pieces of user equipment (UE). Yet it is required to be closer to the Internet boundary. NFV offers a cost-effective way to ungroup these roles and move some of the PGW functionalities away from the Internet boundary and closer to the subscriber. That lessens the unnecessary traffic burden on the network, reduces the overall latency for the user-to-user traffic, and simplifies the network as well. With traditional hardware, operators had to pay for all of the device functions even if they were not using some of them. Through the use of modularity, operators can choose to completely drop the functions they aren't using and always add them back if necessary.

Overall, the advantages of transforming a mobile network's packet core to an NFV-based deployment include lowering capital and operational expenses and

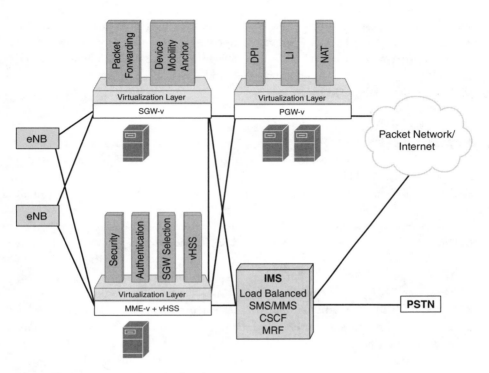

Figure 3-24 *Virtualized Evolved Packet Core*

providing simplification. The transformation can be done in phases, and a hybrid implementation can exist as an interim option; for example, a new virtualized-MME (MME-v) implementing all of the MME subfunctions can be added in parallel to the physical MME appliance, and eNodeB can be moved to the this MME-v gradually. Once the transition for a function is complete, other optimizations and benefits can be planned by using the VNFs that implement the subfunctions.

Virtualizing the IP Multimedia Subsystem

To work with circuit-switched domain, the IP multimedia subsystem (IMS) is added to EPC. The IMS functional block has many subfunctions grouped together. For example, IMS performs call session and control functions (CSCF) through the use of an SIP server and proxy and media resource functions (MRF) such as playing ring tones or conferencing voice mixing. The challenge here is no different than that of EPC, the need to scale or upgrade one of the sub-blocks has forced operators to look for a full replacement of the IMS hardware and search for a vendor that can work smoothly with the remaining EPC infrastructure and meet the current and future growth requirements. The NFV solution, which decouples hardware from software and then offers modularity that allows choosing the functions to implement from a range of vendors, makes a very good use case for mobile operators to choose virtualized IMS functionality (IMS-v).

Virtualizing C-RAN

In the LTE, the radio access layer is referred to as Evolved UMTS Terrestrial Radio Access Network (E-UTRAN), and the nodes are called Evolved Node B (eNodeB, or eNB). The eNB has one or multiple remote radio heads (RRHs), which perform all of the radio functions for the cell cite. This RRH connects to a baseband unit (BBU) to handle and process these signals and connect with the EPC. Before 3G networks, BBU was part of same device that performed RRH, but once 3G allowed it to be split up the BBU could now connect with multiple radio sites and expand its domain.

More recently, Centralized-Remote Access Network (C-RAN) was introduced, which moved BBU to the central office (CO) and allowed it to connect to multiple RRH via dark fiber or other similar means. For a mobile network operator, this brings many advantages; the users continue to stay within the same BBU's domain for a much larger number of cells allowing for possibilities, such as a Co-Operative Multipoint (CoMP), which allows users to connect with multiple RRHs and utilize the available capacity in better way. On the other hand, this also means that BBU has a more crucial role in the network, by serving a much bigger area and many more customers. That makes the BBU a good fit for a device that can benefit from NFV. This allows the BBU to be deployed with resiliency at a protocol level (presuming that each of its protocols is being implemented as a separate VNF). Even if the entire BBU is packaged as a single VNF, it still offers a cost-efficient, high-availability implementation by presenting resiliency without requiring deployment of duplicate BBUs. One other problem that an NFV implementation solves is the running expense that RAN/C-RAN requires. In mobile networks the C-RAN is considered one of the main contributors to operating and ownership expenses [7], and one reason is that these systems have to be overprovisioned for peak demand rate. This is solved by the NFV-based deployment of BBU. When the number of customers in its domain increases and decreases based on time, day, and event (as this clients are all mobile), a virtualized BBU can follow the demand pattern by using elasticity. Also the hardware can now be shared between different BBUs that may be collocated in a central office, as they can share the NFVI infrastructure while serving separate sets of RRH. Additionally, if a control protocol needs to be added or modified to interact to a new generation of mobile devices, a virtualized BBU doesn't need to be replaced. The VNFs can implement their functions and simply update. Figure 3-25 shows the view of

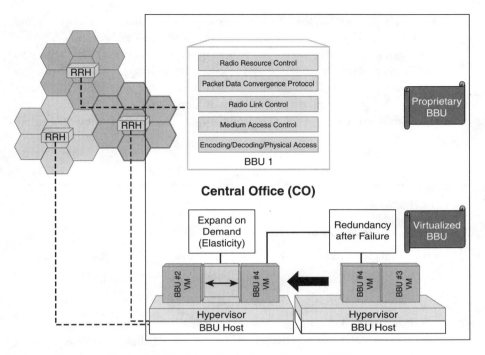

Figure 3-25 *eNodeB In C-RAN, using Physical and NFV-Based BBU*

eNodeB with the BBU and RRH functionalities, and shows a comparison of physical proprietary BBU versus virtualized BBU options.

Summary

NFV has its roots in server virtualization and shares a lot of parallels with it. However, notice that in NFV the goals and targets are prioritized differently. In this chapter, we studied the design criteria and goals that an NFV network should focus on. Understanding the common roots with server virtualization helps, but the differences in goals compared to network functions virtualization are subtle and important. While server virtualization strives to achieve business continuity, fault tolerance, and the agility of growth, NFV gives top priority to high availability (achieving five to six 9s), agility of service deployment, NEBS compliance, and carrier grade service. Similarly, the expertise of designing a classical network is important when it comes to designing NFV networks, but to get the most from the benefits of NFV, a new set of rules, criteria, and goals must be at the forefront of planning and designing.

Despite the great benefits that NFV brings, deployments based around NFV can provide a number of challenges. This chapter examined those challenges and noted that NFV deployments are much different from those of a classical network. It is critical to anticipate them ahead of time and plan ways to work around them and solve them.

This chapter also looked at how NFV is finding use cases in various aspects of networking. The design criteria and challenges combined with the benefits and market demands are resulting in NFV finding value for implementing traditional network functions.

References

Please refer to the following for additional information:

[1] https://tools.ietf.org/html/rfc6325

[2] http://www.ieee802.org/3/ad/public/mar99/seaman_1_0399.pdf

[3] http://www.code42.com/crashplan/medialifespan/

[4] http://www.ciscoknowledgenetwork.com/files/477_11-11-2014-CiscoGCID raftDeck2013-2018_CKN.pdf?PRIORITY_CODE=?TB_iframe=true

[5] http://www.gnu.org/philosophy/free-sw.html

[6] https://tools.ietf.org/html/draft-krishnan-nfvrg-real-time-analytics-orch-01

[7] http://www.cisco.com/c/en/us/solutions/collateral/service-provider/ visual-networking-index-vni/VNI_Hyperconnectivity_WP.html

Review Questions

Use the questions here to review what you learned in the chapter. The correct answers are found in Appendix A, "Answers to Review Questions."

1. What is the typical life cycle for servers and storage devices in a data center?

   a. one year

   b. ten to fifteen years

   c. three to five years

   d. depends on the users' demand

2. List three types of license management that are commonly used?

    a. cloud-based

    b. in-house

    c. fog based

    d. built-in to the device

    e. MANO layer managed

3. What are the four main levels to implement redundancy in an NFV network?

    a. VNF level redundancy,

    b. host OS level redundancy

    c. hardware level redundancy,

    d. infrastructure level redundancy

    e. hypervisor level redundancy

    f. protocol level redundancy

4. What does the acronym YANG stand for

    a. Yocto Assisted Next Generation

    b. Yet Another Next Generation

    c. Yet Another New Generation

    d. Yanked Assisted Network Generation

5. What does the term introspective firewall refer to?

    a. It refers to firewall in the hypervisor, protecting the path the data takes to reach each VM.

    b. It refers to the physical firewall that is protecting a virtual server

    c. It refers to a virtual firewall that is protecting a physical server

    d. It's a virtual firewall that is protecting the VIM functional block

6. What are the two main components of E-Node-B?

    a. Packet Gateway (PGW) and Servicing Gateway (SGW)

    b. Evolved Packet Core (EPC) and Packet Gateway (PGW)

    c. Remote Radio Head (RRH) and Baseband Unit (BBU)

    d. Mobile Media Server (MMS) and Packet Gateway (PGW)

    e. Mobile Media Server (MMS) and Servicing Gateway (SGW)

7. Between a virtual machine and container, name any two advantages of one over the other.

   a. Container: faster boot time and lightweight; virtual machine: better isolation and portability

   b. Container: slower boot time and lightweight; virtual machine: weaker isolation and portability

   c. Container: better isolation time and portability; virtual machine: weaker isolation and faster boot

   d. Container: better isolation and portability; virtual machine: faster boot time and lightweight

Chapter 4

NFV Deployment in the Cloud

Cloud-based service offerings have seen an increase over the recent years. Network functions virtualization (NFV) is benefiting from this shift to the cloud because it allows network functions to be implemented anytime and anywhere they may be needed. The deployment, management, and orchestration of the network functions play a major role in NFV implementation in the cloud. These deployments generally deal with massive scale. They are highly automated and work with a range of vendors and device types.

The main topics covered in this chapter are:

- Architecture and deployment of cloud-based virtualization infrastructure
- Management and orchestration in NFV framework
- Orchestration, deployment, and management of NFV infrastructure
- The tools commonly used to orchestrate and deploy NFV infrastructure and Network Services
- Life cycle management of virtualized network functions

What's in a Cloud?

The term cloud is often used to represent an entire infrastructure that comprises servers, networking, storage, the operating system, and the management applications. This cloud infrastructure can be confined to one location or spread over multiple geographically diverse locations, providing a single virtualized platform for deploying applications and virtualized network functions (VNFs). This infrastructure may be privately owned and operated by one company that uses it to host its own applications and VNFs, hosted by a group of companies, offered publicly as a commodity, or there may be a combination of public and private ownership. To the end user, the applications and network functions that have traditionally been running on their local environment are now pushed out to these hosted resources, which may be in close proximity or a very remote location that is not physically accessible to them, but this distance and visibility is immaterial—hence the term cloud.

Just as server virtualization offers efficiency gain by sharing single server resources among many applications, cloud-based virtualization takes it to the next level and makes it possible to amplify this benefit by consolidating all the hardware resources (local or remote) and managing and operating them as a single entity. Figure 4-1 shows this transformation, reflecting how server virtualization by separate organizations may be moved to the cloud-based virtualization. The National Institute of Science and Technology (NIST) provides a precise definition of cloud (or cloud computing, which is another way to refer to this same concept):

> Cloud computing is a model for enabling convenient, on-demand network access to a shared pool of configurable computing resources (e.g., networks, servers, storage, applications, and services) that can be rapidly provisioned and released with minimal management effort or service provider interaction. (http://www.nist.gov/itl/cloud/)

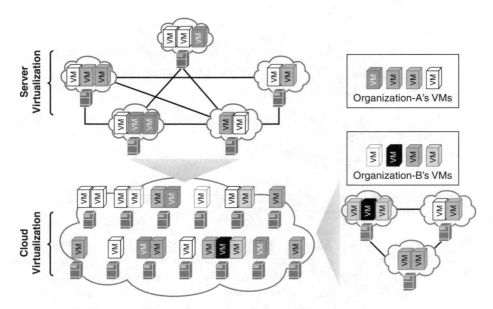

Figure 4-1 *Server Virtualization versus Cloud-Based Virtualization*

Characteristics of Cloud

Based on the previous definition of the term cloud, any infrastructure that is not local to the user may qualify as a cloud. However, a more precise classification for a cloud demands that the infrastructure and service offer some essential characteristics. NIST defines five essential characteristics for a cloud [1]:

- **On-demand deployment:** It should be possible for the user to deploy a new cloud service without requiring any human intervention by the service provider. For example, if users want to add extra capacity to the cloud-hosted storage, they shall be able to do that on their own, as needed.

- **Broad network access:** A cloud environment should be accessible and available through the network. This access may not always be through the public Internet and may be contained within an intranet, but since one of the goals of moving a service to a cloud is to make it easily accessible to authorized users, the availability over the network is implied and required. Since a variety of hosts may be used on the client side, the cloud service shall be able to work with those hosts and offer an environment that can work with wide range of devices over the network.

- **Scalability and elasticity:** A cloud-based service should not be confined to physical device limitations. It should be possible to expand the amount of resources that the service offers. Of course, this will require that the underlying infrastructure that hosts the service is available to meet this requirement, but for a user of the cloud service the limitations of the physical infrastructure should be masked out, and scalability and elasticity should be easily achieved. A good example of this is the storage services available through Rackspace— the user of the service can expand the amount of storage needed and would simply expect that the storage servers are predeployed and available to meet those requests.

- **Pooling of resources:** The cloud infrastructure should be able to pool resources across physical boundaries. Unless required by regulations or security policies, the infrastructure should be able to pool resources not constrained within a physical geography. This characteristic is important to meet the elasticity requirement of the cloud service that was mentioned earlier.

- **Resource monitoring**: Since resources allocated to the cloud are elastic and found in diverse locations, the utilization and usage of those resources can become obscure, resulting in inefficiencies. Therefore, one requirement for cloud-based service is the ability to monitor and measure resource utilization across the cloud deployment.

Cloud-Based Services

With the possibility of creating infrastructure to offer cloud services, many possibilities for new business models open up. A number of companies have started various types of cloud-based services, and these companies generally are referred to as cloud service providers (CSPs). A number of applications are also available to facilitate the deployment of a contained cloud type environment within an organization.

Generally speaking, most applications and services running either on a local computer or on a server in a data center can be moved to the cloud-based model, as long as resources that the application needs (for example, computing, networking, and storage) are available.

There are multiple cloud-based services offered by the CSPs that cater to different application requirements and business needs. Let's examine some of the commonly referenced categories of cloud services.

Infrastructure as a Service (IaaS)

A cloud offering that provides the basic infrastructure to host the application is referred to as infrastructure as a service (IaaS). This type of offering leaves decisions regarding the use of the infrastructure to the users and empowers them by offering a flexible amount of resources they can pool together to run their operating system and applications on those resources. Rackspace, Amazon Web Services (AWS), and Microsoft Azure are a few popular names that offer IaaS.

Platform as a Service (PaaS)

This offering provides the customer the ability to host the application without the need to manage the underlying infrastructure and software, such as the operating system and the hardware running this application. Customers utilizing this service do not need to worry about the infrastructure and can view it as a black box, while managing only the application they will deploy on this platform.

Software as a Service (SaaS)

Another very common and widely used service is software as a service (SaaS), which is offered by the likes of Microsoft, Google, Salesforce, and many others. In this service, predeployed software (for example, the MS-Office suite in the case of Office365) is available in a cloud-hosted environment. The users of SaaS simply employ the software over a network connection and have no need to install the software/application or manage it on their local computer. The upgrade and patches for the software are all handled in the cloud by the providers and from the end-users' perspective, they are just utilizing this application with the provider maintained software.

Figure 4-2 shows these three variations of cloud-based services. As the figure shows, in the case of IaaS the provider manages the underlying cloud infrastructure, while SaaS offers a complete solution where the user simply employs the software's environment. PaaS offers a middle ground between IaaS and SaaS and offers a platform managed by the CSP that the user can consume and build their environment and applications on top of this service.

These three basic categories are defined [1] and understood well across the cloud services industry. However many other categories have evolved. Some of the other popular cloud-based services being offered include:

- **Storage as a service (StaaS)**: Google Drive, iCloud, box, dropbox, and others are some very popular examples of this type of service, where the CSP doesn't offer a computing or networking resource and offers purely storage services that can be used to store user data.

- **Backup as a service**: Some companies, such as AT&T, Amazon, EMC, and Fujitsu, offer storage service in a different way by making available a remote, encrypted, highly available, and secure backup storage, dubbed backup as a service (BaaS).

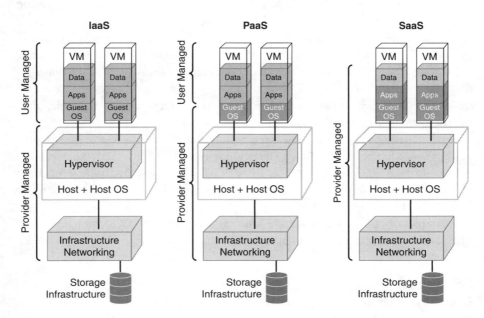

Figure 4-2 *Cloud-Based Services*

Cloud Deployment Models

The main advantage of a cloud-hosted service is that it pools the needed resources and uses them as common shared entities, which can be scaled, upgraded, made accessible, and managed without very tight geographic and physical boundaries. Therefore, cloud-based hosting is available through publicly offered services deployed by massive data centers, or through basic services offered through a small number of servers accessible to a limited group of users. Consequently, this leads to different deployment and sharing models for such services, based on the targeted users, type of application, type of service, and scope of access that the deployment should need. Let's examine the four general categories in which cloud deployments are categorized.

Public Cloud

For many medium and small organizations, managing their own cloud is not a cost-effective option. Public clouds offer these companies the means to use virtualization through publicly available resources. These resources, offered by CSPs, can host their applications, storage, networks, databases and similar items on a cloud infrastructure that is maintained, managed, and operated by the CSP. Opting for a CSP-based public cloud versus maintaining a private cloud is very much analogous to renting versus buying a house. With public cloud, the overhead of maintaining the entire hardware infrastructure (comprising computing, networking, and storage, etc.) and the tools that are required to manage them, operational costs, etc. is completely offloaded to the provider. The user is simply a tenant in the CSP's cloud implementation and shares the resources with other tenants. Other advantages that a public cloud offers is the broader network access (since the cloud is accessed through public Internet), data backup, and vendor backed service guarantee.

In all these ways, a public cloud is the best option when costs and overhead must be kept low. On the other hand, public clouds present some level of vulnerability because of possible security breaches or hacking. There have been many incidents of security compromises resulting in stealing of publicly hosted (but not publicly available) data.

Examples of public clouds include Amazon Web Services (AWS), Google Cloud, Microsoft Azure, Rackspace, and many others.

Private Cloud

A private cloud is most suitably described by the virtualization of an organization's application and networking into one or multiple locations, which are managed, operated, and utilized by the organization itself. This approach offers complete independence, isolation, and privacy, but it also brings in the overhead necessary to acquire, manage, and operate the cloud infrastructure and virtualization tools on top of managing the virtualized devices and network.

This may be desirable for large organizations, where the overhead cost is outweighed by the advantages of the cloud. Especially organizations dealing with financial and military information may require higher levels of security and isolation and avoid putting their data and compute in a publicly accessible domain.

While private clouds offer much more control over the level of isolation, they do not have the cost benefit of offloading the management, maintenance, upgrade, and deployment of the infrastructure.

Several platforms available today offer implementation and management of privately hosted clouds. The choice between these could be based on licensing costs, roadmaps, availability of support, and ease of use. Some of the more commonly used platforms for deploying private clouds are VMware's vSphere and OpenStack (open source).

Hybrid Clouds

Hybrid clouds offer the best of both public and private worlds. In the case of hybrids, the cloud can be setup to use CSP-offered resources for part of the services that are running in the cloud, while continuing to use privately hosted cloud services for more sensitive applications. This allows the hybrid cloud to scale much better compared to a privately hosted cloud, yet it still allows some level of management and control by keeping some data and applications on the private cloud. The combination of hybrid of the two clouds operates as one entity, and the boundaries and distinctions are managed and defined purely by the cloud administrator. To the end-user, the hybrid cloud is seen as one cloud where applications are run, data is stored, and networks configured. Most private cloud management and deployment tools are able to interact with public clouds using published application programming Interfaces (APIs) and present the hybrid cloud model to the user.

Community Clouds

A community cloud is best defined as a combination of private clouds that is shared between a closed group. The operations, management, and maintenance of the cloud may be a shared responsibility within the group, or it may be delegated to one of the members or to a provider. A community cloud is therefore a middle ground between public and private, since it is not limited to one company or organization, but it is not offered or available publicly either.

Figure 4-3 compares the cloud deployment models described. Each of the clouds shown, whether in the public or private restricted domain, are expected to be

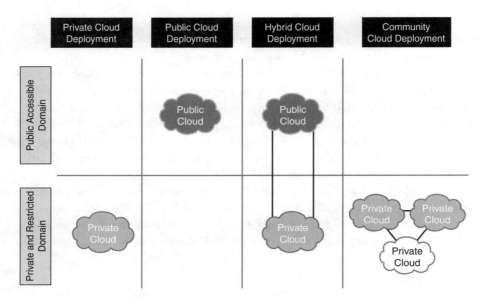

Figure 4-3 *Cloud Deployment Models*

compliant to the basic definition of a cloud. These clouds are not restricted to one location or one physical infrastructure, and each of them may span across regions. For example, the private cloud deployment may be spread over multiple continents but managed as a single cloud.

NFV and Cloud

Virtualization of network functions has use cases for all of the cloud deployment categories described earlier. Many service providers are deploying infrastructure to host services that they offer to their customers. Service providers can use a private cloud to offer a set of services to their consumers; for example an Internet service provider (ISP) may implement a private cloud that has predefined templates for Customer Gateway (CGW), firewall, and perhaps even optional add-ons like content storage, remote management, or others. This combination of networking and data applications can be offered as a package to its Internet customers, who can then request these functions at any time. The service provider's (SP's) private cloud simply spins up new virtual machines dynamically, based on the customer's request. Many other examples of NFV cloud–based services that are being tapped are services such as virtual customer premises equipment (vCPE), virtual distributed denial-of-service (vDDoS) scrubber, virtual Broadband Network Gateway (vBNG), or Virtual Provider Edge (vPE) router. All of these are candidates for a privately deployed service provider cloud that hosts services for its customers. On the public cloud, the strict requirements of latency and throughput must be considered when hosting with NFV. For market trials or a proof of concept, a public cloud could be an option to show the capabilities of the newly introduced product.

The initial tools and software for deployment and orchestration of applications in the cloud were focused towards standalone applications, as the underlying virtualization infrastructures were from OpenStack and VMware. These applications generally use a single connection to a common (virtual or physical) local area network (LAN) to communicate with each other or externally. Additional, these applications are deployed once and may need reconfiguration or tweaking of their parameters. Deployment and orchestration of NFV, however, is a bit different since the VNF may require multiple connections between each other for implementing the NFV topology. It may require reconfiguration based on changes in the network (for example, change in the prioritization of a traffic, blocking a specific traffic stream, adding more routing neighbors, etc.), that necessitate awareness of other VNFs that are part of this topology.

To deploy NFV in the cloud, the cloud orchestration and deployment applications have to take these additional requirements into account. These applications are not only required to deploy a virtual machine to act as a VNF, but also perform service orchestration and network deployment roles. To understand these requirements that the NFV deployment tools need to fulfill, let's revisit ETSI framework's definition of the management and orchestration block and then analyze the software and tools that fulfill each of these conditions.

Revisiting ETSI Management and Orchestration Block

Chapter 1, "The Journey to Network Functions Virtualization" described the ETSI Framework Architecture for NFV and the blocks defined in it. In that architecture, deployment, orchestration and management fall into the Management and Orchestration (MANO) block's responsibility. This chapter provides more details into the NFV deployment and the popular tools and methods used for implementing these functional-blocks.

Before taking a closer look at these, as a quick refresher let's list the functions of MANO blocks and the purposes behind each of them as shown in Figure 4-4.

MANO blocks are composed of the following:

- Virtualized Infrastructure Manager (VIM)
- Virtualized Network Function Manager (VNFM)
- Network Functions Virtualization Orchestrator (NFVO)

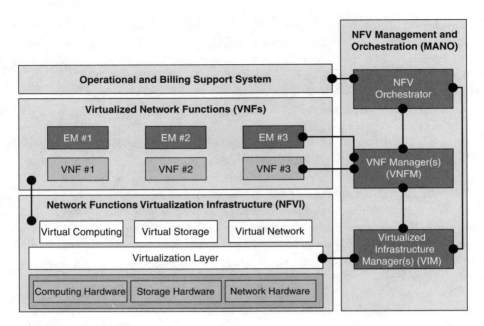

Figure 4-4 *ETSI NFV Architecture Framework*

A VIMs interacts directly with the NFV Infrastructure (NFVI) Block (physical devices, host OS, and Virtualization Layer) and is tasked with deploying and managing these NFVI elements. Software that is implementing VIM functionality must be able to maintain an inventory of the physical resources as well as keep track of their utilization and the allocation of these resources to virtualization pools. It should be highlighted here that because networking hardware and the virtualized networking pool are being managed by VIM, it is one of the VIM's roles to orchestrate the virtual links connecting the VNFs.

VNFM has the responsibility for creation, deletion, and updating of VNF resources, essentially controlling the VNF's life cycle.

The NFV Orchestrator (NFVO) performs resource and service orchestration, working directly with VIM or engaging the VNFM Block. As a refresher, service orchestration implies that NFVO will coordinate the service components deployed (VNF, links between VNFs, connectivity information between them) and manage the entire service's life cycle. Note that resource orchestration by NFVO implies that it will oversee the allocation of resources, and monitor the allocation needed for the services it's managing. In the ETSI framework at the time of this writing, these NFVO functionalities are bundled together. However, ETSI has indicated that they may split these two functionalities into two separate functional blocks at a later time.

Table 4-1 summarizes these roles.

Table 4-1 *Responsibilities of MANO Functional-Blocks*

Functional-Block	Responsibilities
VIM	• Maintaining hardware repository (storage, computing, and networking)
	• Keeping track of the allocation to the virtualized pool for these resources
	• Interacting with and managing the hypervisor
	• Keeping track of hardware utilization and state
	• Working with other functional-blocks to implement VNF connectivity through the virtual network
VNFM	• Managing VNF's life cycle
NFVO	• Resource orchestration
	• Service orchestration
	• Working with other blocks to orchestrate the network and keeping an end-to-end view of the network

MANO Data Repositories

In addition to the functional blocks mentioned earlier, ETSI also describes grouping for the operational and orchestration data, which it refers to as data repositories. These repositories store information used for orchestrating, run time instance's environment, as well as resources being utilized or available. ETSI architecture defines four groups of repositories, as shown in Figure 4-5. Each of this repositories are discussed in detail in the next section.

NFV Service Catalogue

The NFV Service Catalogue (NS Catalogue) is a collection of repositories that defines the parameters for the end-to-end deployment of a network service. The term network service is often misused in various contexts. For purpose of the text here and for NFV in general, network service implies the combination of network functions interconnected to offer a network-based service to the end user. The description of network service is therefore a description of these network functions, their connectivity and topology, and the specifications for their operation and deployment: for example, a virtual private network (VPN) service or an Internet gateway service comprising Network Address Translation (NAT), firewall (FW), or other functions.

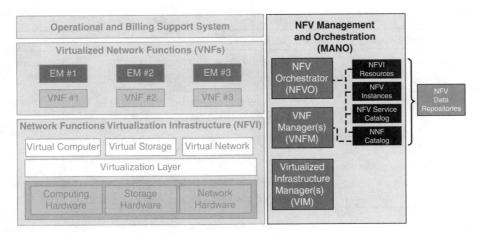

Figure 4-5 *MANO Data Repository*

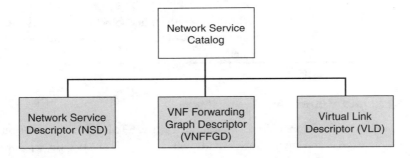

Figure 4-6 *Network Services Catalogue*

NS Catalogue is used by the NFVO functional block when orchestrating a network service. The information contained in the templates that the NS Catalogue bundles together is used to define the exact parameters for the VNFs, links, life cycle, scalability, and topologies that need to exist for offering the network service. ETSI refers these repositories as *Descriptors*. The NS Catalogue groups together three types of descriptors or data sets as shown in Figure 4-6, which are described next.

Descriptors and Catalogues

A descriptor is a repository of templates that are used to define the orchestration parameters. These descriptors can be listed out using a data formatting language such as Yet Another Next Generation (YANG) or XML.

A catalogue represents a grouping of the descriptor repositories. Multiple versions of descriptors can exist in a catalogue.

Virtual Link Descriptor (VLD)

A Virtual Link Descriptor (VLD) offers a deployment template for the resources needed to interconnect the VNFs that are part of a network service and the service endpoints. In addition to the virtual end-points, the VLD also defines the resources needed to connect the VNFs to the physical network function (PNF) devices if those physical devices are playing a role in providing the network service. By defining these parameters, the orchestration part of MANO (NFVO) knows which type of interfaces need to be requested for implementing the service. When NFVO passes this information about link requirements along with the other parameters, like VNF resources, down to the VIM (which is the MANO functional block that is managing the infrastructure) then the VIM is able to appropriately select the host that provides the appropriate resources to meet these needs.

Service Endpoints

If you consider the NFV service as a black box, the service endpoints would be the entry and exit points for that black box.

VNF Forwarding Graph Descriptor (VNFFGD)

While VLD describes the parameters for the links to connect the VNF, PNF, and endpoints, it doesn't describe how those links shall interconnect these entities. This information is described by the VNFFGD template, which carries the topology information using the links described in the VLD. For example, the VLD may describe that you need two interfaces capable of 100G and 1G capability, and then the VNFFGD describes that the 100G link interconnects the two VNFs for data, while the 1G link connects to both of them for management traffic.

Network Service Descriptor (NSD)

NSD describes a network service and pieces together the templates that define the deployment parameters for the entire service. Some examples of the parameters that are defined in NSD are the scaling policy and life cycle event. The scaling policy determines the conditions under which the service needs to be scaled and the actions needed to achieve the scaling. The life cycle event defines the scripts, actions, and behavior for the various life cycle events of the service. NSD defines the service at a high level, in addition to parameters relevant to the service, it also cross-references other descriptors that it use to constitute the service , such as the VNF Descriptor, VNF Forwarding Graph Descriptor, Physical Network Function Descriptor, and Virtual Link Descriptor, as shown in Figure 4-7.

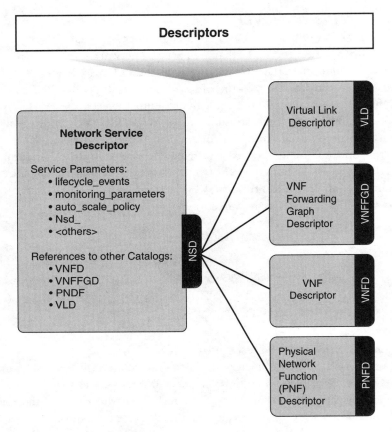

Figure 4-7 *Network Services Descriptor*

VNF Catalogue

The VNF Catalogue is the repository of VNF packages. Each VNF package corresponds to a VNF Descriptor (VNFD), which is used to define the deployment parameters for the VNF, such as CPU resource, memory, and storage requirements, as well as operational behavior such as lifecycle_events (which describe the behavior for life cycle events of the VNF) or policies for elasticity. A VNF catalogue is composed of multiple VNF packages as shown Figure 4-8.

The VNF Package also contains additional information about the image for the VNF and its initial configuration parameters. This VNF Package presents the

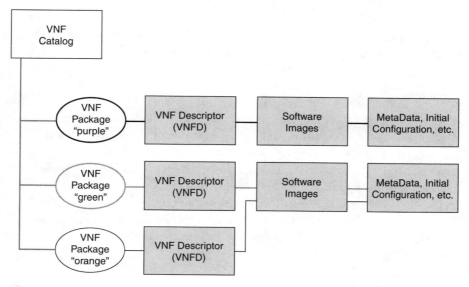

Figure 4-8 *VNF Catalogue*

complete picture of the VNF, by combining the deployment and operational parameters (from the VNFD), the image to be used for it, and the configuration that it should be deployed with. Take the example of a VNF image that can function as a virtual router. This same image can be used to deploy a virtual route reflector (high memory and high CPU requirements) as well as a virtual Provider Core router (low memory and high CPU requirements). These parameters are defined in the VNFD and therefore both of these implementations could be distinct packages, differentiated by the VNFD. The VNF Catalogue can have multiple VNF Packages (each package has exactly one VNFD and vice versa).

The information in the VNF Catalogue is used by both NFVO and VNFM. NFVO uses it to manage the life cycle of the VNFs. For example, when instantiating a new VNF that is part of a service, it communicates the requirement combined with the other pieces of information from NS Catalogue (such as VLD) to the VIM functional block. The VIM functional block then selects and allocates the appropriate needed resources. Similarly, the VNF Catalogue information is also accessible to VNFM, which is the MANO functional block responsible for managing the VNF.

NFV Instances Repository

The two repositories described so far, that is, the NS Catalogue and VNF Catalogue, are used for deploying a network service. Once an instance of a network service is deployed, the information about its running state is stored in the NFV Instances repository. The information in this repository is grouped together and are called *Reports*. The repository has reports for network services (NS Report), VNF states (VNF Report), etc. Any change in the running state of the VNF, links, network service, etc. is updated in the corresponding report in the NFV Instance Repository. For example, changes in the network service state are updated in Network Service Report, changes in the Virtual Link state are updated in VL Report, changes in the topology state are updated in VNFFG Report, and other changes are updated in the corresponding report data structures. Figure 4-9 lists the types of records that ETSI has defined in its NFV architecture at the time of this writing. These records and the parameters that the records group together are listed in depth in ETSI's architecture document [2].

> **Reports**
>
> Reports are repositories of data structures that represent the run-time data for instances created.

NFVI Resources Repository

One of the roles of NFVO described earlier was resource orchestration. This requires NFVO to keep an updated view of the infrastructure resources that are available and at its disposal. Since VIM is the management functional block that interacts directly with the infrastructure, the information about infrastructure resources is available to VIM and provided by it to a repository called the NFVI Resources repository. This repository is then used by NFVO to get a view of resources available, reserved, and allocated.

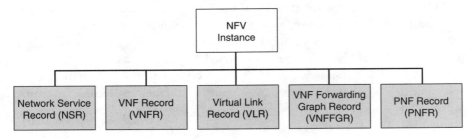

Figure 4-9 *Records Types Defined for NFV Instance Repository*

Note that each VIM has resource information for the NFVI blocks that it is managing, and there can be multiple VIMs functioning in parallel. Therefore the resource information in the NFVI Resources repository is a consolidated view of the resources across the system from all the VIMs.

Putting the Pieces Together

The relationships between the repositories, such as Catalogues, Descriptors, and Reports, and the functional blocks in MANO are summarized in Figure 4-10. As shown, the NS Catalogue and VNF Catalogue are the main sources of data for orchestration of a network service. The NS Catalogue comprises NSD, VLD, and VNFFGD, while the VNF Catalogue consists of VNFD. When an instance of this network service is being created, these Catalogues, as well as the NFVI Resources repository, are utilized by the orchestration functional block (NFVO) for the deployment of this instance. For each of the instances, the reports in the NFV instance repository are created and populated.

Let's take an example to better understand the use of these MANO repositories for the orchestration of an MPLS-VPN service. In this example service, the provider is offering to deploy two virtual PE (vPE) devices as well as a clustered virtual route

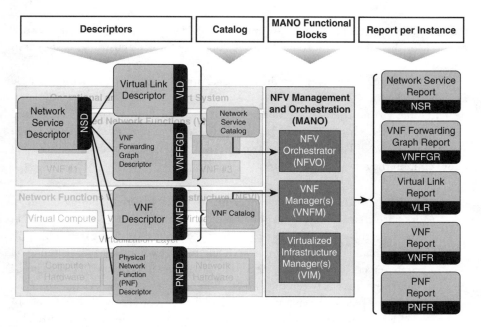

Figure 4-10 *Relationship between MANO Repositories*

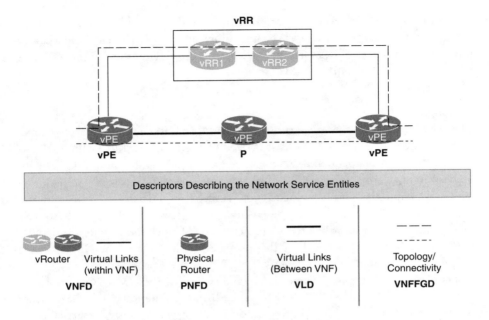

Figure 4-11 *NFV Orchestration for an MPLS-VPN Network*

reflector. The virtual PE devices are interconnected through the physical network core (P) for their data traffic. The deployed topology for each customer is shown in Figure 4-11.

To orchestrate this service, map the NFV descriptors to the entities in the example as shown in Figure 4-11.

The same virtual router VNF image can be used for both virtual PE (vPE) and virtual Route Reflector (vRR) functionalities by defining separate VNFD and then separating the VNF Package for the two applications. In this scenario, the VNFD could contain the following attributes:

- The vRR VNFD may allocate higher memory and lower computing resources to it, since that suits the functionality of a route reflector. Also, as shown in Figure 4-11, this vRR's VNFD may be described to deploy (using the high_availability attribute) two copies of the VNF, and these two copies may be running on separate servers (defined using the affinity attribute). The vRR VNFD also needs to define the links between the two VNF instances. These two virtual machine instances are placed on separate servers, and the interconnecting link and the connectivity point information for links with other VNFs define the vRR VNF. This

VNF is defined using a single package and instantiates one vRR instance. (Note that in this case, two virtual machines are combined to offer one vRR VNF.)

- The vPE VNFD may need high computing power for the deployed instances. It may use the deployment_flavor attribute to define two vPE flavors—defining one of them with higher computing and memory resources more suitable for a central site vPE.

- The links between the VNF instances are defined through the VLD, and in this example the VLD may be describing two different type of links—a low bandwidth link (perhaps 1Gbps) to carry the control plane traffic between the vRR and vPE and high bandwidth links (say 10 or 40 Gbps) for data traffic of the vPE. Since the P router is a physical device in this example, the vPE to P link is describing a VNF to PNF link.

Finally, the topology to connect all VNFs together is defined through the VNFFGD, which classifies the connectivity between the vRR–vPE and vPE–P links shown in Figure 4-11.

A Deeper Look into Descriptors

The descriptors defined by ETSI framework contain various pieces of information. The structure of the information is defined in a hierarchy, and as mentioned previously, Yang or XML formats are some examples of ways to describe the information in the descriptors. At a high level, the information carried in these descriptors can be classified as resource information (for example, capacity for links or CPU resources for virtual machines), connectivity information and information on which parameters should be monitored (also referred to as Key Parameter Index, or KPI).

To get a good idea about how this structure looks and the information contained within, let's take the example of VNFD and describe some of the parameters that it uses. A number of these parameters (called information elements by ETSI) are defined in multiple descriptors and though the definition of that information element is the same, the context changes based on which descriptor it's used in. For example, life cycle_event is used to describe life cycle of VNFD when its employed there, but when implemented as an information element in NSD it refers to the life cycle of the network service.

To communicate a general idea about what type of information elements are defined and how they are used, Table 4-2 lists a few of the parameters defined for VNFD.

For a complete list of information elements for each descriptor and the purpose of these elements, refer to ETSI's documentation.

Table 4-2 *Parameters Defined for VNFD*

Parameter	Definition
vendor	Name of vendor who generated this VNFD
version	Version of VNF software, from the perspective of this VNFD
connection_point	The type of external interface that the VNF offers for connectivity with the virtual_link. For example, connections-points could be management-port and data-interfaces.
virtual_Link	These define the virtual interfaces that are used for connectivity by the VNF. The virtual links reference a connection point that is based on the specification of the VNF. So for the connection points example earlier, the virtual links could be an interface using a e1000 driver and others using DPDK drivers.
lifecycle_event	The behavior (or scripts that shall be used to define those behaviors) in case of certain life cycle events like instantiation, destruction, scaling, etc.
vnf_dependency	If the VNF is dependent on another VNF to offer the functionality, the other virtual function can be defined in the VNFD for this VNF.
monitoring_parameters	This defines the parameters from the VNF that should be monitored to determine its load and if any elasticity and scalability changes need to be made to the VNF. For example, if the VNF is a BGP-RR, then the number of BGP routes, CPU load and available memory within the VNF would be some of the parameters worthy of monitoring. If, say, number of bgp routes are exceeding a threshold, then an instance or memory scaling may be needed for this VNF.
deployment_flavor	This is used to describe different flavors of the deployment for this VNF. Ingredients for a flavor may include vCPU, Memory and Capabilities. For example, in case of a vRR, we may deploy it as a basic level vRR.

FYI: *The term flavor is used by VIM to describe a combination of computing and storage (memory and disk space) resources. These flavors are created and managed by VIM and then made available to virtual machines for their resource requests. In case of a private cloud, VNFM may be able to request VIM to create new flavors as needed. However, in case of a public cloud, the cloud service provider offering infrastructure as a service may have predefined flavors, and VNFM must use one of the available flavors for the virtual machine's creation and resource updates.*

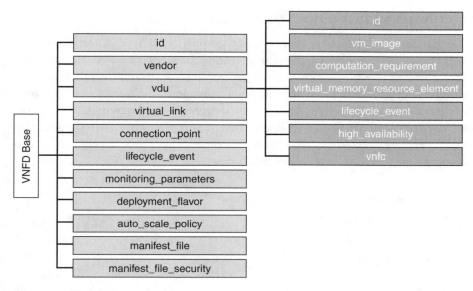

Figure 4-12 *Some of the Information Elements in VNFD*

Figure 4-12 presents a pictorial sample of this for information elements.

Orchestrating, Deploying, and Managing NFV Infrastructure

In Chapter 2, "Virtualization Concepts," the components of NFVI were discussed in-depth. These components, both the hardware and the software portions, form the base of the NFV infrastructure. To orchestrate, deploy, manage, and monitor this infrastructure, a variety of software packages are available today from network vendors and from organizations that represent providers and the open source community. This software is often referred to as a cloud operating system (COS), given that they form the infrastructure for the cloud.

The orchestration and deployment by a cloud operating system is focused on the VNFs, the network connecting them, the storage resources they need to have, and the computing power that should be allocated to them. The choices for the level of hardware virtualization that could be used, the type and amount of networking and storage components that should be allocated to the virtual machine, and other factors come into play for this.

Hardware Virtualization Deployment Options

The hardware, whether it is commercial off the shelf (COTS) or customized vendor-built hardware, is generally shared using the virtualization technologies that were introduced in Chapter 2, "Virtualization Concepts." However, the exact nature of that sharing and the type of virtualization technology could vary and need to be evaluated for each business case, as discussed previously in the context of infrastructure design. The level of security needed and importance of the VNF's function are the key criteria to determine the amount of isolation that should be implemented for its deployment. There are three possible categories:

- bare-metal virtualization
- hypervisor-based virtualization
- container-based virtualization

A bare-metal implementation of a VNF is not really benefiting from virtualization, for it is similar to using a dedicated server for implementing one network function. Bare-metal virtualization provides the VNF absolute isolation and authority on the server resources, but it wipes out most of the benefits that resource sharing capabilities offer. This type of implementation may still be required as part of a bigger NFV deployment to make the cloud appear homogenous to the NFV solution and higher-level tools, yet it provides high isolation to the VNF that is implemented on it.

A VNF implemented in virtual machines, using hypervisor-based virtualization, gives a very good level of isolation, while still benefiting from virtualization and resource sharing. The VNF in this environment needs to run its own operating system (guest OS) and can be completely independent of the host environment. Virtual machines that are sharing a host are protected and secured against infringements on their memory, disk, and CPU space by other virtual machines. Despite the overhead involved in this technique, hypervisor-based virtualization has been the sweet spot for hardware virtualization for NFV.

The container-based virtualization approach offers the least amount of isolation compared to bare-metal and hypervisor-based implementations. In this approach, VNFs share the kernel, binaries, and libraries. This offers a low price point and simplicity (by eliminating the entire hypervisor role and the licensing and management associated with it) but that comes at the cost of reduced isolation. There are limits and bounds placed on containers, restricting the usage of the CPU, memory, disks, and other resources. But since there are many software pieces that are common (including the kernel itself) it is possible for one misbehaving VNF to affect another one in a different container. Although this technique has gained a lot of acceptance and popularity due to its lightweight and agile nature, it not suitable for every scenario because of the low level of isolation and security. In situations where these drawbacks are not an issue, container-based virtualization becomes the preferred choice.

Figure 4-13 shows a comparison between the three hardware virtualization options.

> **FYI:** *The terms orchestration and deployment are often confused and misused. A good analogy to explain the difference between these two terms is to compare orchestration to architectural planning, while deployment is the actual implementation of that plan. Consider a real-estate development: it will involve urban planning activities such as design zones for residential, recreational, and commercial purposes; planning for roads to interconnect those zones and within those zones; and even details of those roads and streets, such as width and routes based on capacity planning. All of these activities are equivalent to orchestration—they define an entire architecture and its connectivity and capacity, but the actual deployment has now to follow these designs and implement the plan.*
>
> *Orchestration in the context of a virtual environment implies determining the amount of resources that need to be allocated, the plan for how these virtual machines will be interconnected, the storage that needs to be allocated to it and its type, and similar factors. Deployment then is the actual implementation and execution of the details that were planned and parameters that were defined during the orchestration process. So when resource orchestration was previously defined as "The allocation, de-allocation and management of NFVI resources to the virtual machine," it implied that that allocations were done in the planning phase. The actual allocation of the resources follows at the time of deployment.*

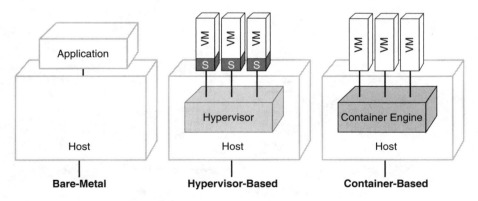

Figure 4-13 *Hardware Virtualization Options*

Deploying Virtual Machines and Containers

There are multiple tools available today that can be used to deploy virtual machines performing networking functions. Chapter 2, "Virtualization Concepts," examined a few different hypervisor options available in the industry. When it comes to NFV, the most popular choices for a hypervisor are Kernel-based Virtual Machine (KVM) and ESXi. Similarly, Docker and Linux containers (LXC) are predominantly used for NFV when using container-based virtualization. The tools that offer NFVI deployment use one of these virtualization modes for deploying VNFs. Therefore, before looking at the tools meant for large scale deployment, let's examine the basics of how these hypervisors can be employed by a command-line interface (CLI) or using very simple tools. Then let's build on top of these concepts and study the mass-deployment NFVI tools.

> **Note**
>
> The content references the term virtual machine in a general context, implying reference to both hypervisor-based virtual machines and container-based virtual environments. Unless explicitly mentioned, the use of the term virtual machine in the following sections refers to both of these technologies.

Using CLI for Kernel Virtual Machine (KVM)

The simplest and most direct way to use KVM is to call it through a Linux command line and pass the arguments to define the parameters to use when instantiating a new virtual machine. Figure 4-14 shows a simple example on how to use KVM through CLI and as shown the parameters passed are for allocating the virtual machine's memory, CPU resources, networking, and the virtual machine image.

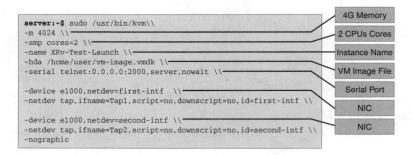

```
server:~$ sudo /usr/bin/kvm\\                                      4G Memory
 -m 4024 \\
 -smp cores=2 \\                                                   2 CPUs Cores
 -name XRv-Test-Launch \\                                          Instance Name
 -hda /home/user/vm-image.vmdk \\
 -serial telnet:0.0.0.0:2000,server,nowait \\                     VM Image File
                                                                   Serial Port
 -device e1000,netdev=first-intf  \\
 -netdev tap,ifname=Tap1,script=no,downscript=no,id=first-intf \\  NIC

 -device e1000,netdev=second-intf \\
 -netdev tap,ifname=Tap2,script=no,downscript=no,id=second-intf \\ NIC
 -nographic
```

Figure 4-14 *Using KVM through the Command Line*

FYI: The kvm *command on a Linux system is a wrapper that calls* qemu-system-x86_64 *with the KVM hypervisor flag set. To see full list of argument that can be passed to use, refer to the documentation for* qemu-system-x86_64 *by using* man qemu-system-x86_64.

This CLI-based method is a very raw way of deploying the virtual machine through KVM. All of the orchestration tools interact with KVM for deployment of VNF when Linux is used as a host OS. But the intricacies and complexities of the KVM usage are masked from the user through the friendly front-end interface. It is good to understand the parameters required to instantiate a virtual machine using KVM to get a better picture of what happens internally when orchestration tools are used, but this CLI mode of deploying a virtual machine is neither scalable nor deployment-friendly, whereas the orchestration tools are generally capable of implementing or supporting automation, allowing scalable mass deployment.

Virsh and GUI Options
Virsh is another CLI-based tool which invokes KVM to create a virtual machine as well as provide enhanced capabilities to update, manage, and monitor the virtual machine environment. Unlike the CLI-based method in KVM, where the parameters need to be passed directly , virsh provides the option to configure the virtual machine parameters in a XML template. Figure 4-15 shows a sample XML file that can be used to instantiate a virtual machine using the virsh interface.

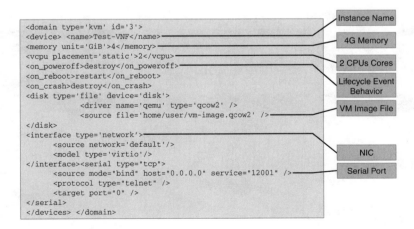

Figure 4-15 *Sample XML File for* virsh

```
server:~$ virsh -help
<snip>
 console                      connect to the guest console
 create                       create a domain from an XML file
 destroy                      destroy (stop) a domain
 migrate                      migrate domain to another host
 reboot                       reboot a domain
 resume                       resume a domain
 shutdown                     gracefully shutdown a domain
 vcpucount                    domain vcpu counts
 dominfo                      domain information
 list                         list domains
 snapshot-create              Create a snapshot from XML
 snapshot-list                List snapshots for a domain
 vol-clone                    clone a volume.
 vol-create-as                create a volume from a set of args
 vol-create                   create a vol from an XML file
<snip>
```

Figure 4-16 *Sample* `virsh` *Command Options*

The virtual machine management and monitoring capabilities of `virsh` are limited, but it does offer many of the basic ways to monitor and manage the virtual machine, such as to reboot it, modify its configuration, view its CPU and memory allocations, create snapshots, or migrate the virtual machine to another host. Figure 4-16 shows a list of the `virsh` options. Refer to the `virsh` command reference for full list of commands and further details. [3]

There is also many open source GUI options to use instead of a `virsh` command-line interface, such as *Kimchi, Virt-manager, mist.io*. Figure 4-17 shows a view of `virt-manager`, which provides a graphical interface to implement `virsh` functions and makes it much more user friendly.

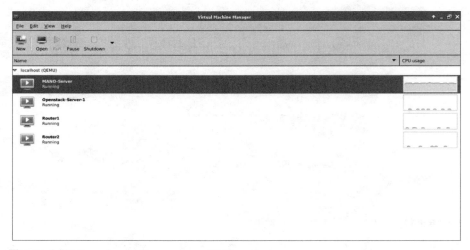

Figure 4-17 *Sample* `virt-manager` *GUI Interface*

vSphere Client

This tool by VMware are is primarily used to deploy, monitor, and manage a virtual machine on an ESXi-based hypervisor. It supports graphical user interfaces (GUI) for direct interaction with the ESXi host and also provides an API that allows other tools to interact with it. Figure 4-18 shows a view of this vSphere GUI. Though vSphere is easy to use and configure for instantiating virtual machines, it doesn't offer a number of advanced functions such as virtual machine migration, cloning, etc., and for those purposes VMware has a full-fledged virtual machine deployment suite that is covered later in this section.

Figure 4-18 *vSphere GUI*

Linux Container Daemon (LXD)

LXD is a tool used to manage and operate a container deployment in a Linux environment. It is built on top of LXC, which was covered in Chapter 2, "Virtualization Concepts." LXD brings additional support of security, plug-in for OpenStack integration, and Representational State Transfer API (REST API) support to facilitate the management of the containers.

The few tools that were discussed are just a subset of the basic tools available for deploying virtual machines and containers. These are useful when deploying in a standalone or simple lab environment, but not intended for deployment in large scale environment. Let's discuss tools that are designed for large-scale deployments and recommended to be used as the VIM.

Software and Tools for NFVI Deployment

NFVI deployment is performed by a VIM functional block. As described earlier, VIM's role is much more than just interacting with the hypervisor. In addition, VIM is also meant to manage the hardware repository, manage, and monitor its utilization, and interface with other MANO functional blocks. Various cloud operating systems that are available in the market today provide implementations of these functionalities along with capabilities to scale and manage large deployments. Some of these are commercial software, while others are developed and managed by the open source community. Many of the commercially available NFVI deployment tools leverage OpenStack or VMware's vCenter and add a management layer on top of them. Some of the popular software choices for NFVI deployment are introduced in this section. OpenStack is used as an example for a more detailed anatomy of the capabilities of the NFVI deployment software.

VMware's vSphere Software Suite

VMware offers the vSphere software suite as its virtualization solution. The key components of vSphere suite are the vSphere hypervisor ("ESXi"), distributed virtual switches, VMotion for virtual machine mobility, and vCenter for management and operations of the virtualized environment.

VSphere is more than just VIM—it has NFVI components in it as well, for it has its own hypervisor, switches, and mechanisms to work with storage (VMware Virtualized SAN). VMware offers three types of switch capabilities to interconnect with the virtual machines: a standard VMware virtual switch, a distributed virtual Switch or DVS (by VMware or Cisco Nexus1000v) and an overlay SDN controller like NSX.

VMware also offers other software suites such as vRealize, which is meant for hybrid cloud management and can work with AWS, OpenStack, and multiple types of hypervisors [4].

OpenStack

OpenStack has become the most popular open source and free tool to deploy cloud infrastructure. The VIM functionalities are a subset of OpenStack's capabilities, and the scope of OpenStack's capabilities is evolving and adapting to the requirements of VNFM and NFVO.

OpenStack started as open source software developed by Rackspace (a cloud hosting company) and NASA, and has evolved into a full-fledged software suite that is meant to build and manage a platform for virtualization. OpenStack comprises multiple modules, which provide the functionality for networking, storage, compute, management, etc. Many service providers adapting NFV have deployed or plan to use OpenStack as the software to deploy the infrastructure for their NFV. OpenStack is discussed in-depth later in this chapter.

Cisco UCS Director

Cisco offers UCS Director (UCSD) as virtualization and management layer supporting both virtual and physical infrastructure for NFV. Because Cisco is a vendor of both physical and virtual platforms, the Cisco UCS Director is offered as a standalone version or a bundled version, providing customers flexibility and choice for their NFVI deployment.

The Cisco UCS Director provides a single pane of glass for the entire NFVI block and acts as a manager interacting with OpenStack or VMware's VCenter-based virtual infrastructure for the compute, network, and storage and with the physical entity such as server, switch, and routers as shown in Figure 4-19. Cisco bundles UCS hardware and UCSD software as an integrated solution for customer consumption and faster deployment of NFVI [5].

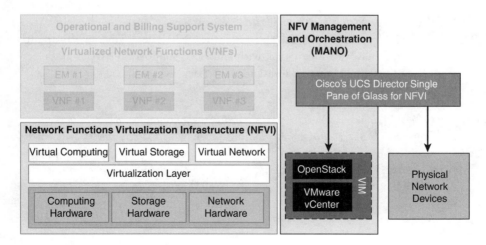

Figure 4-19 *Cisco's UCSD*

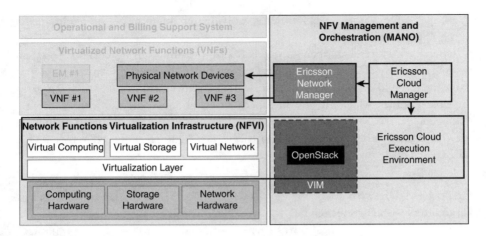

Figure 4-20 *Ericsson Cloud Execution Environment and Cloud Manager*

Ericsson Cloud Execution Environment

Ericsson Cloud Execution Environment is part of the overall Ericsson cloud system suite and it facilitates the deployment of infrastructure as a service (IaaS). The cloud platform supports only the virtualization entity of the IaaS, and for PNF, Ericson has separate management software called Ericson Network Manager. Figure 4-20 shows the two main components of the Ericsson cloud systems suite with respect to the NFVI and PNF infrastructure [6].

HP Helion OpenStack Carrier Grade

HP offers the HP Helion OpenStack Carrier as their NFVI deployment software. It's a commercialized flavor of OpenStack with enhanced support for carrier grade performance, stability, and high availability for NFVI deployments.

> **FYI:** *Often VIM software has the capability to manage another hypervisor's environment. This is useful when dealing with hybrid deployment scenarios. For example, VMware's vRealize works with OpenStack as well as vSphere, while OpenStack also offers the ability to manage VMware infrastructure (using VMware Integrated OpenStack) [7].*

Introduction to OpenStack

NFV and OpenStack are often used together in the same sentence. This is because OpenStack is the most popular among the VIMs and has been gaining mind share and becoming the preferred choice of CSPs. But without knowledge of what OpenStack is and what it can offer, the full context and its applicability to NFV can get fuzzy. Frequent references to OpenStack module names, like Neutron, Nova, etc. make it even muddier unless the purposes of these modules are understood. For this reason, this chapter spends a significant amount of time explaining OpenStack.

Though there is thorough coverage of OpenStack, the concepts explained here serve as an example and are applicable to other VIMs, such as VMware vCenter, etc.

So What Is OpenStack?

In very simple words, OpenStack is a software application that is designed to work as a tool to deploy virtual environments (virtual machines and containers), along with the networking needed to interconnect these virtual environments.

It's written mostly in the Python programming language and needs to run on a Linux environment (as of the time of this writing, there is no plan to make it run on other platforms). It is of course possible to deploy virtual machines and containers without OpenStack, but OpenStack provides a platform and common interface to deploy the entire environment. For CSPs whose business is to offer a public cloud environment, a tool-like OpenStack allows them to let their customers use the front-end interface (typically a GUI interface, which is calling OpenStack APIs in the background) to orchestrate and deploy their entire virtual environment, comprising applications, virtual machines, VNFs, network bridges to interconnect them, etc. Customers who are planning to deploy private clouds also follow the footsteps of CSP and adapt OpenStack for their private cloud deployment.

OpenStack is not the only tool that offers this type of functionality. There are many other ways to deploy and provide a public cloud, as shown in earlier examples. Amazon Web Services (AWS) stands out among them. In fact, OpenStack was designed to mimic AWS functionality. However, OpenStack's popularity and the complexity its terminologies and architecture can create, make it worthy of a bit more focus than other tools. They are examined in this section.

A Brief History of OpenStack

OpenStack has gained a lot of momentum in recent years from its inception in 2010. It started as two components Swift and Nebula. Swift was developed and contributed by Rackspace, which had developed it as an open source software to manage storage, while Nebula was a NASA open source project meant to manage complex data sets. With the two projects combined, OpenStack was launched as a joint effort [38]. Later many other companies joined forces and contributed more code and functionality to OpenStack. Today OpenStack releases and code are overseen by the OpenStack Foundation [8] governing body. The OpenStack Technical Committee oversees the technical aspects and ensures quality, integration, and openness of the contributed code.

> **FYI:** *For both NASA and Rackspace, the original goals were to mimic Amazon's cloud offering of Amazon Web Services (AWS) and develop an open source version for their own and public use. Swift was mimicking Amazon's Simple Storage Service (Amazon S3), while Nebula was mimicking Amazon's Elastic Compute Cloud (EC2).*

The major driving factor behind OpenStack's popularity has been the fact that it is free of licensing costs, community hardened, completely open source, vendor independent, and available to anyone to procure, modify and use. On the other hand, open source OpenStack doesn't have any support model, because it is purely community developed and supported. The OpenStack foundation looks after the inclusions and modifications to the periodic OpenStack releases, but this forum is only to coordinate development and contribution efforts and doesn't offer any formal support for deployment and use. There are many companies that have taken the open source OpenStack, created a customized version of it, and backed it up with a support model. These companies, such as Mirantis, Red Hat, Canonical, and Cisco-Metacloud, are in the business of offering OpenStack deployment and support.

OpenStack was originally built as a tool to deploy application and storage hosting and manage it. As it has evolved into a cloud deployment tool, many cloud service providers (such as Rackspace [9]) are using it for their public cloud offering, while others (like GoDaddy [10]) are using it for deploying their private cloud. In the recent years, however, one of the NFV goals was to achieve vender independence and OpenStack aligns with this very well by offering an option to avoid locking into any particular vendor. The service providers who have been adapting NFV, many of which have evolved from being a traditional telecommunications provider, typically want to build their private cloud (which can host and run their network services) and use OpenStack's attributes of support across a wide range of vendors. The ability of open source and lack of cost have made it a preferred choice for service providers looking to deploy their infrastructure for NFV.

OpenStack Releases

OpenStack follows a time-based release model, where a new OpenStack stable release is made available approximately six months after the previous release and has life of almost one year. The releases are currently named in alphabetical order. Every new release incorporates the code developed and contributed by the community that has been approved and accepted by OpenStack foundation Technical Committee [11]. Figure 4-21 shows the OpenStack release history and roadmap at the time of this writing. Notice the release duration of almost six months and the one-year shelf life.

OpenStack Deployment Nodes

OpenStack is not a single piece of software but consists of multiple modules that are meant to serve different functionalities. The server where OpenStack software is running is referred to as an OpenStack node. Because it is modular, not all components of OpenStack need to run on every node that it is managing. If a server is offering only computing resources to be virtualized, just the computing virtualization management (Nova) module is needed on those nodes, and the nodes are called OpenStack compute nodes.

Similarly, it's possible that some servers may be offering only storage virtualization, so only the storage management module of OpenStack needs to run on them,

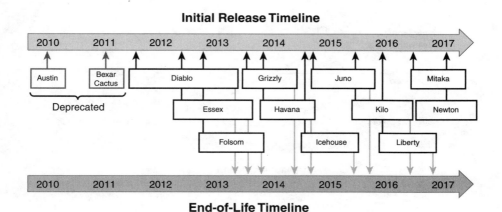

Figure 4-21 *OpenStack Release Timelines*

so they are called OpenStack storage nodes. For network virtualization, there are OpenStack network nodes that may be offering only networking modules to be virtualized and thus only need to run the OpenStack module that is meant for network virtualization management. A few additional node types are also cropping up based on the services being offered, such as an endpoint node for running load-balancing and clustering services or a volume node, which is similar to a storage node. The most commonly referenced nodes, however, are the four types discussed earlier.

In addition to these types of nodes, OpenStack needs an OpenStack controller node to manage its modules and perform centralized functions. These nodes can be spread across different locations and may be geographically distributed. The controller node, is the minimum that is needed for any OpenStack environment and all other node types mentioned can coexist on the same server, can share the same server, or be implemented separately on different servers. If all the nodes are collapsed into a single server, this combination of controller, network, compute, and storage nodes is referred to as an all-in-one" (AIO) deployment of OpenStack. To the end user, the distribution of nodes is not visible and is always seen as a single interface for one OpenStack cloud. Figure 4-22 shows the OpenStack deployments using separate interconnected nodes or AIO deployment.

Also, as shown in Figure 4-22, there can be multiple nodes of the same type within one OpenStack cloud. Since the controller node is the linchpin that holds together the entire cloud infrastructure that OpenStack is implementing, it makes sense to implement multiple controller nodes to avoid a single point of failure. This ensures high

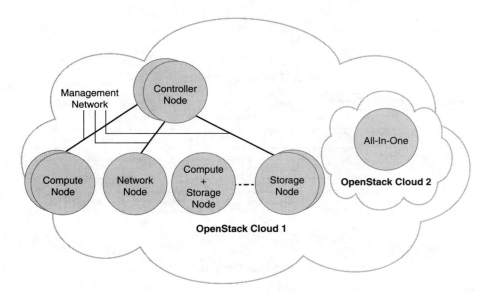

Figure 4-22 *OpenStack Deployment Nodes*

availability for OpenStack, yet adds the complexity of making these multiple controller nodes work coherently. This topic is discussed in more depth later in this chapter.

Figure 4-23 shows the main modules that constitute the OpenStack framework (as of the Liberty release of OpenStack). Each of these is designed to perform specific functions, but they may have dependencies on each other and may be required to interact in the OpenStack ecosystem. An NFV deployment using OpenStack may need some or all of the components shown here, or even additional ones, to build and manage the NFVI layer.

OpenStack creates a cloud environment (called a project or tenant) and offers it to its users to set up their cloud. A user may have access to multiple clouds and have different privilege levels and authority in them.

Within a tenant, the OpenStack user can create their own virtual machines, setup networking for those virtual machines, implement monitoring and analytics, manage storage and images and many other functions that are allowed. The options available in a Tenant environment depend on which OpenStack modules were installed and setup by the OpenStack administrator. In addition to virtual machine management, OpenStack has modules that enable the capability to setup services, such as Dynamic Host Configuration Protocol (DHCP) as a service, Domain Name System (DNS) as a service, or a firewall as a service. Its therefore important to understand the role of OpenStack to fully comprehend the capabilities that it offers. Let's discuss some more the key OpenStack modules.

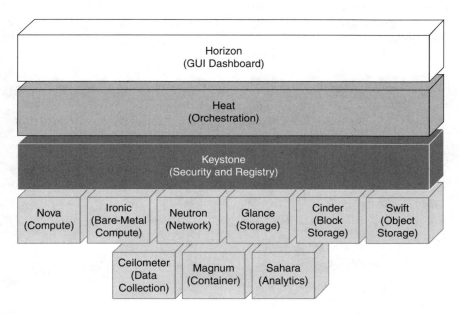

Figure 4-23 *OpenStack Architecture*

Horizon

To interact with OpenStack, each module offers a set of APIs (REST APIs) that can be used to pass parameters and retrieve the responses. The modules also have scripts that act as a wrapper around those REST APIs and offer a command-line tool for passing the parameters or displaying the response, making the interaction a bit friendlier for users and for admins. There is, however, a graphical user interface also available for OpenStack. This graphical interface is implemented using the Horizon module. Horizon is written in the Django web application and provides the dashboard capabilities.

Django Framework

Django is a framework written in Python and meant for web development. It offers an easy way to develop web interface for database-driven GUIs, without the hassle of writing the entire backend.

Most of the administrative functions can't be performed from the Horizon dashboard and still require use of the command line–based wrapper tools. For OpenStack users, however, Horizon provides a decent interface and a graphical environment to monitor and manage their cloud.

Just like the command-line wrappers, Horizon also uses REST API calls in the background. Users (or administrators) can always choose to create their own user interface employing the same API calls and replacing Horizon if they prefer to implement their own dashboard.

FYI: *OpenStack Communication—Because the modules use REST API calls to interact, they are listening to specific port numbers for any REST query that is sent towards them. These API calls could be from the user, from the administrator, or even from another module. These port numbers can be configured individually for the modules and made available to others (along with the IP address) through a central registry. With this context, the modules that are part of an OpenStack framework can be installed on different Layer 3 domains. As long as they have ability to route the REST traffic, which uses HTTP by default and can be changed to Secure HTTP (HTTPS), the OpenStack framework can be distributed across these Layer 3 domains.*

(continued)

Each OpenStack module may be implemented in multiple functional blocks of code, running perhaps as separate processes. When these modules need to communicate within their own functional blocks, they use a more efficient communication method through a messaging queue. A host system where OpenStack is running should therefore have this messaging queue capability installed. Several applications are available for that purpose, and as long as they are compliant with Advanced Message Queuing Protocol (AMQP),OpenStack can use it. The default one suggested is Rabbit Messaging Queue (RabbitMQ), which is an open source implementation of AMQP.

Nova

Nova is an evolved version of Nebula, which was one of the initial ingredients of OpenStack. Nova's main function is to interact with the hypervisor and facilitate the creation, deletion, and modification of allocated resources and image management of the virtual machine. Essentially Nova provides the means to manage the virtual machine's lifecycle. Nova's interface provides the OpenStack user the ability to setup the virtual machines for the cloud. It is therefore an essential OpenStack module in an NFV deployment.

Nova also used to offer a very basic networking function through a submodule called nova-network, but this has been deprecated and replaced by a more powerful implementation through the Neutron module.

Neutron

Neutron facilitates deployment and configuration of network services using Open-Stack. For NFV, the Neutron module plays an important role, for it deals with setting up networking, interfacing with the VNFs to set up connectivity between the virtual machine or VNF and externally to the wide-area network (WAN) or local-area network (LAN).

Neutron evolved from the original Nova network module as a successor and independent module. Neutron, however, needs the Nova module to be present as it relies on it while implementing the network services. Neutron capabilities for networking are limited, but these can be extended and enhanced using a Neutron plug-in. Due to its relevance in implementing networking for the cloud environment and NFV, Neutron is discussed in more detail in a subsequent section.

Ironic

Many applications need a dedicated server, also referred as bare metal, instead of a shared environment. These applications may still be part of a virtualized environment and working along with applications running in virtual machines or containers. OpenStack supports this hybrid or mixed deployment where some applications may need to be deployed on bare metal while others are deployed as virtual machines. Ironic is the OpenStack module, which provisions the bare-metal server and deploys the application on it. It originated from the Nova bare-metal driver project but is now an independent project of OpenStack. By default, it uses Preboot Execution Environment (PXE), and Intelligent Platform Management Interface (IPMI) infrastructure to deploy the application on the bare-metal server. Additionally, Ironic supports the use of vendor plug-ins for vendor-specific APIs, which can enable deployment on bare-metal server using other methods.

PXE and IPMI

PXE, which is an acronym for Preboot Execution Environment, offers a standard way for an administrator to remotely deploy an operating system or full-fledged application on a bare-metal device.

IPMI, which is acronym for Intelligent Platform Management Interface, is a set of specifications to interact with the CPU or firmware of the computing resource hardware. IPMI therefore allows an administrator to directly manage the system without an operating system dependency, even if the OS is not present or the system is not powered up.

Magnum

Just as Nova is used to deploy and manage virtual machines' life cycles, the Magnum module offers functionality to manage and deploy containers. Magnum uses Docker and Kubernetes components for this and offers an API to OpenStack customers to deploy containers in the same way they deploy virtual machines.

Kubernetes

Kubernetes is a container orchestration tool that is developed and made available as open source by Google. Its purpose is to manage clusters of containers. While Docker manages the container life cycle, Kubernetes helps in their deployment and placing the container in new or existing virtual machines.

Keystone

The Keystone module, as its name implies, is the central piece of the architecture and holds every module together. It provides a few important roles.

The Keystone serves as the central registry for the OpenStack services and modules by maintaining a service catalog. Each module that is installed needs to register with the Keystone and once registered gives the Keystone the knowledge of which modules are part of the OpenStack cloud and how they can be reached (IP address to reach it and the port they listening to). When the modules need to communicate with each other (for example, if Neutron wants to talk to Nova) it uses the Keystone to find out if the destination module exists and how it can be reached.

User authentication and authorization is performed through the Keystone. When a user logs in, the authentication credentials are sent over to Keystone, which then determines if this user is valid. It also defines the projects that the user has access to and what the user's permissions are for each of those tenants. The Keystone module can maintain its own database for these authentication and authorizations, or work with existing backend database like Lightweight Directory Access Protocol (LDAP).

Note

In OpenStack, permissions are not assigned to a user, but rather the combination of user and tenant (remember that a tenant is the same as a project and represents one instance of a virtual environment created by the OpenStack User). As shown in Figure 4-24, a user may have access to multiple projects. But it is possible that the same user has administrator rights in Project-A but has very restricted rights in Project-B.

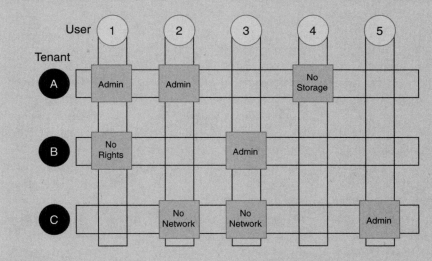

Figure 4-24 *OpenStack User Authorization and Permissions*

An authenticated and authorized user has specific privileges on each module. For example, the user may be allowed to launch a new virtual machine using Nova, but not permitted to connect it to the network using Neutron, or not allowed to use the block storage device to create a storage space for the virtual machine. The permissions therefore need to be checked by each module for what is or isn't allowed. This is done by using authorization tokens, which are allocated and maintained by Keystone.

The token works as a "temporary badge" that is passed to each module that is called by the user and that module can validate the token from Keystone and find out what permissions are allowed. If this user's request for a virtual machine involved creation of network, Neutron disallows that because Keystone notifies Neutron that this token doesn't have permission to create networks.

Glance

To create the virtual machines and containers and run an application in it, a source image for that application is needed. This source image is made available by the application developer, e.g. a Windows virtual machine needs a Windows image file from Microsoft, or an F5 load balancer virtual machine needs to run a load-balancer application image provided by F5. These images can be stored in storage devices, which may be spread over geographical locations, and have different access methods. There are modules that deal with the ways to access storage devices, but for an end user the presence of that image is what really matters. Glance is the OpenStack module that is meant to discover and manage that image repository and image registry. Additionally, Glance can also take an existing virtual machine's snapshot and store that as a template image.

Virtual Machine's Snapshot

Snapshot images are a capture of current running state of a virtual machine. When the virtual machine was created initially, say a VNF for routing functionality, it did not have any customized configuration. The user may configure specific routing protocols in it—for example a full BGP router reflector configuration. The running state of that VNF is now a BGP-RR and can be frozen in time by taking a snapshot. There can be multiple snapshots taken for any virtual machine.

A snapshot has two main purposes. It can be used to create a backup of the current virtual machine state, and the virtual machine can be reverted back to one of the frozen or snapshot stages at any time. For example, if additional address families were added to this router reflector VNF and then it became desirable to roll back those changes, the user could simply tell OpenStack to revert to a snapshot. Another reason to take a snapshot is to replicate the current server state. In this instance, if another route reflector has to be spawned, the snapshot of the first one can be used to do that; in this case, the base image of the VNF is combined with the snapshot when spinning up a new instance.

A virtual machine source image can be used to instantiate multiple running virtual machines. Glance stores information about only the source image and any snapshots of the running images. As shown in Figure 4-25, Glance interacts with the storage location to keep a database of image and snapshot locations, access permissions and other file details.

Swift and Cinder

Cinder is the OpenStack module used to manage virtualization of block-storage devices. Originally Cinder had started as an extension of Nova called Nova-volume and later became an independent module. The common practice for persistence storage for virtual machines that are managed by OpenStack is facilitated by a Cinder module. Cinder block storage devices are called Cinder volumes. The CSPs can offer a catalog of block storage based on service offerings such as database storage, file storage, or snapshots using a Cinder module.

The physical disk for storage of the data used by Cinder can be either local storage or external storage mounted on remote device. The transport mechanism use

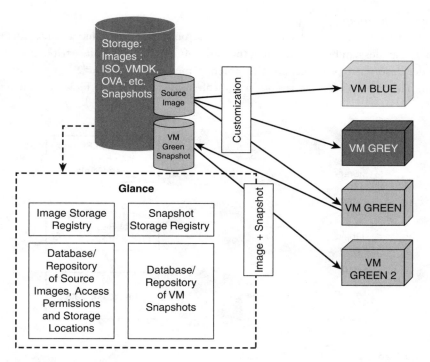

Figure 4-25 *Glance Functionality*

to communicate to the external storage device could be iSCSI, fiber channel, Network File System (NFS), or a proprietary protocol. The Cinder module could be enhanced using vendor-specific drivers to support additional functionality or by vendor-specific drivers using the third-party plug-in. Example of some of the third-party support for storage arrays include EMC, HP, IBM, pure storage, Solid Fire etc.

Swift is another storage module of OpenStack that provides object storage functionality, very similar to Amazon S3. Swift uses HTTP to access the storage device, and because of this HTTP access, the storage need not be local to the compute node and can be located in any remote device, including Amazon S3 or any other platform. With the ability of Swift to store the data on any platform, it offers a cost-effective way of implementing storage on a commodity-based platforms.

The multiple storage options of OpenStack may look complex. The modules are evolving and providing better features and functionality needs. Swift and Cinder do provide differentiated storage offerings based on the requirement of the data. For example, Cinder is well suited for storage of virtual machine persistent data and provides the traditional data storage facility, whereas Swift is suited for highly scalable large volumes of data such as images or media files. Figure 4-26 depicts this.

File System Storage
In this type of storage of data, the information is saved in a hierarchical format, where the files can be located using the path information. The file attributes such as owner, read/write privilege, etc. are stored in metadata and handled by the file system. This type of storage is good for local storage or a LAN. However, since the

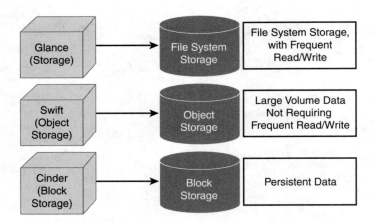

Figure 4-26 *OpenStack Storage Modules*

metadata space is limited, file system–based storage has limitations on scalability and lack of file storage attributes, such as owners and groups, so it is not suitable in situations requiring a high number of files.

Block Storage

Block storage holds the data in equal sized chunks called blocks. A file may be split over a number of such blocks. These individual blocks do not have any metadata associated with them except the address associated per block. It is the application's responsibility to keep track of the blocks that the file is distributed over and combine these blocks when needed to extract the file's contents. This type of storage provides high performance data processing and is typically used for databases or transactional type of data mining, where only a snippet of information is needed for processing. Also, since metadata is not stored, the scalability limits that plague file storage are lifted in the case of block storage, which makes it an ideal choice for storing run-time data. OpenStack has support for block storage. Before availability of that support, the virtual machines used so-called ephemeral storage, which meant the contents of the virtual machine were lost when that virtual machine was shut down.

Object Storage

In object storage, which is also referred to as object-based storage, the complete data or file, along with its metadata, is saved as a single entity. This entity is referred to as an object. In comparison to block storage, object storage doesn't split the file into chunks. When the files are stored as an object, they are combined with multiple attributes such as the unique identifier and applications associated to them. The objects are not organized in any hierarchical format, but are placed is the same level as other objects, forming a flat structure. Using the unique identifier, the server or application can access any object quickly. Therefore this technique offers a useful storage solution for cloud-based architecture. The drawback of object-storage is that if any edit is needed in object storage, the whole object is retrieved for editing and then saved back.

Ceilometer

The word ceilometer is used to describe a device that measures cloud cover and height. The ceilometer module in OpenStack is meant for a similar purpose for the cloud that is deployed through OpenStack. It is meant to collect statistics and usage data for the cloud resources. The data is useful to keep track of utilization, billing, and other tracking purposes.

Heat

The orchestration service of OpenStack is called Heat. This service defines how to deploy the cloud application. In case of NFV this could be the NFV network to be deployed and the resource needed for each virtual machine. Initially Heat closely resembled the AWS CloudFormation service and has grown now to include additional services and offers more features than CloudFormation.

To deploy the cloud, which consists of the virtual machines, the networks, subnets, ports, etc., the composition is defined in Heat as text files called Heat templates. There are two template formats supported by Heat, the Heat Orchestration Template (HOT) that is not compatible with the AWS CloudFormation and is typically formatted using the YAML specification. The second format of template is called Cloud Formation Compatible Format (CFN), which—as its name suggests—is compatible with AWS CloudFormation. The CFN template is formatted using JavaScript Object Notation (JSON) specifications.

YAML

YAML is a markup language. The acronym YAML is recursive, since it stands for "YAML Ain't Markup Language"

The Heat orchestration service does provide the support for both virtual machine–based and container-based cloud deployment. The Heat service typically runs in the OpenStack controller node (the node types will be covered in more detail later) and just like other OpenStack modules, Heat's functionalities can be accessed via a CLI-based client making API calls or a web-based client that can be accessed within in the Horizon dashboard.

The exact format of Heat templates is beyond the scope of this book. OpenStack's documentation [12] provides a good reference for this. At a high level, it is helpful to understand that the Heat template defines parameters (for example, image to be used, resources to be allocated, network types) and which of these ingredients make the virtual environment. This template can then be used to deploy multiple instances of the defined virtual environment. When the deployment is being done, Heat calls Nova for computing, Neutron for networking, and other OpenStack modules for other resources it might need.

FYI: Both YAML and JSON are data formatting and encoding languages. JSON stands for JavaScript Object Notation, defined by RFC 7150. Data encoding doesn't refer to low-level encoding of bits and bytes, but rather to encoding for

(continued)

data structures, variables and their values, and parameters at the application layer. Some other popular ways to encode data are Extensible Markup Language (XML), Protocol Buffers (ProtoBuf) by Google, Thrift by Facebook, and many others. Many open source tools exist to convert between these formats; since essentially they are packaging the same data in different ways, it is possible to translate in between them.

JSON format uses curly braces to enclose data structures and ":" to link key-value pairs as shown in Figure 4-27.

YAML also uses ":" to separate key-value pairs and indentation to define the data structures or object blocks. The same example when translated to YAML is shown in Figure 4-28.

There is much more to both these format, but those details are beyond the scope of this book. Refer to http://yaml.org and http://json.org for details about the formatting and structure.

```
{ "Books":
    {"Technology":

        {   "title" : "NFV with a touch of SDN",
                "ISBN" : "0134463056"
            },
        "Fiction":
            {   "title" : "To Kill a Mocking Bird",
                "ISBN": "0446310786"
            }
        }
    }
```

Figure 4-27 *Example of JSON Encoding*

```
Books:
    Technology:
        title: "NFV with a touch of SDN"
        ISBN: "0134463056"
    Fiction:
        title: "To Kill a Mocking Bird"
        ISBN: "0446310786"
```

Figure 4-28 *Example of YAML Encoding*

Putting it all together

To summarize the key module, Figure 4-29 shows the role of each of the modules discussed earlier. It should be highlighted that OpenStack and its modules belong in the MANO block of NFVI framework, which means that these modules do not deploy virtual machines themselves. For example, Nova can only request the amount of computing resource that needs to be provisioned for a virtual machine, but it's the hypervisor that actually makes that allocation available and spawns the virtual machine. Similarly Glance and Cinder/Swift manage and facilitate the use of virtualized storage, but they don't create the virtual storage on their own.

An example of how OpenStack modules work together is shows in Figure 4-30, which essentially presents the conceptual model of how these modules interact with each other to implement the OpenStack cloud.

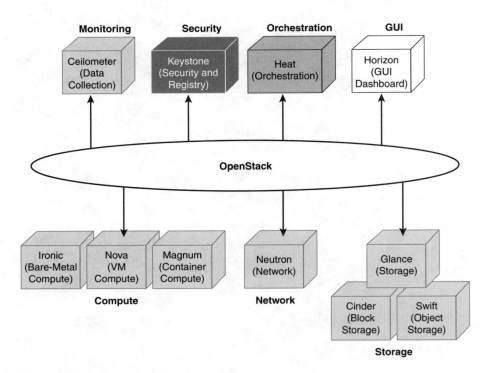

Figure 4-29 *OpenStack Modules Summary*

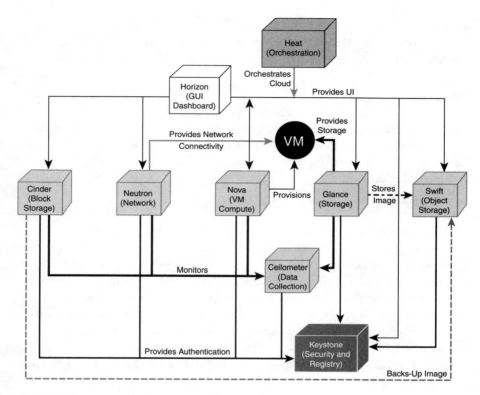

Figure 4-30 *OpenStack Conceptual Architecture [13]*

OpenStack Networking

OpenStack uses a Neutron module to implement networking within the OpenStack cloud. Given its importance in implementing NFVI using OpenStack, the Neutron module is discussed in more depth in this section.

Neutron Basics

Neutron can be used to manage three entities, namely subnets, ports and networks. In simple terms, these three entities jointly represent a virtual Layer 2 network's definition, which has an IP address range defined for any virtual machine that is connected to this Layer 2 network. It is important to be aware of the way Neutron defines these terms.

Subnets

Subnet represents a block of IP addresses that can be assigned to the virtual machines. A subnet block is therefore a Layer 2 broadcast domain and can optionally have a default gateway for external communication. When users of OpenStack want to create their network in their virtual environment, they can define the subnet using Neutron API calls by providing the IP address range that they want their virtual machines to use.

Ports

Neutron refers to the virtual interfaces connecting to the virtual machines as ports. These ports are assigned IP address from the IP pool of the Subnet they belong to. The port therefore puts the Virtual Machine in a particular network. Neutron APIs can be used to create, read, update, and delete (referred to as CRUD functionalities) these virtual interfaces.

Networks

Neutron refers to the entire virtual Layer 2 domain as network. This consists of the subnet that was defined, as well as the ports that are associated with it. An Open-Stack user defines the network prior to associating a subnet and port with it, and this network is managed through OpenStack APIs (or Neutron APIs to be more precise). Users can define multiple networks if they want to use multiple subnets in their virtual environment. Within an individual network, the devices can communicate using Layer 2, but when multiple networks are defined then they are not able to communicate with each other unless they are connected by a router.

Figure 4-31 offers a pictorial representation of these entities managed by Neutron. As shown, the ports are associated with the virtual machines/VNFs. The network comprises ports and subnets that are defined in it, and multiple networks will need a router in between to communicate. The figure also highlights the fact that Neutron and the networking it implements are part of NFV infrastructure.

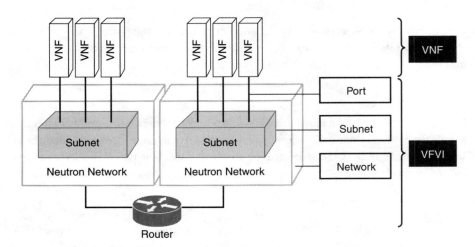

Figure 4-31 *Neutron Basic Entities*

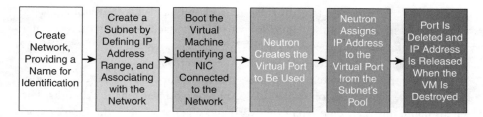

Figure 4-32 *Neutron Configuration Flow*

Neutron APIs can be used by the OpenStack tenant to create and manage their private network within their virtual environment. The process they follow to use these Neutron APIs is shown in Figure 4-32 [14].

Neutron Network Types

Neutron offers a few different types of networks to be created. The important ones to be aware of include the following:

- **Flat:** Flat networks are a single network segment where all the devices are part of the same broadcast domain. As a consequence, a flat network's subnet should use an IP address that is shared and visible to the host and other networks entities.

- **Local:** This type of network is the exact opposite of a flat network. In this case, the network can be segmented and each segment comprises a separate broadcast domain. As a consequence, each segment in the local network consumes a IP address range that is completely local and not visible to other segments in the same network.

- **VLAN:** This type of network uses 802.1Q VLAN tagging to differentiate the networks for external communication. All the traffic leaving the network is encapsulated using 802.1Q, which allows the virtual machines residing in the same VLAN to communicate between each other using a switch (usually a virtual switch, but it can be a physical switch) without requiring a router to interconnect. For any communication outside to other VLANs, the networks can be interconnected using a router (which can be virtual or physical).

Neutron Provider and Tenant Networks

The Neutron network references so far have been focused on configuring the tenant's network using Neutron. However, OpenStack itself also needs a network to be managed by the service provider for connecting the OpenStack servers to the rest of the physical network, as well as connecting between the multiple OpenStack servers.

This network, referred to as the provider network in OpenStack terminology, is provisioned and managed by the administrator of OpenStack. Neutron offers to manage and configure this network as well. Typically, this would be a flat or VLAN network and point to an external gateway for connectivity.

The networks that the tenants or users create for their individual cloud deployments (again, using Neutron capabilities) are referred to as tenant networks. Each tenant maintains their own tenant network and OpenStack uses the Linux namespace methodology to isolate these networks from each other.

Neutron Plug-Ins

Neutron's core networking capabilities can be extended and enhanced using Neutron plug-ins. These plug-ins are additional pieces of software, providing extensions of Neutron's standard basic APIs and can be added by the OpenStack Administrator and made available to the end user. This enables support for wider variety for networking technologies and offers those customers choices to manage their cloud environment's network using these technologies e.g. using Virtual Extensible LAN (VXLAN) or generic routing encapsulation (GRE), or offer services such as a firewall, routers, or load balancers, which they could use in their virtual network.

Figure 4-33 shows some of the commonly used Neutron plug-ins. As shown, there are two broad categories of Neutron plug-ins, that is, core and service plug-ins. To the end user, who is simply using OpenStack's front-end environment and APIs for their cloud deployment, the details about the categories of these plug-ins are not important—they simply need to be aware of the capabilities in the Neutron their CSP is offering. Let's take a look at the plug-in categories in slightly more detail.

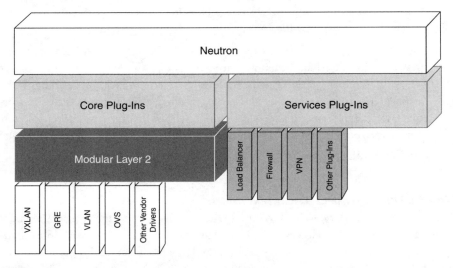

Figure 4-33 *Neutron Plug-Ins*

Core Plug-Ins

This category of plug-ins enhances Neutron's capacities to understand and manage networking protocols and devices. For example, core plug-ins can be used to add the capabilities to use the VXLAN or GRE protocols. The core plug-ins that bring protocol capabilities are called TypeDrivers. Similarly, the capability for Neutron to use these protocols on various vendor devices is brought through another category of core plug-ins, called MechanismDrivers. Figure 4-31 shows some examples of both of these types of core plug-ins. In summary, core plug-ins deal with Layer 2 and Layer 3 capabilities and have the ability to implement these capabilities on different vendor devices (virtual or physical) through Neutron.

Service Plug-Ins

The service plug-ins support networking services and allow them to be managed through Neutron (and effectively allows the OpenStack user to manage, configure and use these services). Examples of the services are routing service implementing routing protocols, Firewall services implementing filtering and blocking of traffic, Load-balance services, etc.

These plug-ins are often developed and provided by network equipment vendors to enable Neutron to work with their VNFs. For example, for a Cisco CSR1000v or Nexus1000v to be managed through the Neutron API, a Cisco plug-in (more specifically, core plug-in mechanism driver) for IOS-XE or NX-OS can be used in Neutron. If the OpenStack administrator (which essentially is the CSP) chooses to use a vendor's plug-in and that vendor's VNF, then the CSP's customers now has the option to use instances of this VNF (which may be a router, firewall, switch, or any other networking function) in their virtual environments. They can manage those instances using Neutron APIs that they can call (note that these APIs may be the standard APIs, or may be extensions to them). For the CSP, this enhances their service offer and differentiates them from the competition by providing advanced networking capabilities in their OpenStack offering. For the vendor, they can generate revenue based on their VNF's usage and licensing.

Note that the vendor equipment managed by Neutron doesn't necessarily have to be a VNF. This networking functionality could also be implemented using a physical device or software that is integrated into the hypervisor. If the networking function is implemented using a physical device, for example a top-of-rack (ToR) switch, then Neutron can still manage that equipment, as long as it has the appropriate plug-ins to interact. In this case, customers of course can't create an instance for use in their own virtual environment, but they can setup the relevant device parameters through their OpenStack environment's Neutron API. In case the network function is integrated to the hypervisor, the functionality it offers can be made available to the CSP's customers in the same way as if it were a VNF, but the tight integration in this case allows for better performance and management capabilities.

> **FYI:** *The type-drivers and mechanism-drivers are not directly used as a plug-in, but rather fall under the Modular Layer 2 (ML2) driver plug-in. By design, Neutron could only add one core plug-in and that means that if one vendor plug-in is used as core plug-in, Neutron couldn't use another one at the same time as a core plug-in. The ML2 core plug-in solves this problem and allows multiple vendor add-ons and different Layer 2/Layer 3 technologies to exist simultaneously. These API extensions are implemented through codes that are referred to as drivers (type and mechanism drivers). We can think of drivers as plug-ins to ML2 and ML2 being a plug-in to Neutron. But to differentiate them for plug-ins, the term driver is used for them instead. For Neutron, ML2 acts as the sole core plug-in and then it acts as an intermediary between Neutron and the drivers.*

Open Virtual Switch

In traditional networks the servers were connected to the networks using physical switches for network interconnectivity. When servers become virtualized, the resulting virtual machines still need to be interconnected. This creates the need for a software entity that would work in the same way as a physical switch. This switch would connect virtual machines with each other as well as connect with the physical interfaces to provide connectivity outside of the physical server. These software modules, called virtual switches, offer this functionality.

Open Virtual Switch (or Open vSwitch, or simply OVS) is an open source virtual switch implementation. It was initially developed by Nicira (now acquired by VMware), and the code was later released as open source software. OVS is a multilayer virtual switch; it provides the standard switching protocols working between virtual and physical interfaces.

Other popular software switches developed by different vendors are Cisco Nexus 1000v, VMware Virtual Switch (Distributed vSwitch or Standard vSwitch). However, given that OVS is open source, the OpenStack community used it as the default switch. Besides, OVS is designed to be controlled by any external controller and in case of OpenStack, Neutron's OVS plug-in makes it easily possible. However, OVS is not a part of OpenStack, and OpenStack can use other available virtual switches as well, as long those switches have a plug-in (more precisely, a ML2 module) available for Neutron to work with them.

OVS provides support for multiple protocols such as 802.1ag, Netflow, Sflow, and IPFIX, and it also supports GRE, VxLAN, Link bundling, BFD, etc. [15].

Note

OpenStack supports Single-Root-I/O Virtualization (SR-IOV) in Neutron through the use of ML2 module for an SR-IOV capable network interface card (NIC). If that is being used, then software vSwitch can be replaced by the virtualized I/O ports that are offered through SR-IOV capable hardware.

Configuring OpenStack Networking

Three basic network entities were described earlier in this section—subnet, port, and network. For demonstrating how Neutron is used to setup a network using these parameters, let's walk through the steps involved. The steps shown here are using Horizon dashboard (in Icehouse release), but just like any OpenStack module, all the steps can be performed using API calls. The use of a GUI dashboard is more human-friendly, but for automated scripts the direct API calls are the most efficient way.

Step 1. Set up the network. Upon logging into the Horizon dashboard, the OpenStack tenant is authenticated from Keystone and can begin to configure a network by providing a network name as shown in Figure 4-34.

Step 2. Define the first of the three entities, that is, the subnet. Both IPv4 and IPv6 ranges can be defined as the subnet as shown in Figure 4-35. The network can now be associated with a new virtual machine that is created, and the

Figure 4-34 *Neutron Configuration: Network Name*

Figure 4-35 *Neutron Configuration: Configuring Subnet Address*

port from this network will be associated with that virtual machine. Therefore, all the virtual machines that associate with this network will be on the same Layer 2 network and be able to communicate.

Step 3. If the virtual machines need to communicate with the outside world or between Layer 2 domains, they need to talk through a router. This is accomplished by using the same GUI in a few steps by creating the router and then connecting it to a routable domain. As shown in Figure 4-36, In this case, it is also connected to the external network which provides reachability outside the cloud.

Figure 4-37 shows the topology once the router is created with the connectivity to the external network.

Step 4. To connect the Layer 2 network to the router, an interface needs to be created on the router, which indicates that this router is connected to the subnet previously defined. This is depicted in Figure 4-38. Once this step is completed, the Subnet now has reachability of the external network as shown in Figure 4-39 and uses the default-gateway that was defined for the subnet to reach the routing interface.

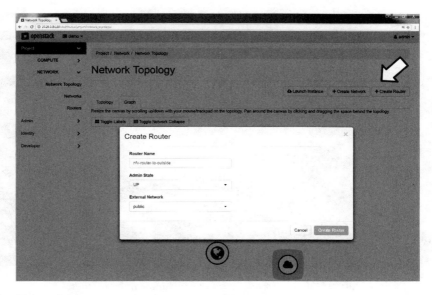

Figure 4-36 *Neutron Configuration: Creating Router*

Figure 4-37 *Neutron Configuration after Router Creation*

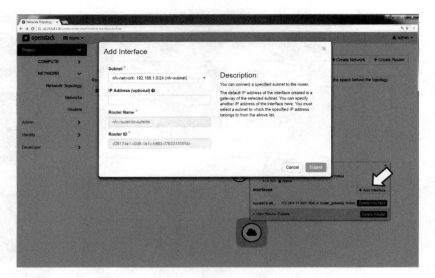

Figure 4-38 *Neutron Configuration: Adding Interface to Router*

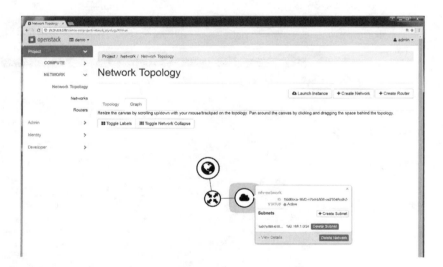

Figure 4-39 *Neutron Configuration: Subnet Connected to External Network through Router*

OpenStack Deployment Nodes Revisited

Earlier in this chapter, the types of OpenStack deployment nodes were mentioned. Only the relevant modules that are part of OpenStack are needed on each of these node types. Figure 4-40 puts this in the full perspective and shows that the modules

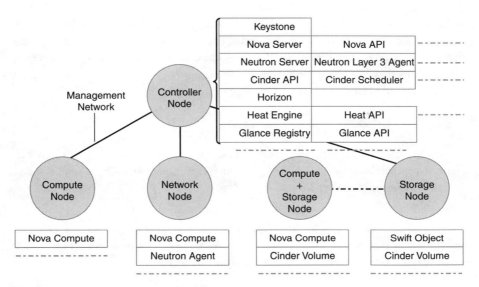

Figure 4-40 *OpenStack Nodes and Modules*

have a client-server model. The controller node runs as the central control for the module's server code, while the client part runs only on nodes that offer relevant virtualization. For example, a storage node needs to run only the Cinder client module (Cinder-Agent), but the Cinder API, which works as the central node for Cinder, needs to run only on the OpenStack controller node. Some components like Keystone, or Horizon and Heat belong only to the controller node. If for any reason the management network's connectivity between the controller node and one of the other nodes is lost, that node is not able to provide its function since it needs the server side part of its module, as well as the essential services such as Keystone to be connected through the management network.

OpenStack High Availability

High availability of an infrastructure is meant to provide mechanisms and design options that keep any single point of failure (SPOFs) in the hardware, application, or operating system from impacting the services running on the infrastructure. In an NFV deployment, the high availability of the network is very critical, and as mentioned previously in Chapter 3, "Virtualization of Network Functions," a carrier-class implementation needs to ensure five-9s availability. An NFV deployment could have failure points in servers, network transport equipment, NFVI components, MANO tools, operational and business support system (OSS/BSS) layers, and the VNFs. These failure points need to be protected. While the considerations related to VNF design were discussed in the previous chapter, this section focuses on high availability for MANO and NFVI layer, particularly in an OpenStack-based infrastructure, as well as the knobs available through these layers to assist VNF and virtual machine redundancy. If the management and orchestration becomes impacted due to a failure, it may not take down the VNFs or the functions they are performing—but it will impact NFV capabilities such as agility, deployment and Elasticity, along with all regular management functions.

> **SPOF**
>
> A single point of failures is an individual element in a system, which can be hardware, software, or an OS, whose failure can impact the whole system and result in downtime or data loss.

This section uses OpenStack's high availability as an example of the types of measures that may be required to protect the MANO block and also takes a look at the design options for implementing a highly available cloud.

High Availability for OpenStack Services

The OpenStack infrastructure doesn't have a lot of measures put in to ensure resiliency, but it does benefit from resiliency and clustering techniques that are implemented in its host operating systems, as well as generic high availability mechanisms.

With the modular infrastructure of OpenStack such as multiple services like Nova, Swift, Glance, Neutron, and Keystone, different variations of high-availability methodologies are possible. This section explores some of the commonly deployed architecture that is currently in use. Each module or service of OpenStack can practically have its own high-availability methodology. As these services are gaining maturity and new features and capability are being added to OpenStack, this high-availability implementation may change overtime and might result in a common framework.

The high-availability for each service of OpenStack can fit into any of the following concepts and should be evaluated against business needs. The overall infrastructure deployment can therefore have any combination of these models.

Stateful and Stateless Services

A service implementation can be stateful or stateless. Stateless services do not require additional handshaking when responding to a request made to them from any of their clients. The queries and requests to stateless services are independent, and responses do not depend on previous history. This makes it easy to replicate the service modules for stateless services and use multiple copies simultaneously to provide redundancy and load balancing. If one of these instances fails, the others can bear its load without causing a service disruption. Examples of stateless OpenStack services include nova-api, glance-api, keystone-api, neutron-api, and nova-scheduler. The CSP can choose to run multiple copies of these, spread them out among different servers or OpenStack nodes, and mitigate the chances of any disruption. The clients making requests to these services can reach any active services that are available and access them at any given time.

Stateful services, on the other hand, require a data exchange or a handshake between the service module and the client making the service request. The response to a subsequent request by a stateful service may be dependent on the response to previous requests by that client. This means that the clients have to connect to the same instance of the service for each request or query that's a part of a transaction. A high availability implementation of these types of services is more complex. Simple duplication of service modules can't easily guarantee that each request by a client will reach the same instance during a session. For these type of services, if duplication of a service module is performed for redundancy, then some level of coordination may be needed between those service modules so that they are aware of each other's state. Some techniques such as active-active redundancy, or active-passive redundancy come into play for such cases. Examples of OpenStack stateful services are database service and message queues.

The stateful and stateless services can be compared to the Transport Control Protocol (TCP) and User Datagram Protocol (UDP) protocols. Just as TCP requires a handshake and is connection oriented, stateful services require the client and service module to establish a connection, and each query and response can be dependent on the result of previous ones. Similarly, UDP's connectionless implementation makes it analogous to stateless services, where each request, query, and response between client and service module communication is independent.

Active-Active and Active-Passive Redundancy

One of the most common methodologies to use multiple instances of stateful services is to implement them as active-passive or active-active instances. In the active-passive mode of redundancy, only one of the services instances is active at a time, while the others stay on standby as backups. This ensures that the client always reaches the same instance (the active instance). If that active instance fails, one of the standby instances take over and starts to handle client requests. The existing sessions with the failing instance may see an interruption in this case and may need to be reestablished.

In case of active-active mode, all the replicated instances are active at the same time. The client requests are handled by using a load balancer to distribute traffic towards the service instance and keeping track of the same session per service.

Single Server Install

As mentioned previously, OpenStack can be deployed in an all-in-one (AIO) fashion, with all the modules on the same server. This single server install can have software-level redundancy by using multiple instances of AIO on the same physical server, however it can't have a redundancy from hardware perspective, since all the services are running on a single physical server. Therefore AIO deployment is useful only for demonstration purposes or lab usage. Production grade deployment demands that the heart of the system (that is, the controller node) be protected along with the modules.

Clusters and Quorum

To implement redundancy for large-scale production deployments, clustering techniques are used. In this case, redundancy is implemented by grouping together multiple controller nodes forming a cluster. Additional levels of redundancy are formed by deploying additional clusters and forming cluster-level redundancy.

In clusters with even number of controller nodes, it is possible that the active controller node may not fail but only lose connectivity with the standby. Any such disruption in the communication between active and standby can result in a situation where the standby falsely detects failure of the active node and assumes active status itself. This sort of situation results in multiple active controller nodes, causing disruption to the service.

To resolve this issue, controller nodes or clusters are deployed in odd numbers, so if an active server fails then the decision to failover to the redundant node is based on the majority rule scenario to keep the data and processes intact. This concept of majority rule scenario is called a quorum. If multiple nodes fail within the quorum and the policy defined enforcing the threshold for the active number of servers to be alive is not met, then the whole cluster is brought down, so that the other cluster can take over all the load.

When using cluster for OpenStack, the common methodology used are the standard Linux cluster management software such as Pacemaker or Veritas cluster server.

In a Pacemaker-based cluster deployment scenario, there are different deployment options with the following three possibilities:

- **Collapsed—all-in-one service**: In this scenario, all services are hosted on a single controller node, and whole node is replicated on multiple servers for achieving redundancy. This implies that the servers need to be powerful enough to host all services at once.

- **Collapsed—distributed service**: The services are distributed across multiple servers, where each server's host has a combination of services, and those servers are duplicated for redundancy. In this case, the amount of computing power required from those servers is less, as the host has a subset of service compared to the all-in-one service scenario. This implementation needs more servers due to the distribution of a set of services per server.

- **Segregated mode—based deployment**: Each service is run as a single service on a server, which provides the flexibility of an individual service to scale up or down as needed without impacting the other services. The redundancy is achieved by replicating each server. The downside is that this type of implementation is that it requires a larger number of servers.

Figure 4-41 depicts the three different service deployment options.

Pacemaker and Veritas

Pacemaker is open source resource manager software for high availability server deployment. Its creation was driven as part of the Linux-high availability project and later became standalone software.

Veritas Cluster Server (VCS) software is a commercial product from the vendor Symantec. This high availability cluster software is supported in the UNIX, Linux, and Windows operating systems. The cluster capabilities span across system software, applications, database, and network file sharing.

Keepalived

Keepalived is open source software that provides a load-balancing and highly available Linux infrastructure to manage the packet flow to the services, based on Layer 4 load balancing to the active service. The high availability in Keepalived is based on the VRRP protocol. In the Keepalived high availability architecture, there is no additional management software to deploy this feature, in contrast to cluster-based scenario.

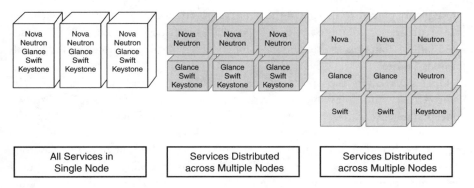

Figure 4-41 *Cluster Deployment Options*

VRRP

The Virtual Router Redundancy Protocol (VRRP) is a dynamic protocol that provides a mechanism to address a single point of failure in the network. VRRP assigns a master device as a virtual gateway to handle all the incoming traffic. In case of the failure of this master device, a backup device takes the responsibility of the master providing the network continuity and highly available network. VRRP standard morphed from the proprietary HSRP (Hot standby Router Protocol).

OpenStack Cloud Redundancy

The redundancy mechanisms of the OpenStack cloud discussed in the previous section are meant to make the OpenStack cloud highly available. More specifically, those methods are intended to protect the availability of the OpenStack controller node. These methods are not visible to the user of the OpenStack cloud, and while they provide a more reliable infrastructure, they do not ease off the requirement of redundancy in the user's design. Users should still take additional measures in their design by implementing redundancy at the application level on the VNFs (routing protocol, VRRP, etc.) as well as designing redundancy between the virtual machines and containers for the VNFs. OpenStack facilitates and assists in making this VNF-level redundancy design by offering a few helpful knobs.

For example, the user may implement virtual machine–level redundancy by creating multiple copies of the virtual machine. These virtual machines may be in an active/standby configuration (one group of virtual machines passively backing up the other group), or the active/active configuration (where redundancy is between processes running on the two groups of virtual machines, while they share the load). In either case, these virtual machines (or groups of virtual machines) need to be strategically placed to minimize the chances of simultaneous failure if the shared infrastructure (or compute node, to be specific) experiences a failure. Without isolated failure domains, the redundancy implemented is voided with a single controller node failure.

OpenStack offers the option of strategically placing the virtual machines by using Affinity and by taking into account the availability zones. Before these two concepts are covered, it is important to first explain OpenStack regions. When the OpenStack sites are distributed but part of a single cloud, then they can be split into regions. Each region has a full set of OpenStack modules, but only the Keystone module is shared across the regions. This allows for grouping within a distributed OpenStack deployment and segregation based on geographical distances. Each region provides an independent API endpoint, and modules have visibility within this region. For example, Glance can only view images that are within its own region and not the images that are present in others. So the modules within a region use the resources that are local to them, and when a virtual machine is being created, Nova provides compute resources and then requests Cinder and Neutron within its own region for networking and storage. Essentially, this means that OpenStack regions can be viewed as independently deployed subgroups of OpenStack modules that are stitched together in a common OpenStack cloud.

Within these regions, OpenStack can define availability zones [37]. These availability zones are subdivisions that represent fault domains. Servers that are connected to the same power feed share availability zone, because if the feed gets disconnected then all of those servers are affected simultaneously. Similarly, servers connected to same upstream switches are all in the same availability zones as those in which they share data path. To maximize high availability of the virtual machine, the redundant virtual machines must be placed in different availability zones. When creating the virtual machines, the user can specify an *availability zone* within its *region and* provide it as one of the parameters passed to *Nova*.

Affinity groups provide another opportunity for OpenStack to offer a way to control the placement of the virtual machines. Affinity groups can be assigned by the provider for each Nova instance and the OpenStack user can request that their virtual machines run in the same affinity group, or they can request that some of the virtual machines not be run in the same affinity group. This allows users some level of control to spread out and distribute their virtual environment over pre-created host groups by the provider.

Figure 4-42 shows the concepts of regions and availability zones.

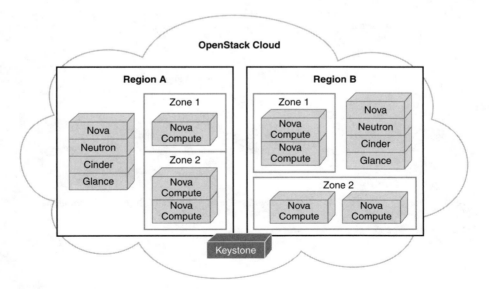

Figure 4-42 *OpenStack Regions and Zones*

Live Migration for VNF mobility

VNF mobility is needed in any cloud deployment for business and operations reasons such as scheduled maintenance windows, consolidation or relocation of servers or data centers, power efficiency by moving VNF to a low-power-tariff data center, moving a VNF from a highly utilized server to a less utilized server, etc. In an OpenStack deployed cloud, using the live migration feature provided in OpenStack, VNF mobility can be achieved in a way that does not impact customers. To achieve seamless live migration, the following design requirements need to be considered during the initial deployment stage of the cloud:

- VNFs should utilize shared storage.

- The same type of hypervisor software should be used on the active and the migrated Node.

- Consider Network bandwidth and Latency during the live-migration.

Figure 4-43 walks through the Live migration process.

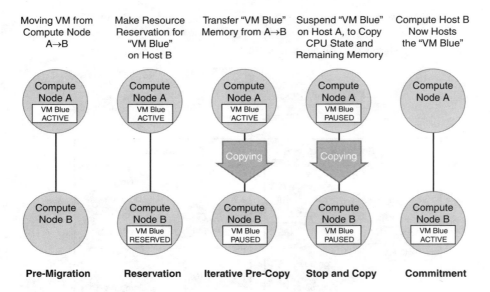

Figure 4-43 *OpenStack Live Migration Process*

Deploying OpenStack

The goal of using software tools such as OpenStack, vCenter and other Cloud Operating Systems (COS) is, as mentioned earlier, to facilitate and automate the deployment and management of cloud applications. However, the COS needs to be deployed and installed. OpenStack, being open, modular, and fast evolving makes it one of the more complex ones to deploy among these. Because it is community supported (the free version), it is harder to make the deployment smooth. OpenStack is available for most common Linux flavors such as CentOS, Ubuntu, Red Hat, SUSE, and Debian, and there are many customized and paid versions of OpenStack available, offering the service centered around deploying, supporting, and sometimes managing a customized OpenStack infrastructure for a private or public cloud. Some examples of these are Red Hat OpenStack by Red Hat, SUSE Cloud by SUSE, Meta-Pod by Cisco, and Ubuntu OpenStack by Ubuntu [16].

The details of OpenStack deployment and use of the available tools are not relevant to this book, but just to gain basic familiarity with commonly used tools, a few are mentioned here.

Devstack

Devstack is meant primarily for non-production or development installations of OpenStack. It's basically a scripted install of OpenStack, which is optimized to quickly create an OpenStack environment for development, testing, and demonstration purposes. Devstack can be installed on a supported operating system and then used to pull a stable OpenStack repository from one of the code repositories. There are also some prebuilt images available that have Devstack built into them and can be installed and then used to pull the OpenStack installation on top of them [17]. Launching Devstack is fairly simple; download Devstack and launch the shell script from its files, as shown in Figure 4-44 [18].

Packstack

Packstack is a tool that is used to perform an automated deployment of OpenStack. It uses Puppet, a configuration management tool, to orchestrate OpenStack deployment.

```
[root@localhost ~]# git clone
https://git.openstack.org/openstack-dev/devstack
[root@localhost ~]# cd devstack; ./stack.sh
<snip>
```

Figure 4-44 *Devstack Installation Procedure*

To install Packstack, it must be added as a package to the Linux environment and then launched to determine the type of OpenStack installation required and then determine which components should be installed. Based on the answers to the interactive questions (or based on the command-line arguments), Packstack creates an answer file that is used by the installation scripts to complete the OpenStack installation process. Packstack can also be installed using the all-in-one option, as shown in Figure 4-45.

> **Puppet**
>
> Puppet is open source software designed to perform configuration management. Its logic is written in its own language and the language files are called Puppet-Manifest. These files determine what the configuration should be for the servers (or virtual machines) that it is managing.

Ubuntu OpenStack Installer

Canonical (the company behind Ubuntu open source Linux) and Ubuntu offer installers for an OpenStack cloud environment. Canonical Autopilot offers support to build a private cloud, while other Ubuntu installers are meant for single and multi node install [19]. These installers use Ubuntu tools like Juju and Metal as a Service (MAAS) to perform OpenStack deployment.

In its simplest flavor, Ubuntu's OpenStack installer can be used to install it on a single machine, with easy-to-follow CLI steps for deployment [20] and a graphical interface for updating and managing the OpenStack environment. Figure 4-46 shows

```
[root@localhost ~]# packstack --all-in-one
Welcome to the Packstack setup utility

The installation log file is available at
/var/tmp/packstack/20160407-183305-c2bBs5/openstack-setup.log

Installing:
Clean Up                                    [ DONE ]
Setting up ssh keys                         [ DONE ]
<snip>
**** Installation completed successfully ******
Additional information:
<snip>
```

Figure 4-45 *Packstack Installation Procedure*

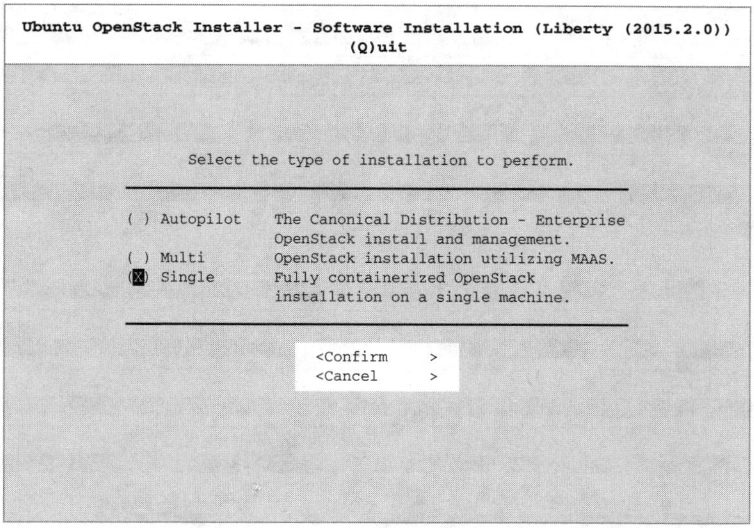

```
Ubuntu OpenStack Installer - Software Installation (Liberty (2015.2.0))
                                (Q)uit



                     Select the type of installation to perform.
       ───────────────────────────────────────────────────────────────
       ( ) Autopilot   The Canonical Distribution - Enterprise
                       OpenStack install and management.
       ( ) Multi       OpenStack installation utilizing MAAS.
       (X) Single      Fully containerized OpenStack
                       installation on a single machine.
       ───────────────────────────────────────────────────────────────

                          <Confirm    >
                          <Cancel     >

```

Figure 4-46 *Ubuntu OpenStack Installer*

the simple GUI to choose the installation type, and once installed, the OpenStack deployment is easily managed using the GUI shown in Figure 4-47.

Juju

Juju is a tool developed by Canonical (Ubuntu) for orchestration and automated installation. Juju isn't meant exclusively for OpenStack, but for deploying any service to the cloud. Juju's orchestration logic is defined by Juju Charms. A Juju-Charm defined for OpenStack can therefore be used to orchestrate an OpenStack deployment.

MAAS

MAAS is acronym for Metal as a Service. MAAS is offered by Canonical/Ubuntu as a tool to provision and deploy bare-metal servers as part of a cloud. Once servers or machines are identified to MAAS, it can go ahead and boot them up, validate their hardware, and be ready to deploy software on them. MAAS uses Juju to perform the provisioning of the software on the system. To Juju, this server may be a virtual machine (MAAS already takes care of the physical aspects) so Juju can go ahead and perform the deployment as instructed to it.

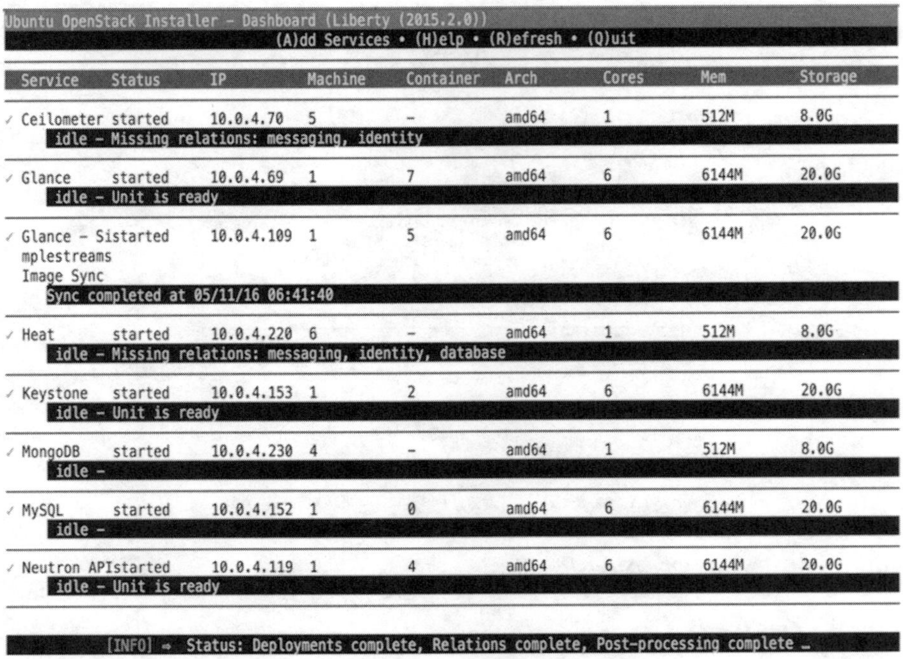

```
Ubuntu OpenStack Installer - Dashboard (Liberty (2015.2.0))
                        (A)dd Services • (H)elp • (R)efresh • (Q)uit

Service    Status      IP          Machine   Container   Arch    Cores   Mem     Storage

✓ Ceilometer started    10.0.4.70   5          -          amd64    1      512M     8.0G
        idle - Missing relations: messaging, identity

✓ Glance    started     10.0.4.69   1          7          amd64    6      6144M    20.0G
        idle - Unit is ready

✓ Glance - Sistarted    10.0.4.109  1          5          amd64    6      6144M    20.0G
  mplestreams
  Image Sync
        Sync completed at 05/11/16 06:41:40

✓ Heat      started     10.0.4.220  6          -          amd64    1      512M     8.0G
        idle - Missing relations: messaging, identity, database

✓ Keystone  started     10.0.4.153  1          2          amd64    6      6144M    20.0G
        idle - Unit is ready

✓ MongoDB   started     10.0.4.230  4          -          amd64    1      512M     8.0G
        idle -

✓ MySQL     started     10.0.4.152  1          0          amd64    6      6144M    20.0G
        idle -

✓ Neutron APIstarted    10.0.4.119  1          4          amd64    6      6144M    20.0G
        idle - Unit is ready

        [INFO] → Status: Deployments complete, Relations complete, Post-processing complete _
```

Figure 4-47 *Ubuntu OpenStack Installer: Monitoring and Status*

Fuel

Fuel is offered by Mirantis and is another open source tool to deploy OpenStack. Fuel offers an interactive GUI to determine which components and modules should be installed and where they should be installed [21].

Using OpenStack as VIM

Earlier the steps involved in configuring a network for the virtual environment were shown, using OpenStack Horizon dashboard GUI. For a complete picture of using OpenStack to deploy VNF, this section showcases the basic monitoring functionalities that OpenStack offers as VIM. It also walks you through the steps involved to construct a VNF that uses the network segment that was deployed earlier. It should be emphasized that when scripts and automation tools are used, or when other functional blocks are instantiating the VNF, they use direct API calls to open source modules, or use CLI (which is a wrapper around the API) to perform these steps.

Step 1. When logged into Horizon, the user can see an overview of the compute node utilization as shown in Figure 4-48. This data is presented only for computing resources, as the OpenStack compute nodes are managing the hardware that is used by NFVI. (The controller node resources are not used for VNF resource allocation.)

Step 2. For a VNF to be instantiated, it needs to be presented as an image. This could be one of the file formats that mentioned in Chapter 2, "Virtualization Concepts," that can package a virtual machine (such qcow2, vmdk, etc.) or a Docker image (for containers), or a read-only ISO file can be provided as a virtual machine image that will be used to boot-up the virtual machine. Figure 4-49 shows these choices.

Step 3. (Optional) On the same screen, the user can also optionally define the minimum disk size and memory allocation that a virtual machine should have been allocated if it is to use this image. These ensure that the VNF doesn't get instantiated with lower than required resources, as that would cause performance degradation or instability. Figure 4-50 shows the menu

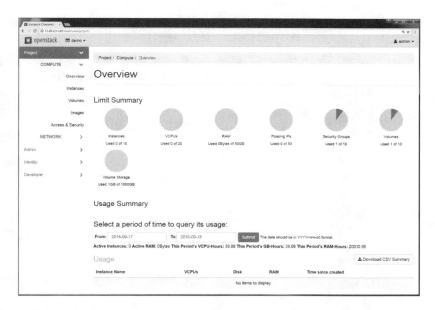

Figure 4-48 *OpenStack VNF Deployment: Compute Resource Monitoring*

Figure 4-49 *OpenStack VNF Deployment: Image Types for Creating Image*

Figure 4-50 *OpenStack VNF Deployment: Creating Image, Location, and Memory Requirements*

options available to set these lower bounds, as well as the two options to load the image file. The image file may exist on any reachable URL address or on the local machine. Once this file information is provided, OpenStack enters this information in Glance database and stores the image in Open-Stack's storage repository. The Glance database can then be viewed using the Image tab, as shown in Figure 4-51.

Step 4. (Optional) The instance tab option can be used to launch the instance, as shown in Figure 4-52.

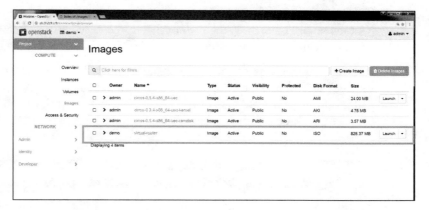

Figure 4-51 *OpenStack VNF Deployment: Glance Database View*

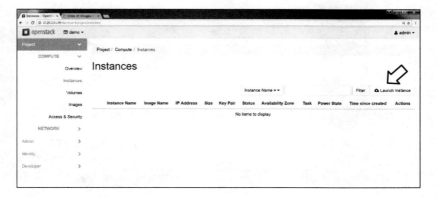

Figure 4-52 *OpenStack VNF Deployment: Launching Instance*

Step 5. VNF can use one of the predefined flavors. These flavors are defined by the OpenStack administrator and offer a specific number of options for computing, memory, and storage space resources. If minimum disk and memory requirements were configured for the image earlier, the flavor selected must meet those minimum requirements. Figure 4-53 shows the selection of flavors and the resulting allocation of Virtual CPU (VCPU), Root Disk, and Ephemeral Disk for the VNF being initiated.

Step 6. Any VNF created should have connectivity to other VNFs or to the external network. Therefore, the association with a network segment is part of the VNF instantiation process. The user can associate the VNF with one of the existing network segments that are owned or shared with that user. As shown in Figure 4-54, the previously created "nfv-network" network is available, and this VNF will be associated with it.

Step 7. The last thing to define is the image that the VNF will boot from. This is the image that was previously uploaded, as shown in Figure 4-55. Another possible option is for VNF to boot from a saved snapshot. At this point, all the resource parameters can be verified, and then the image can be launched.

Figure 4-53 *OpenStack VNF Deployment: Predefined and Customer Flavors for Instances*

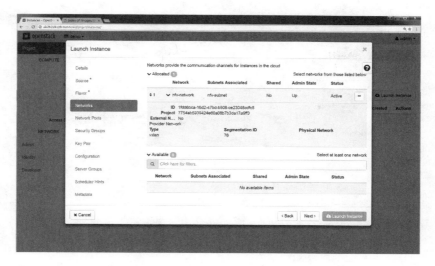

Figure 4-54 *OpenStack VNF Deployment: Associating Network to Instance*

Figure 4-55 *OpenStack VNF Deployment: Image Source for Instance*

The status of the VNF that was just launched can now be viewed from the Instance menu tab, as shown in Figure 4-56. The image was successfully launched and running.

With this newly created instance, associated with the "nfv-network" network, Neutron has now created the ports and shows the association in its GUI, as seen in Figure 4-57.

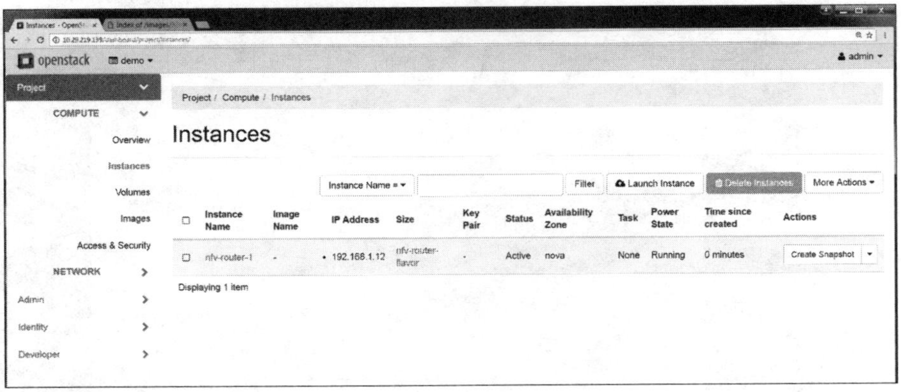

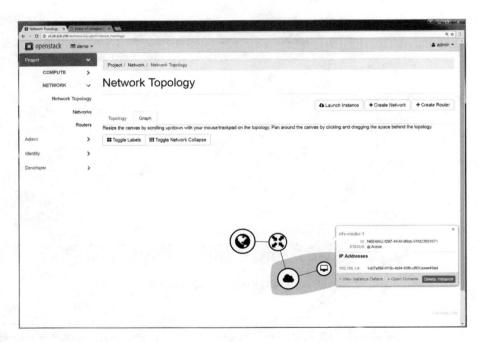

Figure 4-56 *OpenStack VNF Deployment: Instance Status*

Figure 4-57 *OpenStack VNF Deployment: Newly Launched Instance Connected to the Network*

Life Cycle Management of VNFs

The NFVO functional block handles the life cycle of the network service. But for individual VNFs, the life cycle management functionality is the job of the VNF Manager (VNFM) functional block in MANO. The life cycle of a VNF was mentioned previously in Chapter 3, "Virtualization of Network Functions" in context of design and cost considerations. Figure 4-58 shows the VNF life cycle that was presented previously and describes each of the stages and how they are managed.

Instantiation and Provisioning

VNFM interacts with the NFVO block to learn about the VNF that needs to be created or managed for a service. It then uses the information in the VNF Catalogue to determine the resource requirements to instantiate the VNF. The orchestration details in the VNF Catalogue may require one or multiple virtual machines (or containers, or bare-metal servers) to be brought up using a specified image and then programmed with an initial configuration.

VNFM doesn't have any interaction with the infrastructure or hypervisor. One possible path that VNFM can take is to let NFVO handle the resource reservation

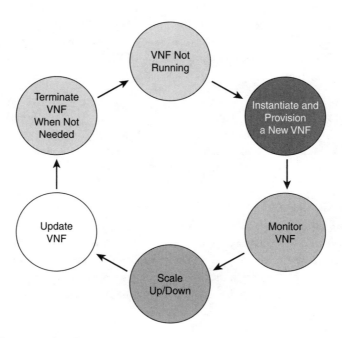

Figure 4-58 *VNF Lifecycle*

request to VIM and confine VNFM's role to determining the hardware resources needed for the VNF or the number of virtual machines required (based on the details it has from VNFD). In this case, VNFM can pass the resulting information back to NFVO, which takes into account its awareness of resources available (through the NFV Resource repository) before requesting VIM to create and allocate the virtual machine resources needed. An alternate path could be that VNFM checks NFVO for resource availability and then makes the resource allocation to VIM directly. To complete the instantiation process, VNFM also configures the VNF with initial configuration.

Monitoring VNF

One of the parameters in VNFD defines the performance indicators and monitoring parameters for the VNF (this element is defined by ETSI as monitoring_parameter). It tells the VNFM about parameters for performance and fault that it should monitor from virtual machine.

Scaling VNF

The monitored parameters are used to determine scaling and healing needs of the VNF. The auto_scale_policy in VNFD defines the action to perform for this, as well as criteria for any such action. Some very common actions are related to mitigating the issue through resource scaling. For example, if CPU consumption is high, then some possible action choices could be to add more computing power (scaling), switch to the redundant VNF (healing), or spawn an additional VNF copy to offload the original one (elasticity).

Updating VNF

Updating the VNF software version, configuration, or connectivity change may be another possible action requirement. These could result from changes made to the VNF Catalogue or a defined life cycle event in the VNFD.

Terminate VNF

A VNF may be terminated once its function is no longer needed or if the system needs to scale down. In this case, all the resources the VNF is consuming get released and returned to the resource pool. The termination action may be defined in the VNFD's lifecycle_policy entity, or initiated by a requester (for example, a user, OSS/BSS, etc.) or be part of elasticity operation to scale down the number of the VNFs when they are not needed.

VNFM Software Examples

Many network vendors, along with the open source community, are offering software to perform VNFM functions. The commercially available options, such as those offered by Ericsson, Cisco, and Nokia, are backed up by their support, service, and roadmaps. In some cases, the software is part of a bundle that the vendor may have qualified and offered. However, in most cases this software is able to work with any VIM and NFVO software by using standard APIs, in light of the openness requirement that NFV demands. Let's examine some of the popular software options and their support and capabilities available at the time of this writing.

Cisco's Elastic Services Controller

Cisco's offering for VNFM is called Elastic Services Controller (ESC). ESC, which is supported software, works with OpenStack and vCenter as VIMs. On the north bound, ESC supports any NFVO that can use RESTConf or Network Configuration (NETCONF) API calls. One big advantage that ESC offers is that it offers support for any third-party VNFs without the need for additional plug-ins [22].

Nokia's CloudBand Application Manager

CloudBand Application Manager is a VNFM tool offered by Nokia. It is part of Nokia's MANO solution, which also has CloudBand Network Director (as NFVO) and CloudBand Infrastructure Software (as VIM). However, it has the ability to work with other NFVO and VIM applications and offers support for several of them, as well as the ability to work with third-party VNFs [23].

Oracle's Application Orchestrator

Oracle Corporation's Application Orchestrator offers a full-fledged VNFM functionality, such as high availability support, elasticity capability and VNF provisioning using templates. On the southbound side it can work with VMware's VIM (vCenter) and Oracle's own VIM tools. The Application Orchestrator software itself is compiled to run on a Red Hat, CentOS, or Oracle Linux distribution [24].

Ericsson's Cloud Manager

Ericsson offers VNFM functionality through its Cloud Manager software. Cloud Manager provides the basic VNFM functions such as a resource utilization, managing both VNF and PNF and using Catalogues to deploy the VNFs and configuration management—to name a few.

HP's NFV Director

HP offers a bundled NFVO and VNFM solution called NFV Director. Its built-in capability offers VNFM functionalities as defined by ETSI, and it offers support for working with other vendor's VIMs and NFVOs. [25]

***

Orchestration and Deployment of Network Services

Orchestration, deployment, and management of network services in NFV are handled by the NFVO functional block in the ETSI framework. As we saw earlier, NFVO uses multiple data repositories to determine the requirements for network services and requirements for the VNFs, defining the links between the VNFs as well as end-to-end topology and finally keeping track of the deployed services' state and infrastructure availability state.

The operations support system (OSS) directly interacts with NFVO, and when the OSS requests any changes to the network services or deploys (or removes) a network service, then NFVO takes care of this request and passes the necessary requests for other functional blocks like VIM and VNFM. To provide the NFVO functionality, many vendor-developed and open source community options are available. Let's examine some of these options and their support capabilities that are offered at the time of this writing.

Cisco's Network Service Orchestrator

Cisco's NFVO offering is called Network Service Orchestrator (NSO), which orchestrates network services using both physical and virtual devices simultaneously. NSO can work with multiple vendor devices and VNFMs, using plug-ins for device CLIs, SNMP, or standardized YANG models over NETCONF.

Telefonica's OpenMANO

Telefonica developed and released OpenMANO, which is an open source management and orchestration tool. OpenMANO has three main parts: openmano, openvim, and openmano-gui. Out of these three, openmano provides the NFVO functionality and interacts with openvim. To manage and use openmano, users can choose either CLI or REST API calls or the built-in GUI interface provided by openmano-gui.

Telefonica has made this product open source, and it is available through Github under open source licensing [26]. OpenMANO forms the core of an open source MANO effort called OSM [27], which is described later in this chapter.

Brocade VNF Manager

Brocade's VNF Manager offers NFVO and VNFM functionalities bundled together as one software package. VNF Manager is based on a OpenStack's open source Tracker project (which is discussed later in this chapter) and can be considered a commercialized vendor supported version of Tracker. VNF Manager integrates with other VNF management tools from Brocade, but it also offers flexibility and vendor-freedom by supporting VNF Catalogues to be defined using Topology and Orchestration Specification for Cloud Applications (TOSCA) language.

Nokia's CloudBand Network Director

When Nokia's VNFM offering was examined, the CloudBand Application Manager was mentioned. The CloudBand Network Director is part of the same product family and performs NFVO functionality [28]. Its supports TOSCA for on-boarding service catalogues and offers both resource and service orchestration functionalities as well as policy engines for analytics and reactive changes to the network service.

Ciena's Blue Planet

Ciena's acquisition of Cyan, the original developers of the Blue Planet software, provides a carrier-grade orchestration system for NFV. It was built with consideration for multivendor support and has an ecosystem of VNF vendors validated and supported by this platform. Blue Planet supports RESTful API and a YANG/TOSCA model-driven approach to interact with other systems that are part of the NFV solution. The Blue Planet platform utilizes the container-based microservices architecture to provide a lightweight and easy integration to other systems.

HP's NFV Director

Mentioned earlier for its VNFM capabilities. HP's NFV Director has both NFVO and VNFM bundled into a single package. It can use its built-in VNFM function or act as standalone NFV orchestrator tool and interface with other third-party VNFMs.

Ericsson Cloud Manager

Just like HP's NFV Director and Brocade's VNF Manager, Ericsson's Cloud Manager NFVO solution is bundled together with its VNFM software. Cloud Manager performs the essential NFVO functions such as resource and service orchestration and repository management, plus it also offers close integration with Ericsson Network Manager for end-to-end network management [29].

OpenStack Tracker

OpenStack was originally focused on a VIM functional block, especially because of its background as an alternative to AWS. As it has started to adapt NFV and ETSI specifications, the OpenStack community has started the Tracker project for performing higher-level management functional blocks. Tracker focuses on NFV orchestration and VNF management functions [30] of OpenStack.

Tracker is open source, and it uses TOSCA for the description of NFV orchestration. Some vendors (such as Brocade) have developed their NFVO and VNFM products by using Tracker, customizing it to their environment and adding their support behind for the end product.

RIFT.io's RIFT.ware

RIFT.io offers an open source engine for performing NFVO and VNFM functions called RIFT.ware. It offers compatibility with ETSI's architecture. Its NFVO and VNFM software has become part of the effort to put together an open source MANO (OSM), which is discussed in depth in the next section [31].

NFV MANO and Open Source Solutions

When NFV was being conceptualized, from the very beginning the affinity with open platforms as well as development of open standards was one of the main drivers. NFV therefore has a close relationship with open source development. As a consequence, many open source projects began to support NFV implementation. Similarly many existing open source projects have been evolving to integrate with NFV architecture, such as OpenStack Neutron and OpenStack Tracker. There are quite a few open source solutions that have become available to offer the entire MANO block's functionality. Some of the emerging ones that have gained popularity and traction are Open Platform NFV (OPNFV) and Open Source Mano (OSM).

Open Platform NFV

Open Platform NFV (OPNFV) is an effort by the Linux Foundation to offer a complete NFV open source solution. While ETSI has described the architecture, the contributors towards it were primarily service providers. Software and tool development, however, is not the forte of service providers, which meant that implementation of the architecture framework was left out for vendors and software developers. In September 2014, the Linux Foundation stepped in and announced its plans to help establish OPNFV as an open platform for NFV.

OPNFV didn't start from scratch. Rather, it has integrated together many individual open source projects that could help realize the ETSI NFV model. At its beginning, OPNFV focused only on the VIM functional block and NFVI block. Therefore the open source software that was selected as the ingredients were OpenStack (for VIM), Linux (for service host), KVM (as hypervisor), Ceph (to handle storage), Open vSwitch (for VNF connectivity), Data Plane Development Kit (for networking performance), OpenDayLight (for management and configuration), etc. Figure 4-59 shows some of the open source software that the OPNFV platform has integrated. Note that some of these, such as Open Network Operating System (ONOS) and OpenContrail, are closer to software-defined networking (SDN) and are discussed in Chapter 5. The fact that the SDN open source software is integrated into Open Platform for NFV reflects the reality that the two technologies are intertwined.

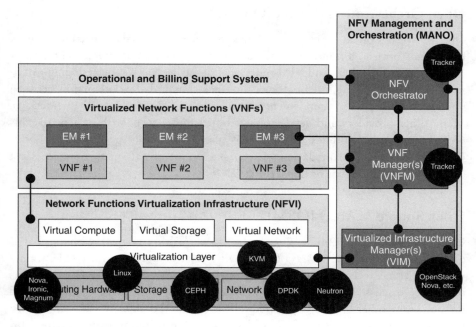

Figure 4-59 *OPNFV Open Source Ingredients*

In late 2015, OPNFV decided to expand its scope and include tools and software covering the entire MANO block, including NFVO and VNFM in its integrated software. By integrating these pieces together, OPNFV aims to provide service providers with a platform that is fully compliant with ETSI's framework, is open and free, and (most of all) has been tested and optimized to provide carrier-class performance and resiliency. OPNFV's first release was called Arno and the subsequent release was named Brahmaputra. These release are lab ready, tested for integration and hardened by OPNFV and providers can take a release and deploy in their environment. Integration was listed as one of the challenges for adaption of NFV. OPNFV directly addresses that challenge making it easier to adapt their integrated and tested release.

Note

OPNFV release names are named alphabetically using names of famous rivers. Arno is a famous river in central Italy, while Brahmaputra is a major river in Asia. The third release of OPNFV is named Colorado, which is the name of a major river in North America.

Open Orchestration Project (Open-O)

Open-O started off as a project by China Mobile and then announced as a Linux Foundation project. It is meant to provide an end-to-end MANO implementation by offering NFVO, VNFM, and VIM functionalities as well as VNF cataloging. Additionally, Open-O aims to define open interface standards for interaction between multiple vendor MANO implementations as well as SDN and NFV interactions. Many other providers and vendors have joined forces to contribute towards this project [32]. As this project matures, it is planned to be integrated into OPNFV (which is also a Linux Foundation project), but the future path of this project is not clearly defined at the time of this writing.

Open Source MANO (OSM)

OSM was launched in February 2016 at the Mobile World Congress, with the goal of offering an open source MANO functionality fully compliant with ETSI's framework. OSM has received contributions from Telefonica's OpenMANO (which was previously discussed and comprises VIM and NFVO functions), Canonical, and Rift.io. Many other big players related to this industry, such as Intel and Mirantis, have also contributed to OSM. Given that it is still in its infancy, the direction this tool takes will be determined in time, but at the time of this writing OSM's MANO implementations has contributions such as [33]:

VIM: Telefoica OpenMANO's openvim

VNFM: Canonical's Juju-generic

NFVO: Riti.io's Rift.ware, Telefonica OpenMANO's openmano, Mirantis' Murano Cataloging and Fuel [34], etc.

Describing Network Service Descriptor

To describe the NSD and other templates, a few different formats and languages have been gaining popularity. Some such examples are OpenStack's Heat Orchestration Template (HOT), TOSCA, Amazon's CloudFormation, Canonical's Juju Charms, etc. These have had mutual influence on each other; for example, HOT and TOSCA have borrowed from each other. There isn't a clear winner between these, though TOSCA seems to have gained more popularity. ETSI doesn't limit its specifications to any of them. Some of the template formats are briefly described in this section with a bit more emphasis on TOSCA due to its popularity. A detailed study of the templates' structure and use is beyond the scope of this book and enthusiastic readers can use the provided references to find more in-depth information.

Juju Charms

Juju is developed and offered by Canonical, as an application for easy deployment and management of preconfigured and predefined applications. Juju uses a data template in a format called Charms to define the components that need to be deployed. Charms package together a combination of files that describe the configuration (usually encoded in YAML) and actions scripts (called hooks) to manage life cycle events such as installation, scaling, upgrading, etc. [35]. Juju itself is considered more suitable as a VNFM, but the charm template could be used for defining NFV descriptors.

HOT

HOT, which is an acronym for Heat Orchestration Template, is one of the templates supported by OpenStack's Heat. OpenStack Heat natively supported CloudFormation-compatible CFN format, and HOT has been meant to replace it. HOT is encoded in YAML and uses a very simple way to represent the data. The fields used in HOT are shown in Figure 4-60 [36].

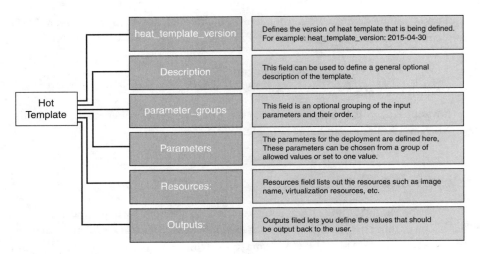

Figure 4-60 *HOT Fields*

TOSCA

TOSCA is an acronym for Topology and Orchestration Specification for Cloud Applications. It's a language that is defined as an open standard to describe cloud-based services, including NFV. Many vendors' NFVO implementations support TOSCA as one of the ways to describe the network service orchestration. Since TOSCA is open and available for anyone to adapt, TOSCA support by an NFVO engine translates to offering flexibility and vendor-independent description of the network service. This freedom offered to the service provider can be one of the factors for selecting a vendor's NFVO application.

TOSCA is defined by an organization called OASIS (Organization for the Advancement of Structured Information Standards), which works on development of various standards. Originally it was encoded in XML, but JSON and YAML encoding are also being explored and will likely become the preferred option. However, TOSCA is not about encoding, but its meant to describe syntax structure.

> **Note**
>
> Encoding of any data can be performed in different ways. An earlier example of JSON versus YAML encoding was provided. Syntax defines the variables, the values they hold, and the relationships between them, while encoding is just a way to communicate this information. If the communication is between applications, encoding such as XML can be easy to use, but if this formatting needs to be human-readable, then a format such as YAML is more meaningful.

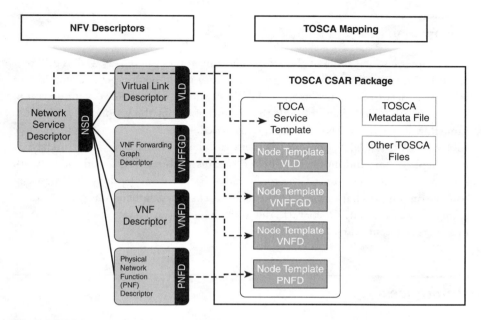

Figure 4-61 *NFV Descriptors to TOSCA Mapping*

TOSCA information is spread across multiple files that are bundled together using Cloud Service Archive (CSAR) format. One of the files in this format is called Service Template (using file extension .tosca). In case of NFV, this service template file is where NSD information is encoded. Recall that NSD has references to VLD, VNFFGD, and VNFD and consequently in the TOSCA description of NSD there are Node Templates defined within the service template file to represent each of these descriptors. Figure 4-61 graphically describes this mapping and relationship

CSAR

CSAR stands for Cloud Service Archive. It's a standard developed by OASIS (the same organization that is behind TOSCA) to define a way to package multiple files together in a compressed file using a specific file and directory structure.

Summary

This chapter covered some of the most important topics in NFV as well as different cloud-based service models and NFV orchestration and deployment. Compared to traditional networks, management and orchestration concepts are very important in NFV networks. The chapters built these concepts from the ground up, using the same flow as ETSI's MANO block, and discussed in depth the roles each of its three subblocks (VIM, VNFM, and NFVO) perform: that is, the management, orchestration, deployment, and monitoring of NFV infrastructure, VNFs, and the network service. This chapter covered the tools and software from vendors and the open source community that implement these subblocks. Special focus was given to open source tools, especially OpenStack, due to its high rate of adaption by NFV service providers in recent years.

References

Please refer to the following for additional information:

[1] http://nvlpubs.nist.gov/nistpubs/Legacy/SP/nistspecialpublication800-145.pdf

[2] http://www.etsi.org/deliver/etsi_gs/NFV-MAN/001_099/001/01.01.01_60/gs_nfv-man001v010101p.pdf

[3] http://libvirt.org/virshcmdref.html

[4] https://www.vmware.com/products/vrealize-suite/resources.html

[5] http://www.cisco.com/c/en/us/products/servers-unified-computing/ucs-director/index.html

[6] http://www.ericsson.com/spotlight/cloud/blog/wp-content/uploads/sites/10/2015/11/Management-orchestration-of-NFV-hybrid-networks-for-Blog-PA2.jpg

[7] https://www.vmware.com/products/Openstack

[8] https://wiki.openstack.org/wiki/Governance/Foundation/Structure#OpenStack_Today

[9] https://www.rackspace.com/cloud/private/openstacksolutions/openstack

[10] https://www.godaddy.com/garage/godaddy/news/building-open-cloud-openstack/

[11] http://releases.openstack.org/

[12] http://docs.openstack.org/developer/heat/template_guide/hot_guide.html

[13] http://www.etsi.org/deliver/etsi_gs/NFV-MAN/001_099/001/01.01.01_60/gs_nfv-man001v010101p.pdf (Section I.1.1)

[14] http://docs.openstack.org/user-guide/cli_create_and_manage_networks.html

[15] http://openvswitch.org/features/

[16] https://www.openstack.org/marketplace/distros/

[17] https://github.com/makelinux/devstack-install-on-iso

[18] http://docs.openstack.org/developer/devstack/index.html

[19] http://www.ubuntu.com/download/cloud/install-openstack-with-autopilot

[20] http://openstack.astokes.org

[21] https://wiki.openstack.org/wiki/Fuel

[22] http://www.cisco.com/c/en/us/products/collateral/cloud-systems-management/network-services-orchestrator/white-paper-c11-734976.html?cachemode=refresh

[23] https://networks.nokia.com/file/52201/info-sheet-cloudband-application-manager?download

[24] http://www.oracle.com/us/industries/communications/com-application-orchestrator-ds-2225363.pdf

[25] http://www8.hp.com/h20195/v2/GetDocument.aspx?docname=4AA5-1082ENW

[26] https://github.com/nfvlabs/openmano

[27] http://www.tid.es/long-term-innovation/network-innovation/telefonica-nfv-reference-lab/openmano

[28] http://networks.nokia.com/portfolio/solutions/cloudband

[29] http://www.ericsson.com/us/ourportfolio/products/cloud-manager?nav=productcategory008

[30] https://wiki.openstack.org/wiki/Tacker

[31] https://riftio.com/product/

[32] https://www.open-o.org

[33] https://osm.etsi.org

[34] https://www.mirantis.com/blog/open-source-mano-osm-to-work-on-nfv-orchestration/

[35] https://jujucharms.com/docs/stable/authors-charm-components

[36] http://docs.openstack.org/developer/heat/template_guide/hot_spec.html#hot-spec

[37] http://docs.openstack.org/openstack-ops/content/scaling.html

[38] http://www.wired.com/2012/04/openstack-3/

Review Questions

Use the questions here to review what you learned in the chapter. The correct answers are found in Appendix A, "Answers to Review Questions."

1. What are the different cloud-based services?

   a. Infrastructure as a service (IaaS), platform as a service (PaaS), and software as a service (SaaS)

   b. SDN as a service (saaS), platform as a service (PaaS), and software as a service (SaaS)

   c. Infrastructure as a service (IaaS), platform as a service (PaaS) and application as a service (AaaS)

   d. Infrastructure as a service (IaaS), hardware as a service (HaaS), and software as a service (SaaS)

2. Which cloud-based model is suited to bring in both the benefit of the private secured cloud and the low-cost public cloud?

   a. Mixed cloud

   b. NFV cloud

   c. Hybrid cloud

   d. Enterprise cloud

3. Mention the three main blocks of ETSI framework responsible for management and orchestration in NFV.

   a. VIM, VNFM, and NFVI

   b. VIM, VNFM, and NFVO

   c. VIM, VNF, and NFVO

   d. VNF, VNFM, and NFVI

4. Is virtual machine life cycle management part of NFVO?

    a. Yes

    b. No

5. In an OpenStack deployment, which module of OpenStack is responsible for the network component?

    a. Cinder

    b. Neutron

    c. OVS

    d. Nova

6. What is the role of VNFM according to the ETSI framework?

    a. Bridge communications between NFVO and VIM

    b. Hypervisor life cycle management

    c. Hardware life cycle management

    d. VNF life cycle management

7. Which is the preferred open source VIM software for NFVI deployment?

    a. OpenStack

    b. Cloudstack

    c. VMware vSphere

    d. XEN

8. The Keystone module of OpenStack is responsible for what?

    a. Authentication and GUI dashboard

    b. Authentication and authorization

    c. Storage and networking

    d. Management and orchestration

9. Which are the two main hardware virtualization deployment options available today?

    a. Virtual machine–based virtualization and Docker-based virtualization

    b. Bare metal–based virtualization and container-based virtualization

    c. Hypervisor-based virtualization and container-based virtualization

    d. Bare metal–based virtualization and hypervisor-based virtualization

10. What are the three types of descriptors that compose the Network Services Catalogue?

    a. VNF Forwarding Graph Descriptor, Network Services Descriptor, and Virtual Platform Descriptor

    b. VNF Forwarding Chain Descriptor, Network Services Orchestration, Descriptor, and Virtual Link Descriptor

    c. VNF Forwarding Graph Descriptor, Network Services Descriptor, and Virtual Link Descriptor

    d. VNF Forwarding Chain Descriptor, Network Services Orchestration Template, and Virtual Link Descriptor

11. New stable release of OpenStack are made available every _____.

    a. 6 months

    b. 12 months

    c. It's a continuous integration and continuous development process (CI/CD)

    d. 3 months

Chapter 5

Software Defined Networking (SDN)

The previous chapters focused on network functions virtualization (NFV) concepts, architecture, and deployment. Software-defined networking (SDN) is a different technology area that is independent of NFV. However, since its goals align very well with those of NFV, the two technologies complement and benefit from each other, bringing a very compelling solution to achieve the common desired results. A discussion about NFV would be incomplete unless it includes SDN. This chapter touches upon SDN, introduces its concepts at a high level, and explores the benefits it brings when combined with NFV.

The main topics covered in this chapter are:

- The concepts of SDN, and the motivations behind it

- Application of SDN in the end-to-end network architecture

- The correlation and cohesion between SDN and NFV

Basic Concepts of SDN

The software implementing the networking function in a traditional network device comprises multiple roles. These roles can be cataloged as independently working functional-planes that interact with each other using proprietary or open application program interfaces (API). The high-level classifications of these roles are as follows:

- **Control plane**: One of the roles is to determine and decide the path which the data has to take as it flows across the device, the decision to allow or disallow a data to transit, the queuing behavior of this data, and any manipulation needed to the data, etc. This is referred to as the control plane.

- **Forwarding plane**: The role for this part of the software is to implement the forwarding, queuing, and processing of the data across the device, based on the instructions provided by the control plane. This role is referred to as forwarding plane or data plane. The control plane therefore facilitates and decides the treatment of data entering the device, while the data plane performs the actions based on those decisions.

- **Management plane**: While the control and forwarding planes deal with the data traffic, the management plane has the responsibility of configuring, fault monitoring, and resource management of the network device.

- **Operational plane**: The operational state of the device is monitored by the operational plane, which has a direct view of all the device entities. The management plane works directly with the operational plane and uses it to retrieve device health information, as well as to push configuration updates to manipulate the operational state of the device.

In the traditional network devices, these planes are coupled together and communicate using proprietary interfaces and protocols, as shown in Figure 5-1.

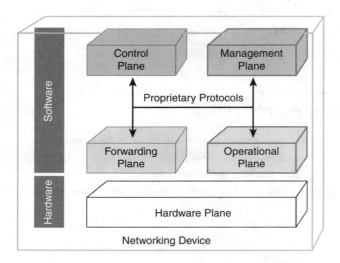

Figure 5-1 *Planes in Traditional Networking Device*

To explain these concepts in context, let's use a router as an example. The management plane, responsible for configuration of the router, provides a mechanism to define parameters such as hostname, IP address of interfaces to be used, routing protocol configuration, thresholds and classifications to be used for quality of service (QoS), etc. The operational plane monitors the interface states, CPU consumption, memory utilization, etc. and communicates the status of these resources to the management plane for fault monitoring purposes. The routing protocol, defined through the management plane, runs on the router, forming a control plane, and predetermines the flow of data traffic to populate the route lookup table (referred to as a routing information base, or RIB) which maps this data against the egress interface of the router. The forwarding plane uses this route lookup table and programs the path for the data transiting through this router.

Since the control plane is bundled into the device software, the resulting network architecture has a distributed control plane, where each node is performing its own control plane computations. These control planes may exchange information between them, for example the routing protocol running on each device interacts to determine the overall network topology or learn routing information from each other. Though the management plane also is localized, network management systems (NMS) have played a role to centralize it by putting another layer on top of the bundled management plane. Protocols such as syslog, Simple Network Management Protocol (SNMP), and NetFlow have traditionally been used to perform monitoring operations, while the configuration is done using proprietary CLI, APIs, SNMP, or scripts. Figure 5-2 presents a pictorial view of this deployment architecture.

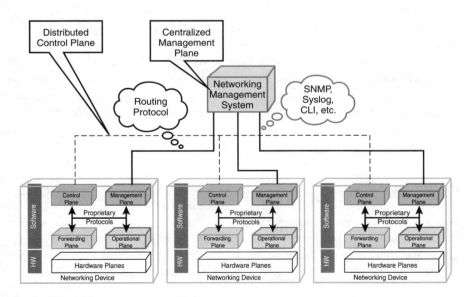

Figure 5-2 *Traditional Network Architecture*

With this background, let's go ahead and introduce SDN.

What is SDN?

In the traditional deployment of network devices presented earlier, the burden of decision-making based on the entire network state falls on each network device independently. This can potentially become a bottleneck whenever the capability to perform the control plane functions hits the device's limitations, even though data plane bandwidth is still underutilized. Also, when a control plane decision involves information from more than one node, for example in the case of Resource Reservation Protocol (RSVP), then additional communication is needed between the nodes to gather this information. This creates unnecessary overhead on the device.

SDN defines a methodology where the control plane can be centralized, moving its functionality from the network device(s) to a central device or cluster. This decouples the forwarding and control planes and offloads the control plane functions from the network devices, allowing the device to perform pure forwarding plane functions. With the separation of the control and forwarding planes, SDN also aims to replace the proprietary interfaces between these planes by open industry-accepted communication protocols. Therefore, SDN makes a vendor-neutral heterogeneous network possible, where the control plane may be interacting with multiple data planes implemented by different vendors.

The objective of SDN is to decouple control plane from forwarding plane, but it doesn't mandate that the centralized control plane be confined to a single node. For scalability and high availability purposes, the control plane may be expanded horizontally, forming a control plane cluster. The blocks comprising this cluster may communication through use of protocols such as Border Gateway Protocol (BGP) or Path Computational Element communication Protocol (PCEP) [1], and act as a single centralized control plane. Figure 5-3 shows the concepts of SDN and the changes that it brings compared to the traditional network architecture. Note that the figure doesn't emphasize the interaction of the planes with hardware planes or the operational and management plane, since SDN's focus is on control and forwarding planes.

Application Plane

In an SDN-based implementation, the control plane may be managed through an application, which can interact with both control and management planes. This application may abstract device information and configuration from the management plane, as well as network topology and traffic path information from the control plane. The application can therefore have a complete consolidated view of the

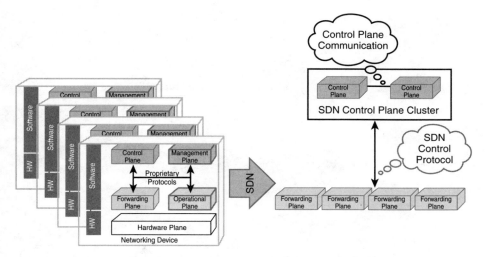

Figure 5-3 *Transition from Traditional to SDN Architecture*

network and use these pieces of information to make decisions that it can pass down to the control or management planes, as shown in Figure 5-4.

An example of such an application could be bandwidth on demand. This application could monitor traffic in a network, and provision additional traffic paths at certain times of the day or when a predefined threshold is crossed. The management plane would have to provide this application with information about the state and utilization of the network interfaces, while the control plane would offer the real-time forwarding topology that is in place. The application then combines the information to determine if additional paths need to be provisioned for the traffic of interest. User-defined policies can be employed to preset the thresholds for this application to take action. The application may communicate its action by instructing the management plane to provision the new path and telling the control plane to start using it.

Figure 5-4 also introduces the concept of northbound and southbound protocols and APIs. These terms are relative to the contexts in which they are referenced, in this case the SDN control plane and management plane. Therefore, the southbound protocols refer to the communication from the control or management planes to the lower layer planes. The interface provided by management and control planes to the upper layer planes, such as application layers, are referred to as northbound APIs or protocols.

Advantages of SDN

When the idea of SDN was originally introduced, its benefits were not compelling enough to make vendors or service providers seriously pursue this direction. Scaled

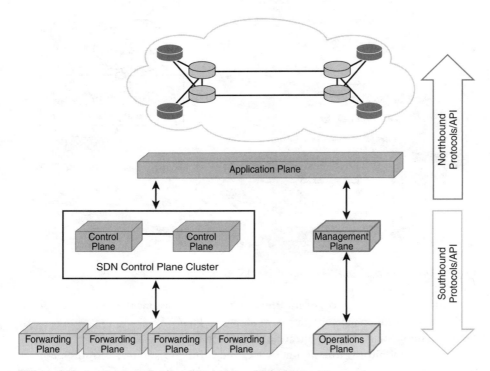

Figure 5-4 *Application Plane and Northbound/Southbound Protocols*

deployments were still using partially automated mechanisms for provisioning and management, and the tight integration of the control and data planes was not seen as a big bottleneck for growth. SDN was therefore initially looked upon as an academia topic and not as a practical, beneficial technological shift. As the networking industry expanded and struggled to cope with the factorial increase in demand, the norms of the networking world started to look like constraints and limitations. NFV is one example of how the industry became innovative and adopted new techniques to break free of the barriers of vendor lock-in. SDN is another such example. It didn't take SDN too long to move from academic world to real world deployments. SDN's adoption has been driven by its potential to implement flexible, scalable, open, and programmable networks. Some of the key benefits of SDN are discussed in the following sections. The benefits are correlated and reflect different aspects of the primary benefit of lowering operational costs.

Programmability and Automation

The ability to control the network through applications is perhaps the most significant of SDN's advantages. Today's networks demand higher agility in network restoration, massive scalability, faster deployment, and operating expense optimization. They simply cannot afford to be slowed down by the lack of speed in human-driven processes. Maximum use of automated tools and applications has become a necessity to meet the network's demands. Automation and programmability capability are needed to support the provisioning of networks, the monitoring and interpreting of device data, and implementing run-time changes based on traffic loads, disruptions, known and unknown events. The methods available through vendors have traditionally been specific to their devices or operating systems (OS) and have offered limited (if any) support for allowing an external device to make decisions based on logic and constraints across the network.

SDN offers a solution by linking applications to the network and bridging the void that existed with manual control and management processes. Since SDN puts the intelligence in a central controlling device (that is, the SDN controller), the programs and scripts that automatically react to expected and unexpected events can be built directly into the controller. Alternatively, applications can run on top of the controller using the northbound APIs to pass down the logic to the controller and eventually to the forwarding devices. The application can handle failures and increasing demand situations, offering quick remediation and restoration. This approach can minimize operational costs by making it possible to significantly reduce service downtime, improve provisioning time, and increase the ratio of devices to network operational staff.

Support for Centralized Control

The centralization of the control plane makes it easy to implement control logic, for all the important information needed is easily available. This consolidated view of the network is made possible by SDN It simplifies the logic for controlling the network and reduces operational complexity and cost.

Multivendor and Open Architecture

SDN breaks the dependency on vendor-specific control by being a proponent of standardized protocols. The traditional proprietary methods that vendors offered to access and configure devices are not easy to program and present a hurdle when applications and scripts are developed to automate some of the configuration and management processes. Especially in a mixed-vendor (or even mixed-OS) environment, the applications have to take into account the changes and differences in the device interfaces. Also, if there are any differences in how the vendors have implemented a control plane standardized protocol (perhaps due to difference in interpretation) it could result in interoperability issues. These challenges have existed in classical networks, but as SDN removes control from the devices, leaving behind only the data plane, it implicitly solves the issues of control plane interoperability in a mixed-vendor deployment.

Off-Loading the Network Device

The control plane of network devices can take up significant amount of resources, especially when the devices are running multiple protocols to communicate various types of information between them (for example, internal routes, external routes, labels, etc.) and then store this information locally as well as run additional protocol logic to use the data for path calculations. This creates unnecessary overhead for the devices and limits their scalability and performance. SDN's approach, which takes all of this overhead out of the devices, allows them to focus on what they are primarily built to do (forward data) while freeing up the processing and memory resources on devices. This can translate to reducing the cost of the devices, simplifying the software to achieve better scalability, and optimally using the resources.

SDN Implementation and Protocols

As explained earlier, the concept behind SDN is separating the control plane and splitting it off from the forwarding plane. A straightforward way to make this happen is to implement a control plane in an external device (that is, referred to as SDN controller) and leave a forwarding plane on the devices that are in the data path. This is exactly how most people initially visualize it, and this is the view that was presented earlier in this chapter. However, if you look more deeply into the SDN philosophy, the fundamental goals of centralized control and offloading the data plane can be achieved in various ways. A few possible implementations are introduced in this section. Let's first formally introduce the SDN controller.

Introduction to SDN Controller

The SDN controller is an independent device that acts as the SDN control plane and communicates its control plane decisions to the networking devices. The controller also retrieves information from those devices to make educated control plane decisions. For its communication with the devices, it uses protocols that are referred to as SDN control protocols. They are discussed in detail later in this chapter.

The SDN controller (or controllers, if more than one is used) don't have to be geographically colocated with the network devices, but they should be able to communicate with the network devices they are controlling. Various open source and commercial flavors of SDN controllers are available. They are examined in a later section.

SDN Implementation Models

It is not always technically feasible for vendors to completely separate the control plane from the networking devices and leave them to perform purely forwarding functions. Therefore, vendors have taken different approaches to implement SDN, which are not exactly in line with the SDN implementations that have been discussed so far. Service providers may have operational challenges that make it difficult to completely transform their networks to SDN and therefore they have good reasons to accept one of these alternative implementations of deploying SDN. As long as the SDN benefits are not compromised and the implementation stays true to the idea of the separation of planes, these approaches are valid ways to implement SDN. There are three ways being used to implement SDN.

Open (Classic) SDN

In this approach, the classic way of control and forwarding plane separation is implemented. Since the network devices that vendors have been building haven't had a way to make this happen, the support for SDN is added by replacing the local control plane with an SDN support layer. The new code is meant to work with the SDN controller and the forwarding plane of the device. It brings in the capability for the device to communicate with an SDN controller using one of the SDN protocols. It also has the capability to directly manipulate the forwarding plane. Figure 5-5 shows this transformation.

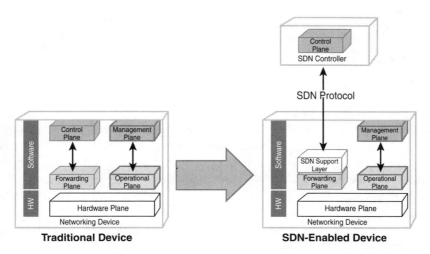

Figure 5-5 *Open SDN*

Hybrid SDN

Many vendors have taken the approach of modifying the device's control plane with an SDN support layer and claim their devices to be SDN ready. However this doesn't necessarily mean that the local control plane of the device has ceased to exist. The local intelligence may still be used with the control plane implemented through the external controller. Since in this implementation the device runs its own (distributed) control plane and the external SDN controller complements the device's intelligence by modifying the routing parameters that these protocols use or modifying the forwarding plane directly, then the approach is referred to as hybrid SDN. Figure 5-6 shows the hybrid SDN method. Note that the major difference here in comparison with the classic SDN approach is the use of a local control plane on the devices.

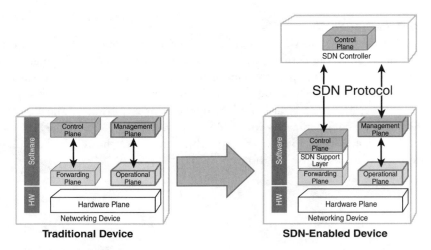

Figure 5-6 *Hybrid SDN*

SDN via APIs

Some vendors have responded to SDN by offering API access for provisioning, configuring, and managing devices. These APIs therefore allow applications to control the device's forwarding plane and are equivalent to the southbound APIs that controllers use with network devices. However, since the APIs can be directly plugged into the application, the need of an SDN controller, which uses standard southbound protocols, may not be present in this implementation.

This is a shift towards a more collaborative and open direction compared to the proprietary command-line interface (CLI) that vendors have been using. However, the implementation may not be truly open, since these APIs may not be compatible across vendors, and hence the proprietary aspect is not completely eliminated. Applications using this API-based SDN approach must be aware of which vendors' equipment they are communicating with so they can use the correct API.

The argument in favor of this approach is that the goals of SDN are still being met by allowing the applications to influence forwarding decisions and the APIs are openly available to anyone who wants to build an application and use the APIs. This makes the network programmable, but not necessarily flexible (because of proprietary southbound APIs). Some vendors have solved the flexibility problem by offering their own controllers, which use the proprietary APIs southbound (towards the networking devices) and standards-based APIs northbound to the applications. Figure 5-7 shows a few scenarios of the implementation of SDN via APIs.

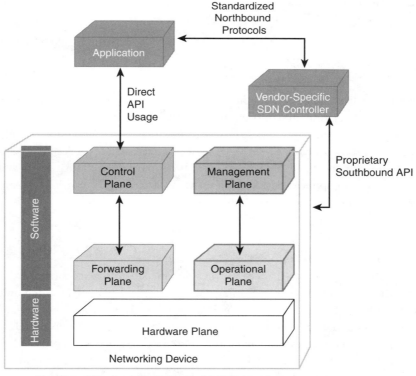

Traditional Device with Published API Support

Figure 5-7 *SDN via API*

SDN via Overlays

Another way to split off the control plane from a network is to create an independent overlay-network on top of the existing one. In such an implementation, the underlay-network still has a control plane, locally managed in the traditional way. But to the overlay-network, this underlay-network is simply providing connectivity and forwarding the data. To the user of the network, the presence of underlay-network, its topology, and its control-plane are transparent, and the overlying network is the network the user interacts with. The user can now employ an external controller to manage the overlay-network and doesn't need any SDN-specific support from the devices that form the underlay-network. This implementation of SDN networks still meets the fundamental criteria, with the only limitation being that the underlay-devices should support the protocol that is being used to implement the overlay-network. Earlier in this book the concept of a virtual network was discussed, and that is exactly what the overlay-network is. Some examples of this implementation are Virtual Extensible LAN (VXLAN), backed by a group of vendors, and Network Virtualization using Generic Routing Encapsulation (NVGRE), supported by Microsoft.

SDN Protocols

Irrespective of the methodology to implement SDN, some type of protocol has to be used for communications and information exchange between the forwarding devices, applications, and controllers. These protocols can be grouped into northbound and southbound protocols from the SDN controller's perspective. As described earlier, southbound protocols are between the control plane device, such as the SDN controller, or even applications, and the forwarding plane. The northbound protocols are used for applications to talk to the SDN controller.

Southbound SDN Protocols

The southbound protocols can be further subdivided into two categories. This classification is based on the reasoning that the control plane can communicate directly with the forwarding plane, or it may indirectly influence the forwarding plane by using a management plane to alter device parameters. The protocols that directly interact with forwarding plane are referred to as SDN control protocols. The protocols that use management plane to alter the forwarding plane can simply be referred to as management plane protocols. Figure 5-8 gives a pictorial view of this categorization of SDN protocols.

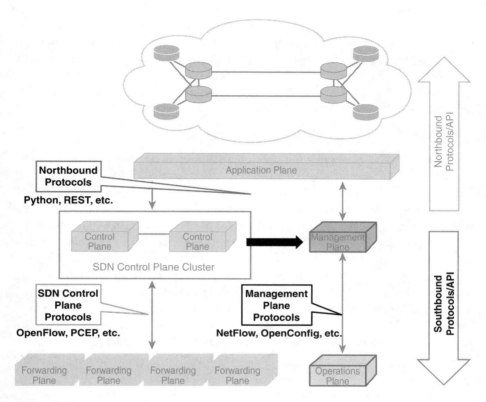

Figure 5-8 *SDN Protocols*

SDN Control Plane Protocols

The control plane protocols operate at a low level on network devices and program the device hardware to manipulate the data plane directly. OpenFlow, Path Computation Element Communication Protocol (PCEP), and BGP Flow Spec are the most commonly referenced ones among the SDN control plane protocols. This section briefly examines these protocols.

OpenFlow

Communication between the control plane and forwarding plane in the traditional vendor-developed network device takes place within the same device. These devices use proprietary communication protocols and internal procedure calls. In the SDN environment, because the control plane and forwarding plane are decoupled, a standard protocol with multivendor support was needed for communication between them. OpenFlow was developed for this purpose. OpenFlow was the first open source control protocol for communicating between the SDN controllers to the network devices to program the forwarding plane. OpenFlow has evolved from the initial lab version and matured into production-grade software with version 1.3 and higher.

OpenFlow maintains what it calls a flow table on the device, which contains the information of how the data needs to be forwarded. The SDN controller can then use OpenFlow to program the forwarding plane of an OpenFlow-enabled switch by altering this flow table.

To program the forwarding information and set up the path across the network, the OpenFlow architecture supports two modes of operation, reactive and proactive. The reactive mode is the default method of implementing SDN using OpenFlow and assumes that there is no intelligence or fragment of a control plane running on the network devices. In this mode, the first packet of the data traffic received on any of the forwarding nodes is sent to the SDN controller, and then the SDN controller uses this information to program the flow across the whole network. This creates the flow table on all subsequent devices in the path, and they switch the data traffic accordingly. In proactive mode, the SDN controller is preconfigured with some default flow values, and the traffic flow is programmed preemptively as soon as the switch is brought up.

As the SDN controller and switches exchange the flow of information over the network, it is recommended that a secure channel, such as Secure Socket Layer (SSL) or Transport Layer Security (TLS), be used for the OpenFlow communication between them.

Figure 5-9 shows the OpenFlow architecture.

FYI: OpenFlow focuses purely on control and data plane relationship. But the programmability advantage that it brings to SDN is somewhat diluted if the management and operations planes on these devices still have to be managed in the old-fashioned way. Originally OpenFlow was developed for switches, and its management aspect was minimal. However, to reap the full benefits of programmability, the management plane should also have an interface that applications can use. To complement OpenFlow, two different protocols are available for management and configuration provisioning: OpenFlow Configuration and Management Protocol (OF-Config) and Open vSwitch Database Management Protocol (OVSDB).

Path Computation Element Communication Protocol

Path Computation Element Communication Protocol (PCEP) is defined as a protocol that can work between two devices, one forwarding using Traffic Engineering (TE) while the other performing all of the computations for determining the traffic engineering paths. It is defined in Request For Comment (RFC)

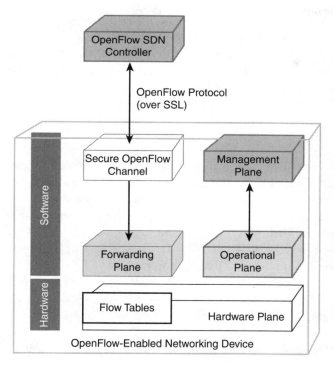

Figure 5-9 *OpenFlow Architecture*

4655. The RFC defines the device running a Traffic-Engineering (TE) protocol as a Path Computation Client (PCC). The device which does all the computation is referred to as a Path Computation Element (PCE), and naturally the protocol between the PCE and PCC takes up the name PCEP. The PCC can be any legacy routing device that has been enabled to work with PCE. Traditionally, the routers perform their own computations and exchange information between each other for that purpose. In the PCEP model, the router (acting as a PCC) does the forwarding and label imposition, disposition, etc. but it leaves the entire computation and path decision-making process to the PCE. If there are multiple PCEs working collectively, PCEP may also be used as a communication protocol between them. To learn the Link State Database (LSDB) information from the network, the PCE device could establish a passive IGP relationship with the devices. Since this limits the vision of the PCE to the area boundary, an alternative approach proposed is to use a new BGP extension called BGP Link State (BGP LS) that could be used to provide the LSDB information to the PCE.

PCEP is designed around SDN use-case for traffic engineering. So it applies to RSVP-TE, Generalized MPLS (GMPLS)–based TE, and more recently to Segment Routing TE (SR-TE). The role of the PCEP, PCC, and PCE remains the same in all these cases. For example, the PCC can request the PCE to perform path computations with specific constraints, and the PCE can respond back suggesting the possible paths that meet the required constraints.

BGP Flow Spec

BGP Flow Spec (BGP-FS) is an addition to the BGP protocol. It defines a method to advertise a flow filtering rule by a BGP router to an upstream BGP peering router. A flow filtering rule consists of criteria to match specific traffic and then to take certain actions on it, including dropping the matched traffic [2]. BGP-FS is standardized, defined in RFC 5575, and is supported by multiple vendors. It defines a new type of BGP Network Layer Reachability Information (NLRI), which can be used to create a flow specification. The flow specification is essentially the match criteria, such as source address, destination port, QoS value, packet length, etc. For traffic that matches, the system can take actions such as rate-limiting, QoS classification, drop, redirect to a Virtual Routing and Forwarding (VRF) instance, etc.

Putting this in SDN's context, the SDN controller could form BGP neighborships with the forwarding devices. As long as BGP-FS is supported on all of them it can be used to manipulate forwarding behavior by applying the traffic filtering rules sent to those devices from the controller using BGP-FS. In fact, BGP-FS was originally intended for dealing with redirecting or dropping distributed denial of service (DDoS) volumetric attacks. In that scenario the controller (after detecting an attack) tells the routers facing the attack-traffic to drop the matching traffic or deflect it to traffic scrubbing devices.

Management Plane Protocols

These protocols operate on the device configuration and in turn indirectly influence the forwarding plane. They assume a hybrid SDN approach. Therefore the devices are running their own control plane protocols, which are then influenced by external applications using the management plane protocols. Let's examine some of the protocols that fall into this category.

Network Configuration Protocol (NETCONF)

Network Configuration Protocol (NETCONF) is an Internet Engineering Task Force (IETF) standard protocol (defined using RFC 6242) that has been adapted by many network vendors with the purpose of supporting a programmatic interface to network devices. NETCONF uses a client-server model and applications act as a client to configure the parameters on the device acting as a server or to retrieve operational data from the server. The configuration or operational data being exchanged through NETCONF is formatted in a pre-defined structure that is described using YANG data models [3]. SDN controllers such as Cisco Network Service Orchestrator (NSO) enabled by Tail-f, Open Daylight (ODL), Cisco Open SDN controller (OSC), and Juniper's Contrail use NETCONF as the southbound protocol. NETCONF and YANG are discussed in more depth later in this section.

YANG

YANG, which stands for Yet Another Next Generation, is a data modeling language that was previously discussed. YANG was originally developed to work with NETCONF, but it is not limited to it.

RESTCONF

RESTCONF is an alternate approach to NETCONF that also uses the YANG data modeling language to interpret the configuration and operational data exchanges between the device and applications [4]. RESTCONF's operations are similar but not identical to the operations defined for NETCONF. RESTCONF finds its roots in the Representational State Transfer (REST) API, which has been commonly used by cloud service providers (CSPs) to program the compute infrastructure. It adapts the principles and operations similar to REST APIs to communicate to the network device providing an alternative to NETCONF for accessing configuration and operational data using YANG models. Due to its commonalities with REST APIs (which may already be in use by the provider for managing computing resources), the use of RESTCONF offers the convenience of a common interface for both the computing and network infrastructures. For example, it supports operations such as OPTIONS, GET, PUT, POST, and DELETE.

REST API

REST stands for Representational State Transfer. The REST architecture defines a mechanism for stateless communication between two entities in a client-server relationship. APIs that conform to the REST architecture are called RESTful APIs. The terminology RESTful API is often further shortened and called RESTAPI.

The most common choice of transport protocol for REST-based communication is HTTP. REST uses a small set of verbs for its operations (called REST methods), the common ones being POST (to create an entry), GET (to retrieve an entry or data), DELETE (to delete an entry or data from the server), PUT (replace an existing data or entry), and PATCH (modify an existing data on the server).

For encoding its verbs and other associated information, JavaScript Object Notation (JSON) has been the most popular choice for REST. However, XML and other methods can also be used as long as the server is able to decode this information and understand the request.

OpenConfig

OpenConfig is a framework that supports a vendor-neutral programmatic interface to the network device. It was started by a forum of network operators such as Google, AT&T, BT, etc. driving this effort in the industry to create a practical use case-based model to programmatically configure and monitor a network device.

OpenConfig uses YANG modeling as the standard for the data being transported. It doesn't specify any underlying protocol for the operations, but NETCONF has been adapted by a few vendors to support the OpenConfig framework. OpenConfig also offers support for monitoring of the network by supporting streaming telemetry data from the devices.

Streaming Telemetry

Streaming telemetry is a new approach of collecting the data from the network device, and contrasts with traditional network monitoring methods such as a SNMP, syslog, and CLI. The traditional methods have been predominantly polling based or based on events. Streaming telemetry uses a stream of information in a push model from the network device, sending out the necessary operational status and data information to the central server(s). It may be programmed to send data periodically or based on specific events.

XMPP

Some of the SDN controller vendors, such as Juniper contrail and Nuage networks have used eXtensible Messaging and Presence Protocol (XMPP) as the communication protocol between the central controller and the Network device. XMPP is an open source, free, and extensible protocol that provides a real-time exchange of data based on XML. XMPP was developed as an alternative to the vendor developed instant messaging system and has further gained traction in other technologies. Some of the main features of XMPP are as follows:

- open and free
- IETF standard–based protocols
- secure, supporting Transport Layer Security (TLS), and Simple Authentication and Security Layer (SASL)
- decentralized (Any organization can implement its own XMPP systems and enhance them for specific needs.)
- flexible and extensible, using XML to build custom features

Interface to the Routing System (I2RS)

I2RS is an IETF working group that is supporting the hybrid SDN implementation. Its aim is to provide a way to programmatically access, query, and configure the routing infrastructure on network devices. I2RS's stance is that the control plane doesn't need to completely moved out of the network device, as proposed by initial SDN proposal. I2RS suggests that issues such as lack of programmability, automation support, and vendor lock-in can be addressed by allowing a common way to influence the distributed routing decisions, monitor the devices, push policies to the devices, etc.

I2RS defines an agent and client. The I2RS agent runs on the network device and interfaces with the routing components such as LDP, Border Gateway Protocol (BGP), Open Shortest Path First (OSPF), Intermediate System to Intermediate System (IS-IS), RIB-manager, and the device's operational and configuration planes, etc. The I2RS agent provides read and write access to the I2RS client that is running on an independent device. This allows the I2RS client to manipulate the routing parameters or retrieve routing information by querying the I2RS agent. The I2RS client can also subscribe to event notification from the agent, so any subscribed routing element changes are communicated in a push model from the agent to the client.

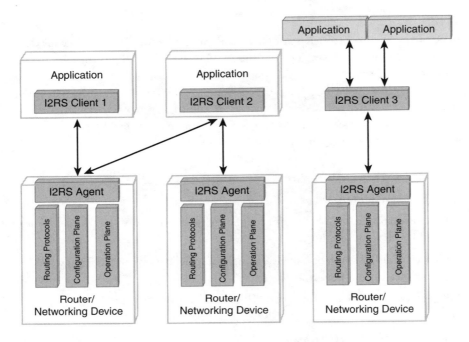

Figure 5-10 *I2RS Deployment Architecture*

The architecture for I2RS defines the agent to be capable of supporting and processing requests from multiple external clients. The I2RS client itself may be embedded code in an application or sitting between the routing device and the application, as shown in Figure 5-10.

Northbound Protocols

These protocols are used as the interface between the SDN controller and the application on top of it, as shown in Figure 5-11. The applications are usually meant to perform service orchestration or make and implement decisions based on logic or policies defined in the application. The communication between the SDN controller and application is not any different than communication between two software entities, so it doesn't require any special new protocol. The existing commonly used protocols are used for northbound communication, such as RESTful APIs or libraries in programming languages like Python, Ruby, Go, Java, or C++.

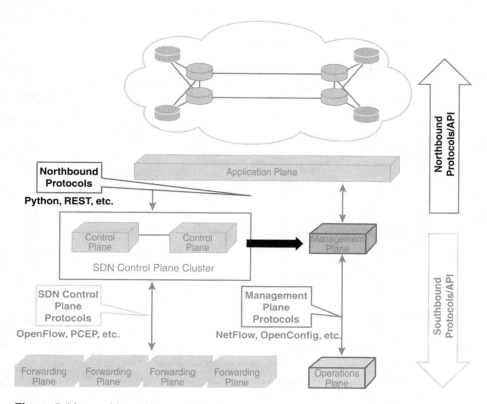

Figure 5-11 *Northbound Protocols/APIs*

Revisiting NETCONF, RESTCONF, and YANG

As mentioned previously, NETCONF and RESTCONF both use the YANG data modeling language for information exchange. The description of these protocols is not complete without mentioning the encoding techniques and transport mechanisms that they use. Let's first take a look at the relationship between all of these elements. As shown in Figure 5-12, the data (operational, configuration, user data), combined with programmed logic coupled with analytics, forms the applications recipe. If the application now intends to configure the device, it can structure that configuration information using a data modeling language such as YANG. Once the information is structured, the configuration protocol (for example, NETCONF) defines the type of operation that needs to be performed using this data. For example, if configuration data is being sent out, NETCONF may perform an edit-config

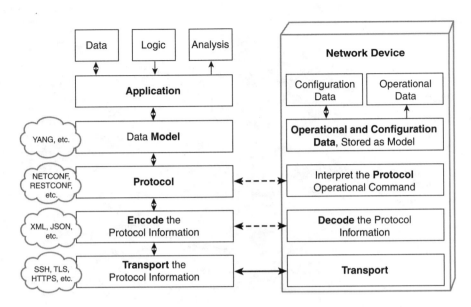

Figure 5-12 *Southbound Protocol Communication*

operation. The protocol's operation and the data mode information need to be encoded. Finally a transport protocol, such as Secure Shell (SSH), HTTPS, TLS, etc., has to be used for communicating information.

The network device needs to have the capability to communicate using the same transport method. Similarly, the device needs to decode the data and then pass it on to the protocol code to figure out the type of operation that must be performed. The device is expected to understand the data modeling language being used and present its configuration and operational data in the defined structure. Since both the application and the device are using same data models, they are able to easily interpret the parameters and fields associated with this data that is exchanged.

> **FYI:** *The differentiation between the data model, protocol, and encoder can become challenging for readers new to these concepts. For example, YANG data modeling may be represented using a JSON format, but that shouldn't be mixed up with protocol encoding. An analogy that might make this useful is to compare these with communication between humans. If we look at the categories in reverse order, and map those to what we use in our day-to-day verbal communication, the analogy will look a bit like the following:*
>
> * *transport medium: air*
> * *encoding: phonemes and sounds*
>
> *(continued)*

- *transport medium: air*
- *encoding: phonemes and sounds*
- *protocol: language being used, such as English*
- *data model: grammatical structure (if the sentences are not properly formed, the words of the language will not make sense)*
- *application: tongue and ear, or human speech and hearing organs in general*
- *data logic analysis: the human brain*

With this context, let's now look at NETCONF and RESTCONF. Both of these are popular and widely used protocols for configuring networking devices using a standard and common application that can work across platforms and vendors. In both cases, YANG is the data modeling language used, and the protocols are standardized through their respective RFCs. NETCONF favors the use of XML as the encoding technique, while RESTCONF is more commonly used with both JSON-based and XML-based encoding. At the transport level, NETCONF standards suggest a protocol that can be secure, authenticated, provide data integrity and security, etc. and though it's flexible it does make SSH as one of the mandatory options to be available. For RESTCONF, the popular choice is HTTP, but others methods such as HTTPS are also commonly used. Figure 5-13 shows this relationship between all of these blocks and the predominant choice for RESTCONF and NETCONF implementations.

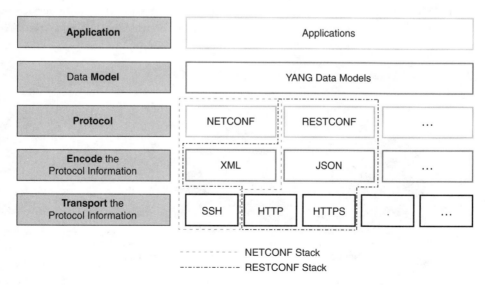

Figure 5-13 *NETCONF and RESTCONF as Southbound Protocols*

A Bit More about YANG Models

In an ideal world, the YANG models would be completely standardized for all features and categories of operational data. In fact, efforts are continuously being made under the IETF banner to have common standard YANG models for different features and configurable parameters. While these models, which can be referred to as IETF YANG, would seamlessly work across vendors, this common support would come with the drawback of not being able to support vendor-specific enhancements to the configuration parameters or operational data. These models can and should support the least common denominator. As shown in Figure 5-14, a separate set of YANG models were therefore developed (or modified using the standards-based models) by vendors. These models, referred to as native YANG models, are more tailored to the vendor's implementation. These YANG models are then published on public repositories and are available to application developers to import and use them. This approach breaks away from a standard-based approach but provides a realistic method while still offering the needed flexibility and openness. A third category of YANG models is driven by providers, under the OpenConfig banner who felt that the IETF's standardization was sometimes taking too long to meet their needs or was too heavily influenced by vendors. These providers stepped forward to develop and publish their own YANG models to fill the gaps.

The YANG models that have been mentioned are specific to network elements. They can represent a configuration of features or structures for operational data (for example, bit rates for interfaces or route scale for a protocol). The models work at the network element level. For completeness, it should be mentioned that YANG models can also be used to define a complete network service. Such service-level YANG models describe the structure and parameters for the entire service (for example, L3VPN service or VPLS service) and can be used by the orchestrator

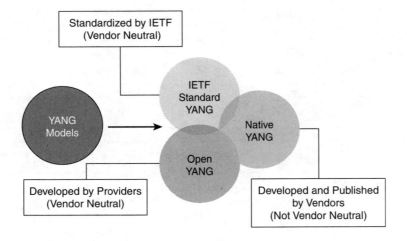

Figure 5-14 *YANG Model Categories*

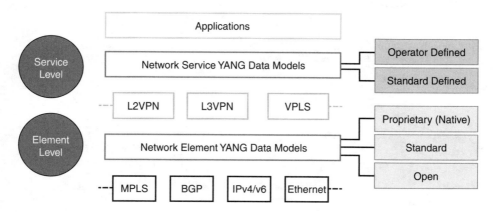

Figure 5-15 *YANG Model Classifications*

to implement the entire service. There are quite a few such models that have been defined through the IETF drafts, while in many cases the vendor or provider develops their own flavors to match the specific service deployment needs. Figure 5-15 shows a relationship between these two classifications of YANG models.

SDN Use-Cases for Different Networking Domains

Initially SDN was conceived as a solution to solve data-center scalability and traffic control challenges. This new technology made its way into other segments of the network, finding different use-cases and applicability in those areas as well. The protocols and the technology used by SDN vary based on the solution it brings to the challenges in each segment. Based on this, SDN is classified into five domains, as shown in Figure 5-16. SDN's role in each of these domains is discussed in detail.

SDN in the Data Center (SDN DC)

Data centers have existed since the mainframe era but have seen factorial growth in size and capacity in the last decade. This growth has been fueled by the advent of the Internet, cloud, and the consequent trend of providers to maintain an online presence to match consumer demands. It has resulted in large-scale data centers housing thousands of servers, deployed on dozens of acres, and consuming multi-megawatt power.

Problem and Challenges

The growth of these data centers has been a driving force behind the virtualization of servers. While it brings efficiency in space, power, and cost, the network architecture to interconnect these virtual servers brought new challenges. One of the

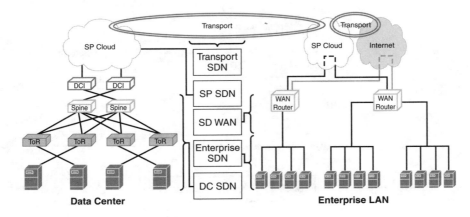

Figure 5-16 *SDN Domains*

challenges has been the limitation of virtual LAN (VLAN) scalability limit of 4096. The virtual servers are typically in the same Layer 2 domain, and VLANs are used to segregate between them to support multi-tenancy. Additionally, the use of cloud-based hosting by businesses created the need to span that business's VLAN domain across multiple data centers, further tightening the available VLAN space.

To relieve this constraint, the Virtual Extensible LAN (VXLAN) protocol was introduced. VXLAN offers to provide a Layer 2 adjacency between the virtual servers using a Layer 3 network. It creates an overlay network using the VXLAN IDs that can scale up to 16 million segments, thus solving the scalability problem. However, it brings a new challenge—to manage, monitor, and program this entire overlay network.

Figure 5-17 shows the VxLAN-based overlay network

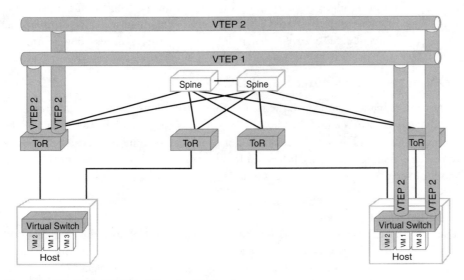

Figure 5-17 *VXLAN-Based Overlay Network*

SDN Solution

The VXLAN overlay network's end points (that is, VXLAN Tunnel End Points, or VTEPs) are either on the top of the rack (ToR) switch or on the host's virtual switch. In both cases, the VTEPs need to be programmed and associated with the tenant's virtual machines. The virtual machines in these massive data centers are deployed using orchestration tools. Examples of such tools were discussed in Chapter 4, "NFV Deployment in the Cloud," such as OpenStack, which can be used to deploy VMs in an automated fashion. These virtual machines therefore can be deployed on any of the physical servers, but for its connectivity to the rest of the network using VXLAN, an additional mechanism is required that should have visibility into the entire network. This is where SDN comes in, as it has a view of the network and can coordinate with the virtual development tool to program the forwarding plane (which is on the ToR or virtual switch) for the VTEP and VXLAN information. As shown in Figure 5-18, the SDN controller (more details about it are presented later in this chapter) communicates to the switch to create the VTEP interface based on the VMs that are provisioned on servers the switch is serving. Since its possible that the virtual machines may move between a physical server or get torn down, VTEP information may need to be reprogrammed or deleted. This is also taken care of by the SDN controller.

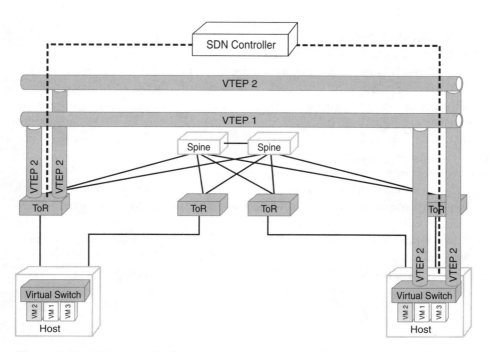

Figure 5-18 *SDN Controller Provisioning VXLAN Network on Virtual and Physical Devices*

SDN in Service Provider Cloud (SP SDN)

Routing devices in service-provider (SP) networks can be classified as provider edge (PE) and provider (P) devices at a high level. The PE-routers are directly connected to the customer networks and are therefore using large number of interfaces with specific features on these interfaces for classification, QoS, access control, failure detection, routing, etc. These routers carry a considerable amount of customer routing information and ARP caches, forming the perimeter to the service provider network. These devices further aggregate their traffic to the *P*-routers via high bandwidth upstream links.

The P routers are not heavy on features and are relatively much lighter in scale. However, they require the use of high bandwidth links between each other that are spread across various geographically distributed POPs. In most SP networks, commonly offered services such as voice, video, data, and Internet use common core links and core routers. These links carry converged traffic data from a large number of customers that these providers may be serving, and any disruption to the high-bandwidth links could impact a high number of consumers. Therefore, to avoid failures and offer carrier class availability, the links and the core routers that these links are interconnecting are deployed with physical redundancy.

Problem and Challenges

With redundant links, nodes, and paths available to the SP traffic, often the shortest available path between the nodes may not be the best path for cost-per-bit or may not be capable of carrying all of the traffic at once. It is, therefore, common practice among SPs to use traffic engineering techniques to steer traffic towards specific paths based on criticality, cost, delays, and network state. This enables SPs to optimize the cost and guarantee better performance. Figure 5-19 shows a generic view of SP network and exemplifies the use of traffic engineering tunnels to steer traffic away from an optimal-route towards a path that is preferred by the customer.

As mentioned, the optimal routing path may not be the preferred traffic path (either because of cost, latency, bandwidth availability, etc.), and specific traffic engineering techniques are used for overriding routing protocol behavior to meet the needs. MPLS Traffic Engineering (MPLS-TE) has been the most common technology used for achieving this goal. More recently, Segment Routing Traffic Engineering (SR-TE) has also been offered for this purpose. In both these protocols, the end-to-end view of the network link bandwidth, link preference, shared failure groups (such as links that may be sharing the same transport gear), switching information

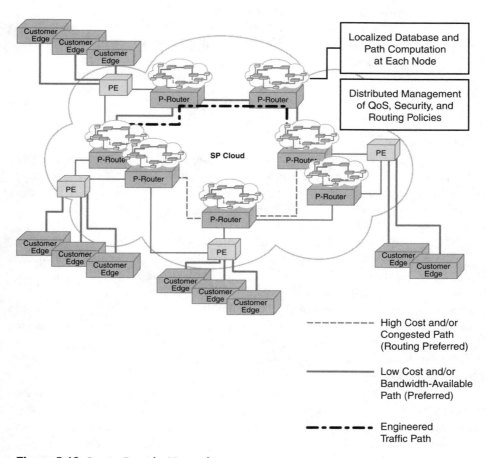

Figure 5-19 *Service Provider Network*

for the engineered traffic-path, etc. is not available to each node. Special protocols or protocol extensions are used to coordinate between the nodes for exchange of these information and decide the full traffic engineering paths. Each node makes the computation of the path and the decisions, and thus the data required for it has to be kept on all of them. This overhead takes away device resources, as it is CPU intensive and consumes memory, as well as requiring end-to-end coordination due to the distributed nature of the implementation.

Another challenge in SPs is scope of impact to the network and services in the event of a potential failure. Though mechanisms like Fast Re-Route (FRR) can be implemented, when coupled with capacity planning and QoS guarantee requirements, the overall network design can become quite complex and hard to optimize.

SDN Solution

The challenges for managing and designing traffic engineering across the network can be solved in an optimal and efficient way through the use of a central controller that has a vantage point view of the entire network's link state and can track the bandwidth allocation and allow the controller to handle the decision-making process.

SDN is perfectly suited for this role. In the SDN-based solution, the routers do not need to make the decisions or keep the database required for these decisions, which reduces the memory and CPU resource overhead. The central SDN controller could go beyond the basic decision-making criteria based on traffic and link utilization. It can be designed to interact with a higher-level application to use policy-based traffic re-routing. Examples of such policies are pre-emptive traffic re-routing before the maintenance window, changing traffic direction based on time of day or special events, or dynamic change of bandwidth allocation for specific traffic flows to meet temporary requirements.

The central controller could also play a role in managing the feature-rich PE routers. The new customers that are provisioned on these routers could be configured to have consistent QoS, security, and scale and connectivity experience based on their Service Level Agreement (SLA) requirements. If these requirements change at some point (for example, the customer requests a higher preference for any specific data stream), then the changes can be easily and consistently pushed down to the entire SP network edge routers from the centralized SDN controller, as shown in Figure 5-20.

SP network security and high availability are other critical business aspects that can benefit from an SDN-based solution. For example, if a provider network is experiencing a volumetric distributed denial-of-service (DDoS) attack (either to the customers it is hosting or to the SP network itself), then the central controller can be used to deflect the attack away from the standard routing path and redirect it towards either a central or distributed set of scrubbing devices, protecting the SP infrastructure.

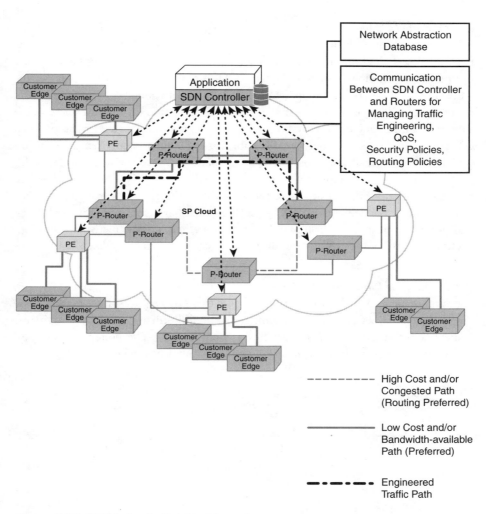

Figure 5-20 *SDN in Service Provider Network*

SDN in Wide-Area Networks (SD WAN)

Enterprise and business customer networks are spread over geographical regions, with multiple branch offices connecting to the head office locations. These sites utilize dedicated leased wide-area network (WAN) circuits, such as T1 or T3, or dedicated lines from a virtual private network (VPN) service provider to connect between different offices. These links or services come with large price tags and increase the operational expense for the networks. To reduce the cost overhead, companies have been shifting their connectivity towards secured Internet links, made possible by the use of new technologies such as Dynamic Multipoint VPN (DMVPN) or MPLS VPN. The overlay network can be set up dynamically with added encryption for data protection, enabling the use of a shared Internet connection for the enterprise's private traffic. Internet connectivity, however, may not guarantee SLA. Also, despite the encryption, it may not be considered suitable for exchanging highly sensitive corporate data. Therefore, this approach reduces the bandwidth requirements on the dedicated link yet doesn't completely eliminate the need for private WAN links. Based on the SLA required or the sensitivity of the data, the traffic can be steered to either the Internet link or the dedicated WAN links. Using this shared Internet provider link in addition to the primary dedicated link, the customer has a cost-effective way of connecting different branch offices and the head office, as shown in Figure 5-21.

Problems and Challenges

For large-scale WAN deployments with perhaps hundreds of sites, maintaining interconnectivity between the branch offices while still utilizing split connectivity of dedicated and interlinked links becomes a complex task. The policy that decides which traffic types can be deflected to the Internet link needs to be managed on each

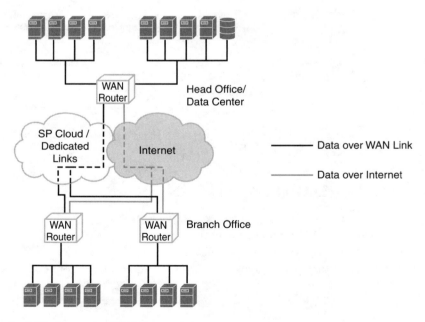

Figure 5-21 *Enterprise WAN Connectivity*

location as well, and this alone can become a management overhead. Optimizing these policies based on real-time measurements or making them dynamic with frequent changes isn't easily possible either. The cost and performance benefits were clearly visible, but without the presence of a management system that could centrally manage the flows and configure the WAN routers, achieving this result wasn't a feasible goal to pursuit.

SDN Solution

Using the SDN model of centralized network topology for the deployment, the WAN network with multiple links of connectivity can be abstracted to a central management system, which is termed a controller. The controller can monitor the SLA on the Internet links and instruct the branch or head offices to utilize the right links for the data. It also makes it possible to manage the traffic flows based on traffic type and nature of sensitivity and to split the traffic to efficiently utilize the dedicate circuit and the Internet link. Additional advantage of link utilization on the remote routers can be taken into consideration to make the decision of traffic flow egressing the source router. Therefore, the operational expense savings that were otherwise very hard to realize are now achieved using the SDN-based solution. This solution is referenced as SDN for WAN, or simply SD WAN. Vendor's offerings such as Viptela's vSmart, Cisco's IWAN, or Riverbed's Steel-Connect are some examples of commercial offerings of SD WAN. Figure 5-22

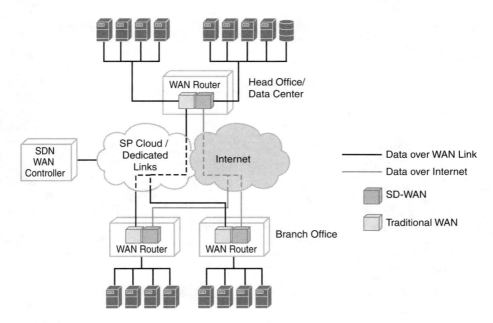

Figure 5-22 *SD WAN*

offers a pictorial view of this solution. As shown, a central SDN WAN controller manages the WAN routers to monitor performance for uplinks and alter their traffic flows using centrally managed policies based on link performance, nature of traffic, time of day, etc.

Enterprise SDN

An enterprise network consists of network devices spanning local LAN and WAN connectivity. Depending on the scale of the enterprise's business the local-area network (LAN) could consist of wireless and wireline for connectivity to the computers, printers, voice/video end points, and other network device. To connect to the remote branch office or data-centers, the WAN connectivity can have a dedicated WAN link or Internet link. There are multiple services deployed in the network, such as a voice network for internal office and external world communication, a data network connecting the local users, and data storage in a private data center or public cloud. Large-scale enterprises segregate their networks based on departments like engineering, finance, marketing, sales, and partners. Figure 5-23 shows a pictorial view of this enterprise network.

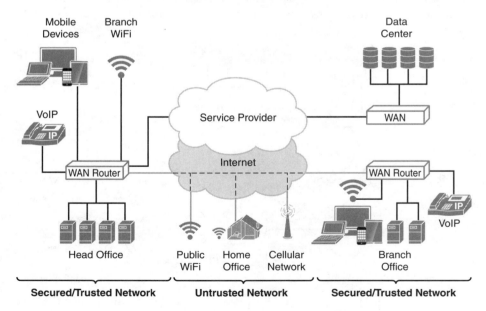

Figure 5-23 *Typical Enterprise Network*

Problems and Challenges

The requirements for enterprise network may need different policies depending on whether it is accessed from LAN or WAN. A high level of security and flexibility is essential to deploy and manage this type of network architecture. With the adoption of private cloud–based architectures by enterprise, the network access, firewall, and security practices need to evolve to benefit from this private cloud deployment. With so many new types of business agility models such as BYOD (bring your own device) and the proliferation of computing devices (laptop, mobile devices, tablets, etc.) and the ability to access the network anywhere from any device, enterprise IT department needs to support all of this architecture without compromising the network. The security policy to access the network is very dynamic and complex in nature. For example, the user access devices, like laptops running multiple Oss, need different security procedures, the network transport layer needs VPN and encryption, and data privacy is needed on the servers at the data center. The user policy needs to be provisioned at all of the user access points, and the QoS policy need to be deployed across the entire network.

With the fluid nature of network access by the user implementing the wireless and mobile device network transport, all of these policies need to follow the access ports on the edge network to which the user would connect.

SDN Solution

The enterprise challenges are being addressed using SDN's centralized model of the network view and its ability to program the network from a single source. For BYOD, the SDN controller can detect the presence of the device's entry on the network and based on the user or device, the appropriate profile can enforce the access policy on the device and as well program the edge and transport of the network with the appropriate policy enforcement. With this approach that creates a dynamic policy from a central source, the enterprise customer now can provide its users/employees or partners the ability to access the network from any location without the need to be physically present at a single office/desk. Without the SDN model, it would have been a cumbersome job for the IT personnel to configure QoS/security, etc. on the network dynamically, based on each device or user. If the organization has thousands of employees and is spread across multiple locations, such dynamic configuration is an almost impossible task with traditional methods. Additionally, to protect the enterprise network from any DDoS or other security attacks, SDN plays a significant role. In this role, when any signature of an attack is detected or learned from any source, the SDN controller can mitigate this security risk across the entire enterprise network and safeguard the business data. One such example is the use of BGP flow-spec to handle DDoS attack traffic. Once the attack traffic is identified, the BGP server running on the SDN controller can be made aware of this, and the server can then use BGP-FS to instruct the edge devices peering with it to drop or deflect (for scrubbing) all the traffic that matches the attack traffic's profile. Without this method, today this is being done by injecting a static route (which can only be used to match based on traffic destination) for a remote triggered black hole (RTBH) to tweak each edge device's routing to divert traffic towards scrubbing centers.

Enterprise networks are embracing the new network architecture in combination with SDN. It is bringing business benefits such as the self-service IT, lower operational expenses, security, and compliance with scale and agility.

Bring your own Device (BYOD)

BYOD provides the ability for the employees to bring any personal device of their choice, such as a laptop, or smart phone, to the office and access the company network with the same privileges as if using a company-provided device. This is also referred to as IT consumerization.

Transport SDN

Transport networks provide the Layer 1 infrastructure for connectivity to network points of presence. Typically transport networks are used by CSPs to interconnect datacenters or by a network service provider to form a network between their core routers. This transport network may be owned by the same provider or an independent transport network provider. Such networks consist of optical fiber links, optical switches, optical multiplexers (MUX) and demultiplexers (DEMUX), optical regenerators (REGEN), etc. and carry many logical circuits. The logical circuits sharing the physical media are separated through the use of different wavelengths (or lambdas, as they are commonly referred to), and these wavelengths/lambdas can be added to or dropped from the transport network at the ingress or egress points for the logical network. Figure 5-24 shows a simplified view of the transport network.

In today's transport networks, the functions of MUX and DEMUX are combined into single device that can be reconfigured to determine the lambdas that should be added or dropped. These are called reconfigurable optical add-drop multiplexers (ROADMs). In a transport network, ROADMs perform a very similar function to what switches (Layer 2 switches, or even label switched routers) perform in an IP network. Since the optical link carries multiple wavelengths at a time and uses the wavelength to determine the appropriate switching action,

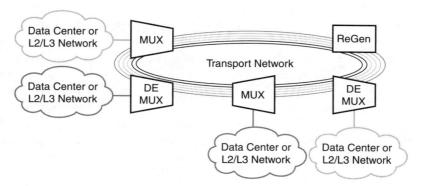

Figure 5-24 *Optical Transport Network*

the resulting network that uses ROADMs, REGEN, optical links, etc. is also referred to as a wave division multiplexing (WDM)–based switched optical network, or WSON [5].

Problems and Challenges

Just as a switch maintains a MAC table or an MPLS router maintains an label forwarding information base (LFIB) table, the ROADMs also needs to maintain a table to determine the switching, adding or dropping of a wavelength from the composite optical signal. Historically, the switching decisions were managed manually and locally on the devices, resulting in long provisioning times for any new circuit that had to be configured. To make the process automation-friendly and enable the devices to exchange control plane information, a few different protocols were developed independently. Most mentionable among those are Generalized MPLS (GMPLS) by IETF and Automatically Switched Optical Network (ASON) by International Telecommunication Union (ITU). The two had similar goals but different approaches. GMPLS was developed as a protocol based on MPLS-TE and related protocols in an attempt to generalize the MPLS protocol to work with an optical network. ASON, on other hand was developed as a new approach towards automation-friendly control plane architecture for optical networks. Different vendors sided with variations of these options, and due to interoperability issues across the vendors, a vendor-heterogeneous deployment continued to face challenges in providing an end-to-end information exchange for allocation and management of wavelengths across the transport network. In a vendor-homogenous deployment, the information exchange is limited and not centralized, which has similar inefficiency challenges as seen in the SP core network implementation.

> **FYI:** *The wavelength selection process is an important step in an optical transport network; it is necessary to choose a wavelength that is available to reach the destination. It is possible to start the connection using one wavelength and then at some point in the network convert to another wavelength by performing optical-to-electrical and electrical-to-optical transformation. However, such an implementation increases the complexity and cost of the network while impacting its speed, due to conversion and processing by electrical components. The network should be kept purely optical end-to-end as much as possible (therefore using higher power transmitters and high quality fibers to avoid regeneration).*

Aside from wavelength availability, other factors that influence the choice of lambda are the signal degradation or impairment, signal error rate, etc. [6]. These are measured at each hop, and an exchange of this information with other devices in the network can be utilized to determine the switching decision. Unless all of these pieces of information about the transport networks are visible, the devices (ROADMs or switches) can't take an optimal, quick, and automated decision on how to switch the circuits.

SDN Solution

The centralized control plane solution offered by SDN using abstracted network information helps tackle the challenges mentioned earlier. By abstracting the wavelength and signal information from the optical devices, a controller implementing transport-SDN has a complete view of available wavelengths and the quality of signal received at each hop. It could then compute the most appropriate and suitable path to be used for switching a signal between the source and destination, and program the ROADMs, switches and repeaters (signal regenerators) along the path. The use of SDN in the network not only drastically decreases provisioning times from weeks to minutes, but also opens up possibilities for faster service restoration, detection and remediation of service degradation and optimal utilization.

At the time of this writing, there are several efforts underway, both by providers and vendors towards standardization and implementation of transport-SDN solutions. Since each vendor may present a different interface to extact information or send instructions to it, efforts have been made to develop a common set of YANG models to fulfill this purpose and provide a common interface [7]. Other efforts made in this direction have used OpenFlow with the participation of vendors offering this support in their equipment [8]. On the standards development, Optical Interworking Forum (OIF) has published a framework for common APIs for transport SDN and proposed next steps [9]. Other standardization efforts being made in this direction are the extensions to the PCEP protocol that have been proposed to ensure PCEP interoperability with GMPLS networks [10], as well as mechanisms to consider WSON network's health when performing path selection decisions [11].

Revisiting SDN Controllers

Now that we have covered the role of the SDN controller and the various protocols that these controllers use, let's take a look at some of the popular SDN controller options that are available today. Both the open source options, as well the commercial ones that network equipment vendors are offering are examined in this section. While going through these options, reader should consider that it is desirable that any SDN controller is capable of the following:

- Provide the ability to communicate with a wide range of networking devices. This could be made possible by supporting multiple SDN southbound protocols.

- Provide open and/or well-documented northbound APIs to make it easy for to develop applications that could interact with the controller.

- Keep a global view of the network.

- Provide the ability to monitor network events, and offer the capability to define reactive actions in response to those events.

- Provide the network the ability to perform path computation and decision making.

- Offer highly availability features.

- Provide modularity and flexibility, so that the network can be programmed and customized for changing needs or new protocols. Ensure it is scalable, so it can grow as the need grows.

Some of the popular SDN controller options available in the industry will be discussed next.

Open Source SDN Controllers

Many open source SDN controllers are available, with contributions both from vendors and open source communities. Just like any open source software, these controllers do not have any licensing costs associated with them, and anyone can retrieve the code and use it as-is or modify it for their needs. This advantage comes at the cost of dependence on the open source community for support and feature development. Let's examine a few popular controllers.

OpenDaylight (ODL)

The OpenDaylight foundation was formed by a forum of network vendors to offer an SDN platform that is open and supports a multivendor network. The foundation helped develop and maintains the OpenDaylight SDN controller, which has become the de facto open source SDN platform in the network industry.

ODL uses a microservices architecture, making it modular and flexible with the ability to install only the protocols and services that are required. ODL supports many of the commonly used southbound protocols, such as OpenFlow, PCEP, BGP, NETCONF, SNMP, and Location/ID Separation Protocol (LISP), and northbound APIs such as RESTCONF. This variety of southbound protocols makes ODL suitable for a brownfield deployment, as these deployments may require a specific protocol to be used. ODL is purely a software product and runs on Java as a Java Virtual Machine. Figure 5-25 shows the architectural diagram of ODL.

Since ODL is open source, multiple vendors (HP, Cisco, Oracle, etc.) have contributed and provided software to its code, mainly to enable support in ODL for it to interact with their devices. Some vendors have modified their own copies of the

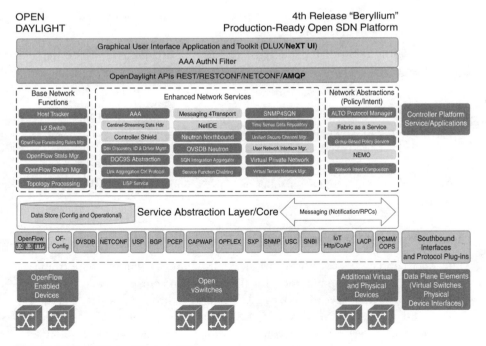

Figure 5-25 *ODL Architecture [12]*

open source ODL and developed additional capability in it, offering it as a commercial product along with a vendor-backed product support model [13].

ODL releases are named following the periodic table, Hydrogen was the first release, which made its debut in early 2014. It was followed by Helium, Lithium, and Beryllium. At the time of this writing, the Fifth ODL release is available, called Boron (B).

RYU

RYU is a community-supported open source SDN controller. The controller is entirely written in Python and is designed to be component-based, with well-documented APIs enabling any application to be easily developed to interact with it. Through the use of its southbound libraries, RYU supports the major southbound APIs such as OpenFlow, OF-config, NETCONF, and BGP [14].

It supports multi-vendor network devices and has been deployed in a Nippon Telegraph and Telephone (NTT) data center. Figure 5-26 shows the architecture of an RYU SDN controller–based deployment.

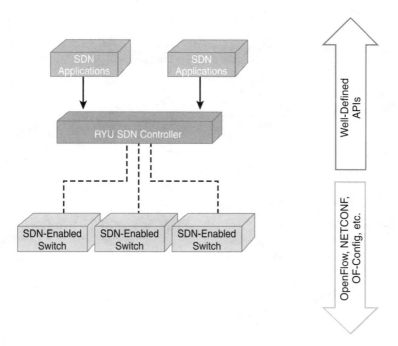

Figure 5-26 *RYU SDN Controller*

Open Network Operating System (ONOS)

ONOS is a distributed SDN operating system that provides a rich capability of high-availability and carrier grade SDN. It was made available as open source in 2014 with the aim of providing an open source platform for service providers to build a software-defined network. Today, ONOS is supported through the collective work of many service providers, vendors, and other collaborators, with new members continuously joining the ONOS community.

Figure 5-27 shows the architecture of ONOS and emphasizes its use of a distributed core that enables ONOS to boast of high availability and resiliency to match the carrier class standards. This distributed core layer is sandwiched between the northbound core APIs and southbound core APIs. Both of these cores serve the purpose of offering protocol-agnostic API to the distributed core from their respective directions. The distributed core takes care of the coordination across the cluster, as well as state and data management from the northbound and southbound cores. It also

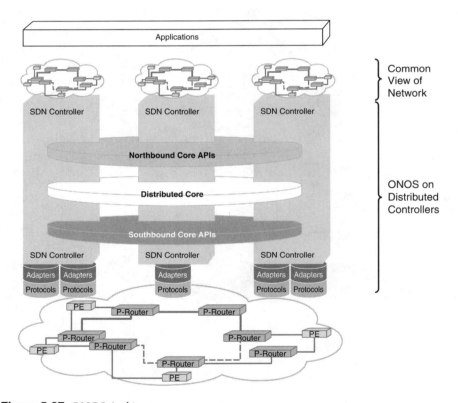

Figure 5-27 *ONOS Architecture*

makes sure that the various controllers across the network work coherently and keep a common view of the entire network view and not just segregated view based on their visibility. The application interacting with ONOS should have this one view of the network. This is where ONOS' strength and benefit of its distributed nature comes in.

On the southbound core APIs, ONOS uses pluggable adapters, which allows it to support many popular SDN southbound protocols, as well as being flexible. The northbound APIs allow for applications to interact with and use ONOS without requiring knowledge of the distributed ONOS deployment.

ONOS releases are named after bird species, even the ONOS logo is that of a flying bird. Its latest release, called Hummingbird is available at the time of this writing. One of the most popular uses of ONOS is its inclusion in a new open architecture called Central Office Re-architected as a Datacenter (CORD) that is designed to facilitate adaption of SDN and NFV by vendors. CORD is discussed in depth later in this chapter.

OpenContrail

OpenContrail is the open source SDN platform developed by Juniper. It was designed to implement SDN via an overlay model. It makes use of network virtualization techniques, where the overlay network forwarding function, like MPLS, or VXLAN, is decoupled from the data forwarding function and the control function is handled by the SDN controller. It is licensed as Apache 2.0 and supports additional features such as analytics, virtual router, and commonly used northbound APIs.

Commercial SDN Controllers

Many different SDN controllers are commercially available, not only from network equipment vendors but also from new entrants into the industry that are looking to acquire a share of the networking market by offering better and more lucrative SDN controller options. As previously mentioned, a number of vendors have used ODL as their base and built their SDN controllers by enhancing it with features, roadmaps, and support. Others have developed their SDN controllers from scratch. This section examines some of the popular options available today.

VMware NSX

VMware NSX is among the first SDN controllers developed by vendors. It began as a development by a startup company called Nicira which was later was acquired by VMware. The NSX platform implements SDN via overlay approach and creates a VXLAN-based overlay network while supporting routing, firewall, switching, and other network functions. The NSX SDN platform is designed to work with any hardware and any hypervisor and presents end-user with all the logical functions of networks, such as logical load-balancers and logical routers, and also provides a programmable and flexible network.

Cisco SDN Controllers

Cisco has developed various SDN controllers to cater to the needs of different market segments. Initially Cisco had an open Cisco Extensible Network Controller (XNC), which was supported through Cisco's own onePK protocol for southbound communication. Later it joined with other vendors and was one of the founding members of the ODL. Cisco supports a commercial version of ODL called Cisco Open SDN controller (OSC), which is built on top of the ODL with standards-based southbound and northbound APIs and protocols.

Cisco's SDN controller solution for the data center and enterprise is called Application Policy Infrastructure Controller (APIC). The APIC flavor for the enterprise is called APIC Enterprise Module (APIC-EM) and is discussed later in this chapter. For the data center, it is called APIC Data Center (APIC-DC), which is part of Cisco's ACI ecosystem. This ecosystem uses a Cisco proprietary solution. Cisco APIC-DC is the central element of the ACI solution providing support for programmability, management and deployment, policy enforcement, and monitoring of the network. It offers both GUI and CLI interface to interact northwards, and on the southbound it supports use of a proprietary protocol, iVXLAN, to implement SDN via a VXLAN overlay, as well as standardized the OpenFlex protocol (which was developed and made open source by Cisco) [15]. Additionally Cisco offers a open- and standards-based SDN controller for overlay management and provisioning system called Cisco Virtual Topology System (VTS), which provides the SDN overlay functionality via the Multi-protocol BGP Ethernet Virtual private network (MP-BGP EVPN). Cisco VTS supports REST-based northbound API to integrate with other OSS/BSS and a extensive list of southbound protocols such as RESTConf/Yang, Nexus NX-OS API, etc.

> **FYI:** *In a VxLAN-based network deployment, where the Layer 2 addresses are carried over a Layer 3 transport, the Layer 2 MAC addresses of the end-hosts are learned by two methods: via flood and learn using data path or using a control protocol to exchange these MAC addresses. In a MP BGP EVPN, the control protocol method is used and the MP BGP provides this functionality of exchanging the MAC address between different VxLAN end-points.*

Juniper Contrail

Juniper offers a commercially supported version of the open source OpenContrail SDN platform called the Juniper Contrail, as shown in figure 5-28. Just like OpenContrail,

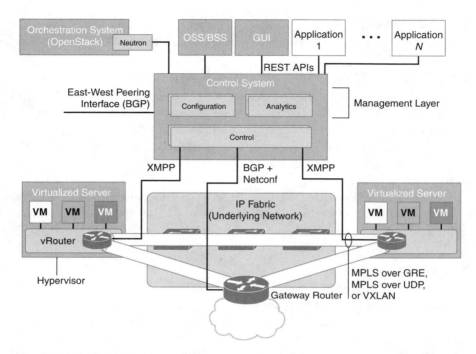

Figure 5-28 *Contrail Architecture [16]*

the commercial flavor offers SDN via the overlay model's support and works with existing physical networks to deploy a network virtualization layer on top of it. Contrail supports use of XMPP for its southbound communication with Juniper's virtual routers (vRouter), as well as NETCONF and BGP.

Juniper has backed out of the ODL project in 2016 and now supports Juniper Contrail and OpenContrail as their SDN controllers.

Big Network Controller

Big Switch Networks was one of the first few names to enter the SDN controller market. Big Switch has contributed three important projects to the SDN open source community:

- **Floodlight:** an open source SDN controller
- **Indigo:** supports OpenFlow in physical and virtual environments
- **OFTest:** a framework that tests OpenFlow conformance on switches.

On the commercial side, Big Switch's SDN controller has evolved from the initial days of the Floodlight project and is marketed as Big Network Controller. It support standard southbound protocols such as OpenFlow, taking a classic SDN approach, and is capable of working with both physical and virtual devices [17].

Nokia's Nuage Virtual Service Platform (VSP)

Nokia's SDN controller solution is offered through Nuage Virtual Services Platform (VSP). This was originally started as Nuage Networks, which was acquired by Alcatel-Lucent and is now part of Nokia's portfolio.

VSP consists of three main elements: the Virtual Services Controller (VSC) is the main SDN controller to program the data forwarding plane and supports OpenFlow as the protocol of communication, VSC talks to the northbound traffic via XMPP to the Virtual Service Directory (VSD), which acts as a policy engine. Similar to open vSwitch, Nuage has a virtual routing and switching (VRS) platform and integrates it with the hypervisor providing the networking functionality.

SD-WAN Controllers

As mentioned earlier, SDN is making its way into different segments of the network. One of the trending areas of SDN use is SD-WAN. Multiple controllers are available from vendors that explicitly target this domain. Since the controllers have a similar architecture, this section examines them collectively. The enterprise WAN market has just started to embrace the SDN technology and in additional to the traditional vendors there are a lot of new entrants trying to capture this market. SD-WAN controllers from some of the big players of today include Cisco's APIC-EM, Riverbed's SteelConnect, and Viptela's vSmart Controller. Some of the unique features that each of these products bring are as follows:

- Cisco's APIC-EM:
  - part of Cisco's intelligent WAN (iWAN) solution as a feature-rich SD-WAN
  - works with any WAN link technology
  - uses DMVPN for site-to-site communication

- Riverbed SteelConnect:
  - Brings in added value to customers utilizing cloud application offerings such as MS Office365, Salesforce, and Box, by using an application database catalogue for steering traffic across different WAN links
  - Uses Riverbed's Steelhead CX platform to provide software as a service (SaaS), dynamically creating virtual machines closer to the branch or end user and thus bringing the benefit of low latency, minimum jitter, and high speed access

- Viptela vSmart Controller:

    - Part of Viptela's Secure Extensible Network (SEN) platform for an SD-WAN solution, which also has the vManage application to manage the network, and vEdge routers [18]

    - Brings plug and play to the access device, with ease of deployment and management

    - The control plane and data plane communicate via a propriety protocol.

    - The controller and the configuration management software are offered free with customer paying for the edge hardware system only

    - Uses L3VPN for site-to-site communication

SDN Correlation with NFV

SDN and NFV are two independent innovative technologies. However, many of SDN's goals are shared by NFV, so the two heavily benefit from each other and support their mutual adoption.

When traditional network devices built by the vendors are considered, the control, data, and hardware planes are tightly integrated together, as shown in Figure 5-29. This makes it impossible to scale them independently. The architecture doesn't offer flexibility to implement new services or the agility to absorb changes. As Figure 5-29 shows, SDN and NFV play a role in breaking this bonding in two different dimensions. SDN's focus is separation of the control plane from a forwarding plane, and it uses network abstraction for an independent control plane to manage, manipulate, and monitor the forwarding plane. On the other hand, NFV's focus is on decoupling the network function from the vendor-built hardware, and it facilitates the use of generic hardware to run the software implementing network functions.

Both SDN and NFV offer different approaches to flexible, scalable, elastic, and agile network deployment. Though these two can be implemented independently, the principles of SDN can be applied to NFV by virtualizing the network function as well as separating the control plane function from the forwarding plane. Figure 5-30 reflects this blended relationship, and in this scenario NFV uses commodity hardware and implements the network function's forwarding plane, while the control plane function is extracted to the SDN controller.

Applications may form a glue to hold this relationship together and maximize the benefits of both technologies to offer a new networking landscape.

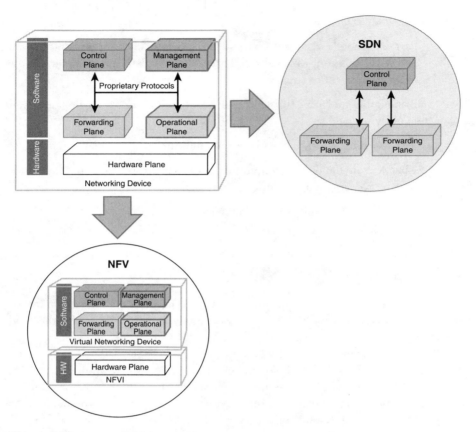

Figure 5-29 *SDN and NFV Focus Areas*

As summarized in Figure 5-31, the combination of these three areas offers the perfect recipe to meet cloud scale requirements of on-demand expansion, optimization, deployment, and speed.

Service providers are therefore moving towards this direction to reap the maximum advantage for their business and rapid implementation of new services for end users. With the industry shift, major vendors as well as new entrants are also supporting this trend to become the leading providers for the new market opportunities. With a significant number of open source tools available in both SDN and NFV, a number of projects are being evaluated to collectively use those tools. One such example is the Open Networking Lab (ON.Lab) and AT&T joint project called Central Office Re-Architected as Datacenter, or CORD. This project is discussed in more detail to showcase and explain the amalgam of the NFV, SDN, and application worlds.

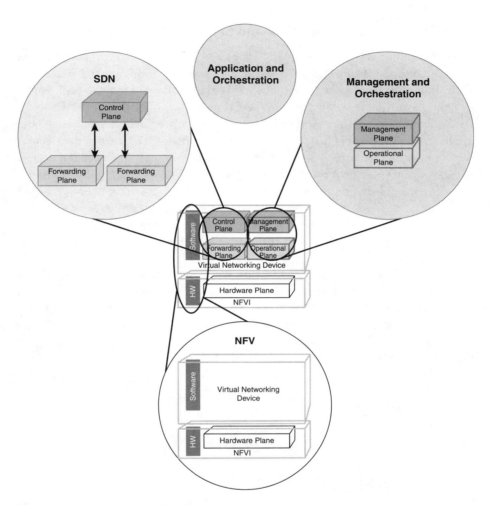

Figure 5-30 *SDN Combined with NFV*

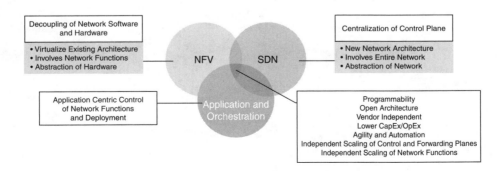

Figure 5-31 *Amalgamation of SDN, NFV, and Application*

CORD—An Example of NFV and SDN Working Together

CORD is a joint effort between AT&T labs and ON.Lab, putting together a new architecture for transforming the way a telecommunications central offices are built. It is considered a platform that would enable scalable and agile deployment of next-generation network services. CORD makes use of both SDN and NFV as core components of the architecture, along with open orchestration tools and application programmability bundled together with concepts from data center deployment architecture. The SND and NFV combination makes it the perfect use-case example of how these technologies collectively are used to revolutionize the design, implementation and deployment of new networking services. Both NFV and SDN focus on open source software and breaking vendor boundaries. That is true for CORD as well, because at its heart the CORD architecture is essentially knitted together from open source software on the merchant's silicon-based generic hardware.

The CORD architecture consists of an entire stack from hardware, software, and service orchestration. ONOS is used as the SDN controller. Network services are implemented by the VNFs running on COTS hardware, OpenStack performs NFVI orchestration, and an open cloud operating system, XOS, stitches this pictures together to make it possible to create, manage, run, and offer services using all these elements. Figure 5-32 presents a generic diagram for the CORD architecture.

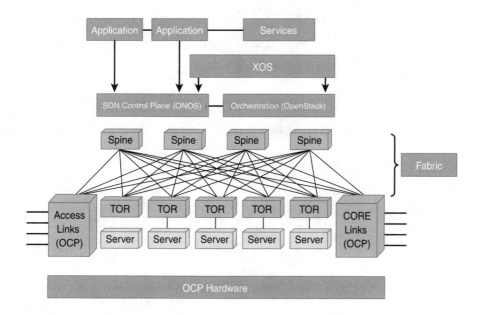

Figure 5-32 *CORD Architecture*

As Figure 5-32 shows, the commodity servers and the underlying network are built in data center-style spine-leaf architecture. The SDN controller and the applications on top of it perform control plane functionality, while XOS and OpenStack perform the service and NFVI orchestration accordingly.

Open Compute Project

The Open Compute Project is a project started by Facebook with the goal of developing specifications for the most efficient design for data center infrastructure resources (computing, storage, networking, fabric, power and cooling, etc.). The project's two years of effort resulted in Facebook's data center in Oregon that was energy efficient and significantly more cost effective to build. This design was later shared with Intel, Rackspace, and others and called Open Compute Project [19].

Different networking segments have started to utilize CORD infrastructure to build use cases for their specific domains. For example, mobile vendors are looking to leverage CORD for mobile 5G-based services, called M-CORD. In M-CORD, the concepts of NFV are applied by virtualizing the Mobility Management Entity (MME), Serving Gateway (SGW), and other elements into their virtual equivalents, while the use of a methodology like SD-WAN optimizes the network usage by deflecting traffic to cached servers or the Internet as needed. Other domains, such as Enterprise CORD (E-CORD), are being tapped to offer customized on-demand networks by using vFW, vLB, as well as SDN concepts to make it programmable and adaptable [20].

Now let's look at the use of CORD in broadband residential access. The traditional central offices that are offering broadband services to the customers are built using architecture inherited from the time-division multiplexing (TDM) era. With an increase in demand, especially with Gigabit access to the subscribers from technology like G.fast and Gigabit Passive Optical Networks(GPON), the central office design needs an architectural shift to keep up with the requirements. The goal behind CORD is to build an infrastructure with scalability and agility and to bring new services while reducing operational and equipment costs.

Figure 5-33 shows a traditional telecommunications architecture implementing a Packet Optical Network (PON). In PON networks, the optical fiber to the subscriber (irrespective of where it terminates) is passive, and the link to the central office is shared among multiple subscribers.

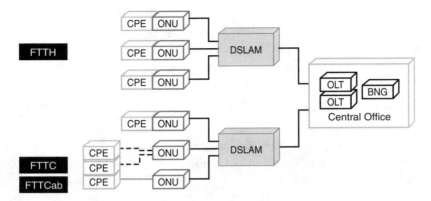

Figure 5-33 *Traditional Telecommunications Central Office*

FYI: PON *access may be deployed to bring a fiber to the subscriber's home, which is called Fiber to the Home (FTTH) deployment. In this case, the customer's data is directly put on the optical link, which is multiplexed with other FTTH subscriber data. In a different implementation, the fiber is brought only to the neighborhood, and then twisted copper wire connectivity is provided to each residence. This is referred to as Fiber to the Curb (FTTC). There are other variants of these as well, for example Fiber to the Basement (FTTB) is similar to FTTC but for multiplex buildings, and Fiber to the Cabinet (FTTCab) uses digital subscriber line (DSL) technology from the customer's premises to a telecommunications cabinet in the neighborhood. Irrespective of the methodology used, the overall architecture can be generalized as described in the main text.*

In PON deployments, the mentionable key functions are as follows:

- Customer premises equipment (CPE) is present at the subscriber or user premises that allows network access, management of local network, and connectivity through an optical network unit (ONU). The ONU's role is to convert between optical and electrical signals.

- The ONU's location may vary depending on which FTTx deployment is used, but in each case the data from the subscriber's (or multiple subscribers') ONUs is multiplexed using wave division multiplexing (WDM) techniques at common equipment that serves as the DSL access multiplexer (DSLAM). DSLAM takes the combined signal to the central office (CO).

- The CO is the hub of the optical connections from various DSLAMs and terminates them at a device called the optical line terminator (OLT). The role of OLT is same as that of ONU, but in the reverse order. The user is then authenticated using the Broadband Network Gateway (BNG) device, and eventually the user is able to reach the network that the CO is connected to.

G.fast & GPON

These two technologies are at the forefront of enabling gigabit access for residential users.

G.fast is successor to very high-speed DSL (VDSL) and it offers speeds of gigabit per second, which is a significantly faster speed that that offered by VDSL. Gigabit Passive Optical Network (GPON) is another residential broadband technology that brings gigabit speeds to subscribers, but it uses point-to-multipoint deployment of FTTH. Providers wanting to utilize existing deployment of copper wire to the home are looking at G.fast; the fiber is brought closer to the subscriber (for example, FTTCab brings fiber to the cabinet) and then G.fast from the subscriber to the fiber location. G.fast, however, works with very short distances of a couple of hundred meters from the fiber termination point. In both technologies, the fiber to the central office is shared between subscribers.

In the transformation of this network by CORD architecture, the CPE is replaced with a virtual CPE (vCPE) and instead of the OLT a virtual OLT (vOLT) is used. All of these transformations make use of the following NFV techniques:

- The CPE virtualization is straightforward. As discussed in Chapter 3, "Virtualization of Network Functions," the CPE virtualization could replace the CPE with a dumb device. The ONT function could be implemented in the same device as well. The vCPE could run new services and subscriber features in the central office.

- The OLT function is trickier to virtualize, because this has a more important role in the hardware. The hardware and software can still be decoupled, but the vOLT VNF requires hardware that is built for this functionality. The solution being proposed for this is to build the hardware with open specifications in collaboration with the Open Compute Project (OCP). Even though this hardware is purpose built, because it is not tied up to a particular vendor and offers open specifications [21] for anyone to build and replicate, its use doesn't break the rules for NFV.

- The BNG role doesn't need to be virtualized by using a vBNG VNF. This is where SDN enters the picture. The SDN controller (hosted on ONOS) manages the traffic flow on the fabric and towards the core network. In traditional network this function was performed by BNG. The authentication and IP address assignment roles of BNG are implemented in the vOLT. Therefore, vBNG is implemented with this combination of SDN-based flow control and the shift of some roles to other VNFs.

- OpenStack orchestration is used to manage the NFV infrastructure, ONOS manages the flow through the fabric (as mentioned previously), and XOS works with ONOS and OpenStack to implement the broadband-based services.

Figure 5-34 shows a view of the CORD implementation for a broadband network. The solution that CORD brings addresses similar challenges being faced today in different domains such as wireline, mobility, business VPN services, Internet of Things(IOT), and cloud. It is able to meet new and growing demands and offers new innovative services with a quick turnaround. With the benefits of SDN and NFV together, CORD provides a platform that has the ability to scale and bring both technology and business benefits to network providers.

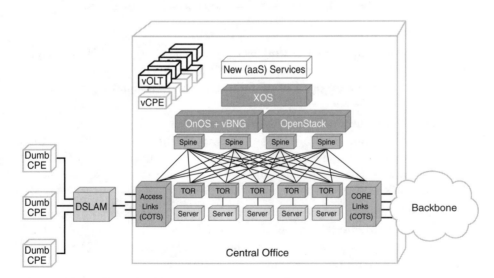

Figure 5-34 *CORD for Broadband*

Summary

This chapter covered concepts of SDN and discussed its benefits and use-cases in different networking domains. The SDN protocols and controllers were covered in significant depth. Most importantly, however, the relationship between SDN and NFV was examined, along with a detailed discussion of how they work together to complement and support each other as demonstrated in the example of a CORD project.

This chapter concludes with a key take-away on understanding interworking, as summarized in Figure 5-35. As the figure shows, SDN works with both physical and virtual devices performing network functions, while NFV works with the physical infrastructure and the VNFs that are hosted on them. The application at the top layer performs end-to-end service orchestration and interacts with both the SDN controller and NFV.

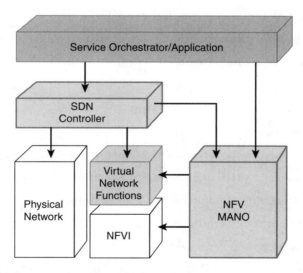

Figure 5-35 *SDN and NFV Working Together*

References

Please refer to the following for additional information

[1] https://tools.ietf.org/html/rfc5440

[2] https://tools.ietf.org/html/rfc5575

[3] https://tools.ietf.org/html/rfc6241

[4] https://tools.ietf.org/html/draft-ietf-netconf-restconf-05

[5] https://tools.ietf.org/html/rfc6566

[6] https://tools.ietf.org/html/rfc4054

[7] http://openroadm.org/home.html

[8] https://www.opennetworking.org/images/stories/downloads/sdn-resources/technical-reports/oif-p0105_031_18.pdf

[9] http://www.oiforum.com/public/documents/OFC_SDN_panel_lyo.pdf

[10] https://tools.ietf.org/html/draft-ietf-pce-remote-initiated-gmpls-lsp-02

[11] https://tools.ietf.org/html/rfc6566

[12] https://www.opendaylight.org/odlbe

[13] https://www.opendaylight.org/ecosystem

[14] https://osrg.github.io/ryu/resources.html

[15] https://www.sdxcentral.com/cisco/datacenter/definitions/cisco-opflex/

[16] http://www.opencontrail.org/wp-content/uploads/2014/10/Figure01.png

[17] http://www.bigswitch.com/products/SDN-Controller

[18] http://viptela.com/solutions/overview/

[19] http://www.opencompute.org/about/

[20] http://opencord.org/wp-content/uploads/2016/03/E-CORD-March-2016.pdf

[21] http://onosproject.org/wp-content/uploads/.../Technical-Whitepaper-CORD.pdf

Review Questions

Use the questions here to review what you learned in the chapter. The correct answers are found in Appendix A, "Answers to Review Questions."

1. Which of the following is an SDN southbound protocol?

   a. OpenFlex, OpenFlow, and XMPP

   b. OSPF

   c. C++

   d. Ruby

2. True or False? SD-WAN reduces the operational expenses for enterprise customers.

   a. True

   b. False

3. True or False? SDN mandates a single central controller for the network.

   a. True

   b. False

4. Which protocol can. be used to distribute route policy from the central server to the edge router for traffic diversion?

   a. MPLS

   b. ISIS

   c. NetFlow

   d. BGP-FlowSpec

5. Which are the main elements of CORD project that is providing the programmability, flexibility, and scaling of the network dynamically?

   a. OSPF and NetFlow

   b. Python and HTML

   c. SDN and NFV

   d. Java and C++ with COTS hardware

6. True or False? SDN needs NFV to function.

   a. True

   b. False

7. Which technology decouples the control plane from the forwarding plane in a network device?

   a. NFV

   b. SDN

   c. NetFlow

   d. Virtualization

8. Which one of the following is a method to implement SDN?

   a. SDN via APIs

   b. SDN via NFV

   c. SDN via cloud

   d. SD-WAN

9. What is CORD is an acronym for?

   a. Central Office Re-Architected as Data Center

   b. Classic Office Redesigned as Data Center

   c. Classic Open Reconfigurable Data Center

   d. Central Office Range Distribution

Chapter 6

Stitching It All Together

The previous chapters have gone through the core topics of network functions virtualization (NFV) design, orchestration, and deployment, as well as the fundamentals of software-defined networking (SDN). This chapter stitches all those fundamentals together and looks at some of the very important finishing touches required when all the pieces work collectively for NFV implementation. The main topics covered in this chapter are:

- Security implementation for NFV deployment
- Enabling virtualized network functions to work together to implement a network service
- The dynamics and details of programmability of the virtual network
- Performance impact and challenges in a virtualized environment

Security Considerations

Security considerations in NFV were addressed in Chapter 3, "Virtualization of Network Functions," from a standalone architecture perspective. This section describes the details of how security considerations need to be addressed for NFV in conjunction with SDN and applications. In this dynamic environment, the security measures must be designed to respond rapidly to threats and provide a high level of robustness. With these three domains, both per domain and common security polices are needed to be implemented to secure the network. Figure 6-1 shows some examples of different security considerations across these domains in a virtualized network.

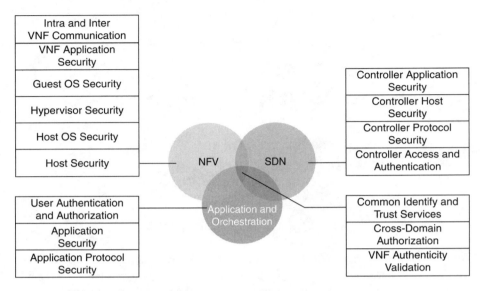

Figure 6-1 *Examples of Security Considerations across Domains*

Let's discuss some of the basic security measures that are necessary. They are as follows:

- **Intra- and inter-VNF communication**: The communications traffic between VNFs can take two paths, one within the same server, using virtual links, and the other between servers, using the physical infrastructure. Security measures need to be defined in both of these scenarios for intra- and inter-VNF communication to make sure the traffic is not compromised.

- **NFV infrastructure**: The host operating system (OS), hypervisor, firmware, and BIOS need to be up to date on security patches for threats against infrastructure vulnerability. The external access to this infrastructure needs to be secured for any attacks such as Transmission Control Protocol (TCP) sync attack, volumetric distributed denial of service (DDoS) attack etc.

- **SDN protocol security**: The traffic from the SDN controller to the NFV infrastructure needs to be secured. Proper measure must be taken and policies for encryption and authorization must be implemented. For example, even though OpenFlow doesn't mandate security as a required field, using the Transport Layer Security (TLS) mode for authentication of the switch or end device to the controller provides the security measure of device authentication. It also secures the control protocol message between the controller to the switch in an encrypted format to prevent eavesdropping and man-in-the-middle attacks.

- **SDN controller security**: As SDN is an application running on a Host or Virtual Machine (VM) environment, the security of the host or VM can utilize a similar measure as described in the NFV infrastructure. For the SDN application, the application needs to be evaluated against any vulnerability and proper measures need to be taken. For example in the case of Open Daylight Controller (ODL) that is a java-based application, any security hole in Java will need to evaluated and patched to ensure ODL is not vulnerable.

- **User and administrator authorization policy**: The user and administrator authorization must be defined with the multiple domain architecture comprising of compute infrastructure, VNF, Orchestrator, SDN components, hypervisor, and applications. Each of these domains may fall into different administrative or operational groups. If the NFV infrastructure is hosting a tenant-based network per customer, then the authentication and authorization of the tenant must be incorporated and provide the needed security to accommodate the customer's access policy.

- **Common security policy**: As the multiple domains are tightly intertwined, a single user may need access on multiple domains with various sets of privileges. The security policies need to accommodate this flexibility such as Single-sign-on authentication and accountability.

Service Function Chaining

Traffic in a network may need to go through a sequence of network functions as it enters, traverses, and leaves the network. The networking functions may vary depending on a number of design factors around the traffic. The sequence of functions that are applied can be considered as linked together in a chain, and since they constitute the network service through their combined effect, this design of arranging the packet path to traverse these network functions in a specific sequence is referred to as service function chaining or just service chaining, as shown in Figure 6-2. Since the resulting picture resembles a line graph while reflecting the forwarding path, it is also referred to as a network forwarding graph.

This concept was previously introduced using the example of a mobile network. This section discusses in detail how the service chaining architecture is defined and implemented as well as the standards driving it in the context of NFV.

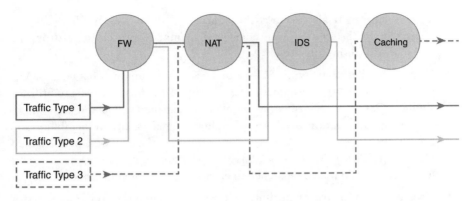

Figure 6-2 *Service Chaining*

Service Chaining in a Traditional Network

Service chaining is not a new concept and is implemented in the traditional network using physical and logical interconnections of network devices. However, since these networks are very rigid, any changes to the path based on traffic classification or any addition or removal of new network functional blocks requires the chain to be altered and can become challenging. If the new network functions require the addition of new hardware, then the change consumes time and resources with the physical installation and then provisioning of the transport link. Another possible approach is the use overlay networks, especially if the hardware already exists, for the functional block can be added by rerouting the traffic-path by configuring the overlay networks. Even though overlay networks can solve some of the physical network limitations of service chaining, they create configuration complexity and still depend on the underlying network topology. Figure 6-3 shows such an example in which two different types of traffic are configured for separate service chains by using Layer 2 vlans. Irrespective of the methodology required or used for achieving the insertion of new network functions, any new service cannot be deployed on today's networks on the fly. This results in a loss of tappable revenue, and restrains vendors to meet the scaling demands of cloud-scale networks for faster and more agile service deployment.

Another challenge with service chaining that uses physical or overlay network technologies has been its inability to offer application level granularity, support for any transport medium, or the interconnection between different overlays. The existing overlay techniques do not facilitate the possibility for the application-level information to be carried along the data path where it could be utilized by the intermediate nodes or the end nodes to influence the packet processing decisions.

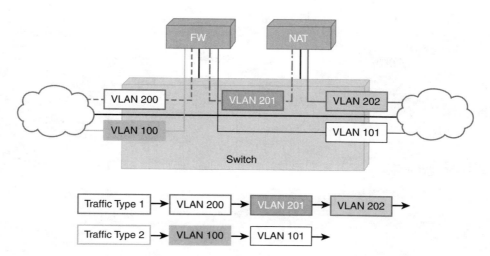

Figure 6-3 *Service Chaining Using Logical Network*

Service Function Chaining for Cloud Scaling

An agile and flexible network architecture that can adapt to the business changes in a faster time to meet market demands requires a service function chaining (SFC) architecture that is able to support new services. These services must be inserted dynamically and with minimum or no disruption to the existing network. Given the industry trend towards virtualization, the architecture should be able to accomplish this on a virtual, physical, or hybrid network. Service function chaining techniques also need to carry information from applications and be able to interpret that information. Several standards and use cases are emerging to make this possible and are discussed in detail in this section.

To meet goals and develop a methodology to implement service chaining in a uniform and compatible way across the network, the Internet Engineering Task Force (IETF) has been driving the efforts to define an architecture for service chaining. This architecture defines the blocks that could collectively make it possible for service chaining to meet the cloud scaling requirements and achieve the goals mentioned previously. Figure 6-4 shows the high-level view of this architecture and the different components that form it. The individual blocks shown are logical definitions of the roles that should exist. Some or all of these roles may be performed by a single physical, virtual, or hybrid device. Each of these components are discussed in detail.

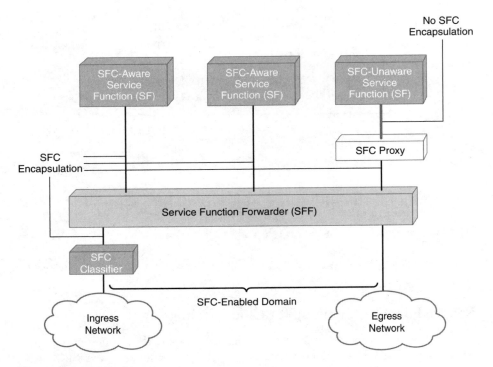

Figure 6-4 *SFC Architecture*

SFC-Enabled Domain

The service function chaining (SFC) architecture refers to a network as an SFC-enabled domain (or simply, SFC domain) when the end-to-end service function chain is supported with a single administration. The SFC domain has ingress and egress nodes, which act as its boundaries. Packets get classified and directed to the right network functions upon entering the domain and when they leave at the egress node any SFC-related information is removed before sending the packet to external network. The SFC domain is therefore just a portion of the network where the network functions related to the service are placed, as well as the mechanism to selectively choose the path of the traffic being processed by these network functions.

Classifier

A classifier's role is defined to be simple and straightforward—classification of the data that enters the SFC domain. The classification of the traffic can be as simple as a source or destination or can consist of different policy driven actions. A classifier adds information in the form of an SFC header on the packet to ensure that the traffic is sent on an appropriate course within the network based on the classification criteria such as service policy or other matching conditions.

> *FYI: The policy mentioned here, just like any other policy, is a set of rules. It consists of a pairing of matched conditions and actions. In the case of SFC, the policy may match on the information contained in the networking layers and then decide which set of network functions should be applied to the packet. Since the match criteria can also match on embedded information in the application layer, the traffic path determination decision can be very flexible and granular.*

Service Function (SF)

The service function (SF) is the logical block that performs a network service or network function on the packets. The service function can interact on the application layer or any of the lower-level layers, and may include services such as a Firewall, Deep Packet Inspection (DPI), caching, or load balancing.

The device performing this service function would ideally be SFC aware, which means it can understand the SFC header and process it. The architecture also allows the possibility for SFC-unaware service functions, where the service function is not able to process packets with SFC information. In such a case, a Service Function Proxy is needed to handle the SFC packets going to and coming from this SFC-unaware SF.

Service Function Path (SFP)

The SF path is a specification of the path definition for classified traffic within the SF-domain. It can be compared to a bus route going around the city. Once a passenger rides on a bus headed for a route, it takes them through the exact set of stops and exact path. Depending on the needs, the passenger can hop off the route at one of the stops and take a connecting bus with a different route. In the same way, the SFC need not be a linear chain of strictly defined hops, but it can rather be sparse and allowing flexibility to diverge in a new flow path. Figure 6-5 illustrates service chaining with SFC path.

Service Function Chain or Service Chain (SFC)

The abstract of the complete topology for a service as well as any parameters or constrains associated for the traffic path is referred as the service function chain (SFC). SFC is therefore not a logical block but rather a consolidated view of the SF path (SFP), the service function (SF), and other logical blocks that are part of the domain. As with the earlier example of a bus route, the SFC can be compared to a map of all the bus stops and bus route maps across the various areas in the city, and SFP can be compared to an individual bus route.

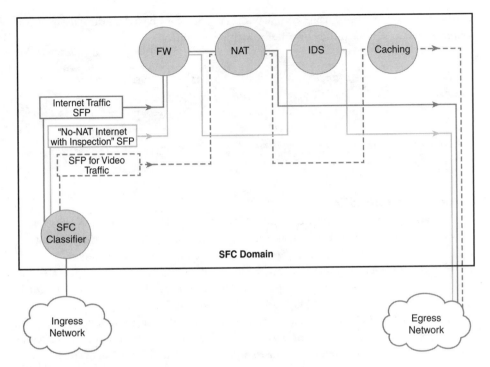

Figure 6-5 *SFC Paths*

Service Function Chain Encapsulation

When the classifier identifies the traffic to be forwarded to the service chain path, additional header information in the data frame is added to it. This additional header is called the service function chain encapsulation. There are multiple possible encapsulation headers, and existing overlay techniques, such as Layer 3 Virtual Private Network (VPN) or segment routing (SR), can be used for this purpose.

These overlay methods depend on the presence of an IP network. IETF is driving standardization for a new SFC encapsulation format under the banner of network service header (NSH), which can work with various other underlying networks. NSH is discussed in depth later in the section.

Reclassification and Branching

The classifier's tagging of an SF Header is based on information available to it at the time the packet enters the SF Domain. Newer information about the packet, especially based on the SF in its path, may require altering the path and diverting the traffic to different path. An intermediate Service function has an option to reclassify the packet and can update or modify the SF Path, The information can result in update of the information embedded in the packet, or the packet's SF Headers, or both. The type of update to SFP resulting in a new path is referred to as branching. An example of this is sending a traffic for parental control functions if the firewall SF has rules which determine that the traffic originating at specific times of day cannot go towards gaming server destinations.

Service Function Forwarder (SFF)

The service function forwarder looks at the SF headers and determines where the data packet with the service header needs to be forwarded so that the network service is able to act on this packet. Once the packet has been processed by the service function, it is sent back to the SFF, and the SFF now forwards the packet to the next network service. Just like other blocks, the SFF is a logical unit and can reside within the service function or outside on a top of rack (TOR) switch. An SF domain can have multiple SFFs. Figure 6-6 shows the SFF functionality in action. The two different classified traffic types are sent by the SFF towards various SFs and return back to it after processing is complete. Compare this view to Figure 6-3, which illustrates the use of Virtual LAN (VLAN)–based overlays to achieve a similar goal. In that case, which is how service chaining is accomplished today, the configuration would be complicated and hard to keep track of, while the same results can be achieved by applying SFC architecture and using a combination of classifier, SF header, and SFF.

Service Function Proxy (SF Proxy)

If the network service is not able to process the service function chain information, it can still be part of the SF domain by putting an SF proxy in the traffic path to and from this service function. The SF proxy removes the service function header and sends the deencapsulated traffic to the service function based on the information derived from the SFC header. Once the service is processed and the packet is sent back to the SF proxy, then the SF proxy reinserts the service function header and path information and forwards the traffic to the SFF for the next steps. The drawback in this approach is that the service function can only perform a local network function, but it can't take any action that could be reflected in the changing of the SF path onwards.

Service Function Control Plane

The service function path is constructed by the service function control plane responsible for the service overlay. This overlay can be a fixed path by providing a static flow for the packets, or a dynamic path based on the network deployment, or can be a

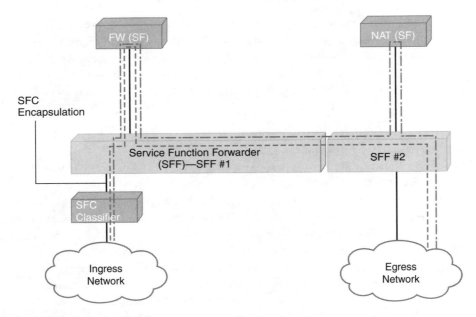

Figure 6-6 *SFF in Service Function Chaining Domain*

combination of static and dynamic path. This control plane can be distributed or can be a centralized function. In a centralized model, a central controller is called the service function controller which will be discussed next.

Service Function Controller

SDN concepts are very much applicable to SFC. The service path can be defined in a central controller be abstracting the network information and applying the policy via the application layer and this central controlled function. The logical block implementing this is referred to as a service function controller. In an SDN-enabled network, this SF controller can be integrated with the SDN controller.

Network Service Header (NSH)

Network Service Header (NSH) offers a standard for SFC encapsulation that is regulated by IETF and supported by multiple vendors in the networking industry. NSH is composed of two major components: the first provides information about the service path the traffic flow takes in the network, and the second carries additional information about the payload in the form of metadata. Applications and higher-level protocols can use the metadata component of NSH to send their information

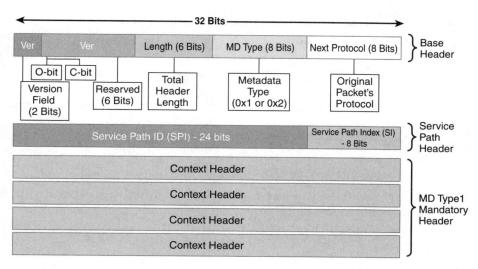

Figure 6-7 *NSH Protocol Header*

along the service path. This information can be helpful in the design making process for the service path selection and any other special handing the packet may need.

NSH protocol's header is defined as a set of three types of headers—base header, service path header, and context header—as shown in Figure 6-7. [1]

Base Header

The base header is a 4-byte header, with the following fields:

- A 2-bit version field is reserved for backward compatibility in future versions.

- A single bit called the O-bit indicates if the packet contains operational and maintenance (O&M) information. The payload of a packet with the O-bit set in its NSH header should always be inspected for operational information by the SF and SFF.

- A single bit called the C-bit indicates that at least one of the type-length-values (TLVs) present in the later part of the header contains critical information. The purpose of this bit is to make it easier for the packet parsing application or hardware to determine if critical TLV information is present by simply looking at the C-bit without having to parse the TLV data.

- Six bits are reserved for future use.

- The length of the NSH header is captured as a 6-bit field in the header.

- 8 bits are reserved for defining the metadata type or option that is being used. Two types are currently defined for NSH—type 1 and type 2. In type 1 metadata for NSH, the header has a fixed format, which helps service forwarding to maintain predictable forwarding performance and also makes it easy to optimally implement in hardware. Support for this type of metadata is mandatory for NSH implementations. The second option, type 2 metadata, uses a variable length, and this can be utilized to carry custom information like application-level hearers, TLV, etc. Type 2 metadata is expected to be supported in NSH implementations. The base header's information just identifies the metadata type. The metadata information itself is in a different header field.

- The last 8 bits of the base header are used to identify the original protocols of the packet. At the time of this writing, the inner packet protocol values allowed are listed in Table 6-1.

Table 6-1 *NSH Protocol Base Header Next Version Field*

Value in Hex	Protocol
0x1	IPv4
0x2	IPv6
0x3	NSH
0x5	MPLS
0x6 to 0xFD	Unassigned at the time this writing
0xFE-0xFF	Experimental values

Service Path Header

A service path header contains information about the service path. It's a 4-byte header, and is composed of the following fields:

- The Service Path Identifier (SPI) is the major portion of this header, using 24 of the 32 bits. The SPI uniquely identifies a service path which the packet will take within the SFC domain. Revisiting the example of a bus route for service function path, the SPI is analogous to the route-number for the bus.

- The Service Index (SI) uses the remaining 8 bits to indicate the location of this packet within the service path. The service path is decremented by every SFC-enabled node that the packet traverses. So by looking at the SPI and the SI values, one can determine exactly which SF the packet is at. It also works in a similar way as the Time to Live (TTL) value used in the IP header for loop detection.

Context Headers

The context header contains metadata and other information embedded by or based on higher layer information. The length of this header depends on whether type 1 or type 2 metadata option is used. If type 1 metadata option is used, then there are four 4-byte context header blocks that are added to the NSH header. For type 2 metadata, this header can be of a variable length or not exist at all.

NSH MD Types

As mentioned in the discussion of the details of a base header, there are two different metadata (MD) options for the NSH header, and the context header contexts vary depending on which MD type is chosen. For type 1, the data within the context header is opaque and doesn't have a specific format. The data contained in the four fields can also be any metadata chosen by in the implementation. The standards suggest, but do not mandate, the following use of the four context header fields:

- **Network Platform Context**: Information about the network device, such as port speed and type used, quality of service (QoS) tagging, etc.

- **Network Shared Context**: The data available to the network node, which is useful if passed to the other nodes in the network. For example, information about the customer associated with the interface, location information of the node, etc.

- **Service Platform Context**: Information about the network service available to a network node that could be useful to share with other nodes. For example, the type of hashing algorithm that was used for load balancing the traffic.

- **Shared Service Context**: This can contain metadata useful to implement the service across the network. For example, if traffic has to get a special treatment throughout the network, perhaps based on the level of service the customer has purchased, then this information can be embedded as a metadata here and help propagate it to all the NSH enabled devices.

When type 2 MD is being used, any number of context headers can be present (the base header's Length field comes really handy here, since the NSH header can now be variable size). In contrast to the mandatory type 1 context headers, the NSH standards define a format for these optional type 2 headers, which is shown in Figure 6-8.

This format specifies the uses of a TLV format, with 8 bits for the Type field, 5 bits for the Length, and 32 bits for the Value field. It also reserves 3 bits for later use, as well as specifies a 2-byte TLV Class field at the beginning of the header. The TLV Class is used to specify the category of the TLV field, such as the vendor this TLV belongs to or some implemented standard that the TLV may be using.

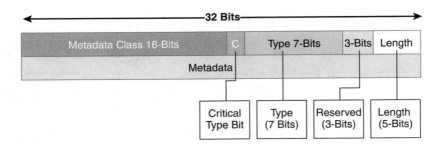

Figure 6-8 *Context Header in NSH Type 2 Header*

The Type values are left open to be defined by the NSH protocol implementation, but its higher order bit has a special significance. This bit indicates that the TLV should always be processed and understood by the nodes that the packet goes through. Therefore, it is mandatory that type values of 128 to 255 be understood across the SFC domain, while types 0 to 127 can be ignored.

TLV

The term TLV (an acronym for type, length, and value) is used in many network protocols. By definition, it packages data using a type field acting as a key, a variable length value field, and a length field to indicate the size of the value field. It's a generic way to pass variable length key-value paired information by a protocol.

An NSH header is inserted between the original Layer 2 or Layer 3 headers and the data payload as shown in Figure 6-9. For service visibility, assurance, and troubleshooting, NSH supports the O&M functionality through the O-bit in its header. The setting of the NSH service path can be distributed, where each network node can define the service path, or it can be based on a central controller, where the controller with its ability to view the network can define the path and have the classifier insert the NSH path during ingress from the service domain.

Metadata

A major advantage that SFC brings is the ability to carry and consume the application-level information in the form of metadata. In its generic definition, the term metadata refers to any set of information about any data, but in the context of SFC, metadata provides the contextual information about the data that is transported through the SFC domain. It's the role of the SFC classifier to insert the metadata in

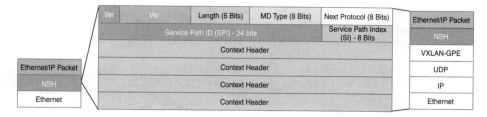

Figure 6-9 *Examples of NSH Protocol Header Insertion in the Packet*

the service header, such as the context header of NSH. The SFC may extract this information from higher layer protocols, such as information contained in an HTTP header or URL. For example, metadata may be used by the classifier to tag the video traffic differently based on its destination. The traffic going towards a preferred streaming content can be put on a high-quality service path. Once the metadata is put in the SFC protocol's header, the nodes in the path (SFF, SF, etc.) read, process, and respond to the data and take the appropriate predefined action.

There are different methods for the exchange of metadata information across the service function chain elements. Some of the methods used are as follows: [2]

- in-band signaling like NSH, MPLS labels, Segment Routing labels etc.

- application layer headers such HTTP

- congruent out-of-band signaling, such as the Resource Reservation Protocol (RSVP)

- noncongruent out-of-band signaling, like OpenFlow and Path Computation Element Protocol (PCEP)

- Hybrid in-band and out-of-band signaling, like Virtual Extensible LAN (VXLAN)

  - **In-band signaling**: If the metadata is carried as part of the packet, this is referred to as In-band signaling. In this case, the metadata can be part of the header or part of the payload. Figure 6-10 describes the metadata signaling flow. The Network Service Header is a good example of this method.

  - **Metadata in Application layer headers**: Metadata in application layer headers can be transported in the application header and is available for the service functions that can consume this Layer 7 information. Some examples of the use of this application layer metadata are the HTTP <meta> tag and SMTP's *X-* metadata. Figure 6-11 shows an example of HTTP.

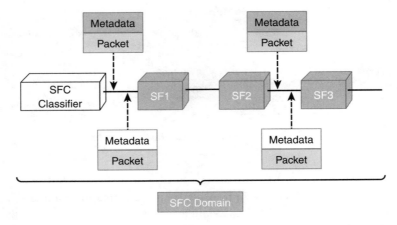

Figure 6-10 *Metadata Using In-Band Signaling*

```
$ telnet google.com 80
Trying 2607:f8b0:4004:80e::200e...
Connected to google.com.
Escape character is '^]'.
GET
HTTP/1.0 200 OK
Expires: -1
Content-Type: text/html; charset=ISO-8859-1
P3P: CP="This is not a P3P policy! See https://www.google.com/support/accounts/answer/151657?hl=en
for more info."
Server: gws
X-XSS-Protection: 1; mode=block
X-Frame-Options: SAMEORIGIN
Accept-Ranges: none
Vary: Accept-Encoding

<meta content="Search the world's information, including webpages, images, videos and more. Google
has many special features to help you find exactly what you're looking for." name="description">
<meta content="noodp" name="robots">
<meta content="text/html; charset=UTF-8" http-equiv="Content-Type">
<meta content="/images/branding/googleg/1x/googleg_standard_color_128dp.png" itemprop="image">
```

Figure 6-11 *Metadata in Application Layer Header*

- **Congruent Out-of band signaling**: Congruent out-of-band signaling occurs when the metadata information is carried in a separate channel and the data is transported in different flow even though both of the packets flow on the same path, as shown in Figure 6-12. File Transfer Protocol (FTP) is an example of using this type of signaling where port 21 is used for control signaling and Port 22 for data transport.

- **Non-congruent out-of-band metadata signaling**: In the previous signaling mode, metadata is being carried by a different flow compared to data flow, but the flow was the same path for both packets flow. In noncongruent

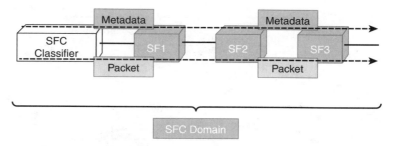

Figure 6-12 *Metadata Using Out-of-Band Signaling*

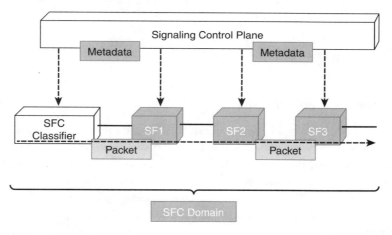

Figure 6-13 *Metadata Using Noncongruent Out-of-Band Signaling*

out-of-band signaling, the metadata signaling takes a different path compared to the data traffic flow. Figure 6-13 shows this model, using an example of a signaling control plane interacting with the nodes and managing the metadata. Some example of using this type of method are Border Gateway Protocol (BGP), route-reflector, PCEP, and OpenFlow.

- **Non-congruent out-of-band metadata signaling**: A network can have a combination of metadata signaling that can consist of the in-band and out-of-band signaling forming the hybrid metadata signaling. As shown in Figure 6-14, the hybrid model is using a combination of in-band and out-of-band models. Some examples of using this type of signaling are VXLAN and Layer 2 Tunneling Protocol (L2TP).

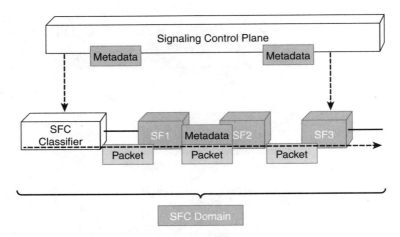

Figure 6-14 *Metadata Using a Hybrid Approach*

Other Protocols for SFC

Though NSH, backed by IETF as explained in the previous section, is the emerging standard for SFC, metadata communication can be done in various ways. Consequently, it is possible to implement the concepts of SFC through a number of other protocols, including some which have been around for a long time. Some examples are the use of MPLS-TE, VXLAN, or Segment Routing Traffic Engineering (SR-TE).

Figure 6-15 shows one such implementation of SFC, using SR-TE. A central SDN controller acts here as an SFC as well, and may be using PCEP to talk to the devices in the network. The SFC classifier attaches a stack of segment routing (SR) labels to the packets, based on the policies predefined for traffic types. The SR-labeled traffic is directed towards devices performing specific functions (acting as SF), based on the outermost label. Once the SF processes the packet, it is directed to the next hop based on the next SR label. If the SFC controller determines that the SF's processing should recalculate the path, it could instruct the SF to insert a new set of labels on the existing stack.

Service Chaining Use Case

Service chaining brings the advantage of controlling a traffic path by classification, based on information from higher-level protocols. The advantages of this propagate to the designer, service provider, and end user.

For the network designer, service chaining gives a powerful amount of control over the traffic and allows sophisticated and finely tuned application-aware policies

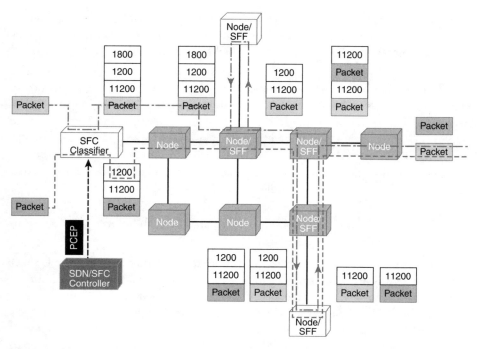

Figure 6-15 *SFC Using Segment Routing TE*

to be implemented for efficient use of the network, which can adapt to time of day, demand fluctuations, network failures, etc.

Businesses can use the metadata information to offer very granular service levels to its consumers, as well as offer new and innovative services. Some possible examples include the following:

- A service can be offered to classify video traffic from home surveillance systems so that it goes towards an encryption function before it is sent off to cloud-based storage or remote streaming.

- A security service on the network can be offered to deflect browser traffic to a Deep Packet Inspection (DPI) device that can identify and warn about malware. The voice, video, and other data traffic can bypass the DPI altogether.

- Providers can offer an alternate solution to software-defined wide-area network (SD-WAN). In that solution, the enterprise needs to implement this solution to optimize its WAN links by using it for selective interoffice communication. The same results can be achieved if instead of maintaining its own SD-WAN solution, the enterprise lets the provider use SFC to classify the traffic and tags it based on destination, source, application type, and any other metadata. This tagging can be used to set up different service paths for the traffic.

The consumer benefits from the new and flexible range of services shown in these examples. SFC in combination with NFV also makes it possible to allow consumers to modify their service agreements on-demand, perhaps using a portal offered by the service provider. Such a portal could permit consumers to add, remove, or modify the network functions that they would like to be included in their service bundle.

A use-case of a parental-control service shows how a new service can be created, designed, and deployed using the following SFC concepts:

- **Requirement**: The service should offer parents the ability to restrict access to the network for devices used by their children.

- **Design**: Each device's browser sends out metadata that identifies the OS version, hardware, etc. Using a plugin, the browser is made to send additional metadata to simplify its identification as a child's device. The service provider designs its classifier to use the specific metadata matches to tag the traffic's SFC headers. Traffic identified as originating from a child's devices is routed through a firewall, while the traffic originating from other devices is allowed to go out unfiltered.

- **Implementation**: The service provider may offer a portal that can be used by the parent to specify the time and destination-aware filters, as well as define device profiles mapped to different policies.

How Virtual Machines Communicate

Virtual machines or containers need to communicate to each other, either within the same host or to physical or virtual devices outside of the hosts. In any case, they need network interface cards for this communication. There are two ways of communication, which were touched upon in Chapter 2, "Virtualization Concepts." One is via the virtualized interfaces, and the other is by using dedicated physical interfaces to a virtual machine. The physical interfaces, of course, is only useful for communication with devices outside of the host. However, since the number of interfaces needed by the virtual machines is generally much higher than the number of physical interfaces available on the infrastructure, interface level virtualization is not avoidable. The NFVI layer takes care of that, along with other virtualization roles it performs, including virtual network interface cards (vNICs) that are made available to the virtual machines. To the virtual machines, these vNICs are treated as real physical interfaces, and they use the interfaces for sending and receiving packets outside of the virtual machine. To make this virtual interface scalable, capable of offering some switching features, and perform packet switching without significant performance degradation, a number of different approaches have been used to offer this service. Some of these options are discussed in this section.

Virtual Switch

Use of virtual bridges is the simplest solution to achieve interface virtualization, but virtual bridges lack features, scalability, and flexibility. To overcome the feature limitations, several other types of virtual switch software are available for virtual machine communication, providing enhanced switching features. Some examples of these are Cisco's Nexus 1000v, VMware's Virtual Switch, and Open Virtual Switch (OVS). Among open source switches, OVS is the most popular option. It can run within the hypervisor and supports a feature-rich set of capabilities (for example, it supports sFlow, NetFlow, and OpenFlow.). Its popularity has made it the default choice for OpenStack and other virtual machine orchestration platforms.

The challenge with this approach is the performance impact when scaled to higher interfaces, because the hypervisor software or kernel has to bear the burden of reading the packet from ingress or egress queues and then queuing and distributing the traffic to or from the virtual machines. This uses a significant number of CPU cycles and makes this approach inefficient for a scalable solution. Additionally, there is also the issue of the virtualization tax that was touched upon in Chapter 3, "Virtualization of Network Functions." These issues become much more significant when the virtual machines are running network functions with VNF directly in the data traffic path. Any performance degradation due to virtualization tax will directly impact end-to-end traffic.

One solution mentioned earlier for avoiding the virtualization tax was the concept of pass-through, where the hypervisor is bypassed and the vNIC communicates to the physical NIC directly with a one-to-one mapping. This helps to avoid the virtualization tax but makes the scalability situation even worse, because one physical interface is assigned to one virtual interface. Typically, the servers do not have a high number of physical interfaces, which limits the number of virtual machines that can use the pass-through mode. In addition, it brings in the challenge of guest OS device driver support that was discussed in Chapter 2, "Virtualization Concepts."

Single Root Input/Output Virtualization and Sharing (SR-IOV)

Single root input/output virtualization (SR-IOV) facilitates interface-level virtualization. The specification presents a standard way for a single NIC to appear as multiple NIC cards available to the host OS. Therefore, it takes the burden of virtualizing NICs away from the Kernel or Hypervisor and uses the NIC's resources to manage interface virtualization. This reduces stress on the host CPU.

> **Note**
>
> To be more precise, SR-IOV allows multiplexing of any input/output (I/O) device that is using the Peripheral Component Interconnect Specifications to interface with system components. SR-IOV was created and is maintained by the Peripheral Component Interconnect Special Interest Group (PCI-SIG).

When virtualization of network interfaces is implemented in the hypervisor or host, the host CPU is interrupted by packets that arrive at the NIC and need to be read and processed. Once processed by the host, the packets need to be queued up to the respective virtual machines they belong to, and to the virtual CPU resources. This indirectly impacts the host CPUs again as it serves the request to read the queues from the NIC and process them again within the virtual machine's context. With SR-IOV, the NIC card takes care of the first of these interrupts and masks it away from the host CPU. First, it creates multiple virtual interfaces and presents those as a physical interface to the upper layer (host, hypervisor etc.). In SR-IOV's jargon, the virtual interfaces are called virtual function(s) (VF). Similarly, the part of the NIC that is acting is and dealing with real physical interface functions is referred to as a physical function (PF). Note that the term virtual function (VF) should not be confused with virtualized network function (VNF). The two don't have much in common except that they are both related to virtualization technologies.

The hypervisor can now allocate these VF interfaces and present them as physical NICs (pNICs) to the virtual machine, connecting them in a pass-through fashion. When a packet arrives at the physical interface, the host CPU is not interrupted. Rather, the NIC takes up the responsibility of reading the packet from the wire, processing it, and then queuing it up to the virtual interface that is allocated to the destination virtual machine. These tasks are all performed by the PF, while the queue belongs to the VF's memory space. To queue the packets toward the correct VFs, SR-IOV uses identifiers such as MAC addresses and VLAN tags that uniquely identify the correct VF.

Figure 6-16 illustrates the SR-IOV implementation.

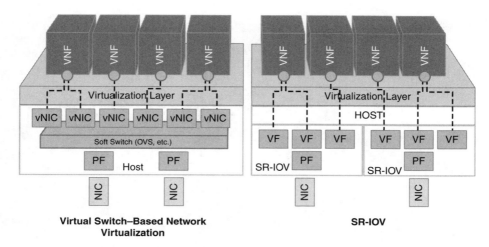

Figure 6-16 *SR-IOV Implementation Compared with Virtual Switch–Based Network Interface Virtualization*

Though SR-IOV presents virtual interfaces to the host, it doesn't hide the fact that they are virtualized. The VFs are only meant to move data between the host and the PF and are not required to act as a regular PCI device. Consequently, the host, hypervisor and virtual machine need to have support for SR-IOV. For example, once the hypervisor provides a pass-through connectivity from the virtual machine to the VF, the VNF must understand that it is talking to an emulated PCI device which doesn't need resource configuration, etc.

One of the drawbacks of SR-IOV is that it uses the PCI bus for packet exchange between the VF and the host's CPU. With service function chaining, the packets may go back and forth on this path multiple times, and the PCI bus' bandwidth can become a constraining factor. [3]

Direct Memory Access

One of the ways that virtual machines can communicate between each other is by using a shared memory space from the host OS. In this technique, a portion of the host's memory is reserved for this purpose and made accessible to the virtual machines. They can then write and read from this memory space, treating it as a PCI device [4]. The memory location therefore acts as a data link for the virtual machines to send packets back and forth.

This method does break the isolation principles of virtualization, because now the virtual machines are using memory space that is shared between them

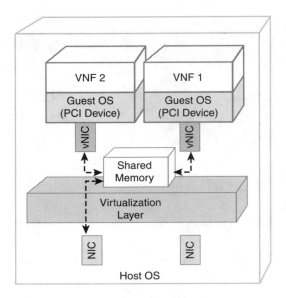

Figure 6-17 *Use of Shared Memory for VNF Communication*

and also doesn't belong to them but rather to the host. Additionally, support from hypervisor is needed to make this mechanism work. Figure 6-17 shows this mechanism.

Enhancing vSwitch Performance

The goal behind the interface virtualization approaches discussed in the previous section, was to provide network interfaces to virtual machines that can be scalable while still offering good forwarding performance. These techniques originate from the server virtualization world, and therefore a limited set of switching features and the performance degradation (compared to native bare-metal performance) are acceptable, as the majority of traffic would be directed to the application. However, in NFV these interfaces are in the data path and their performance directly reflects on the NFV network's performance. Now that the virtual machines are performing network-specific functions and are in the direct data path, performance factors such as interface throughput, latency, and jitter become very significant. A slight degradation in interface performance for one VNF can affect the entire data path and cause degradation of service. Similarly, NFV could benefit from putting some intelligence in the virtualization layer to help with service chaining. For example, if a virtual switch is capable of understanding service chaining information, it can act as the SFF and highly simplify the packet path between the VNFs, as Figure 6-18 shows.

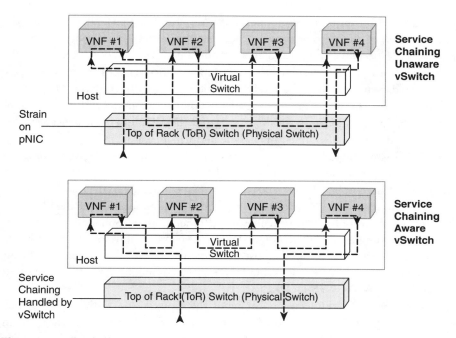

Figure 6-18 *Virtual Switch with Service Chaining Feature Capability*

Among the methods discussed so far, the throughput is worst when a virtual switch is used, because the entire burden is carried by the software path, which is not optimized for packet processing. The throughput achieved by SR-IOV is relatively much better, and that by shared memory methods is the best among the three. However, a shared memory technique has the associated security concern that was highlighted earlier. Neither SR-IOV or memory sharing are optimal for bundling advanced switching features [5]. The virtual switch, though low in throughput, is optimal for implementing these additional features. Therefore, a number of approaches have been taken to achieve higher performance while using these virtual switches bundled with needed features. This section discusses the some of the enhancements to the basic switching methods that have been introduced.

Data Plane Development Kit (DPDK)

Data Plane Development Kit (DPDK) makes use of the fact that the low performance of software-based (virtual) switches predominantly occurs because they are not optimized or designed to handle and switch high packet rates. Before explaining how a DPDK improves this situation, let's revisit the limitations in regular virtual switches.

The lack of optimization for high rates of packet processing results in involving the CPU for most of the steps in packet processing. Since the CPU is multitasking, its availability (especially if it is overloaded) creates a performance bottleneck. The virtual switches are also not designed to use system memory very efficiently. They copy the packet data to a memory buffer, interrupt the guest CPU, copy the data over to the guest memory location, and then again read the data from the vNIC to the application. The buffer allocation, deallocation, and the CPU interrupt processing for memory reads and writes alone can degrade performance. [6]

DPDK was developed to implement an optimal way to provide packet processing in software. It is a set of libraries and NIC drivers created by Intel Corporation, originally released in late 2012. In 2013, it was made available to the developer community as an open source development kit, allowing developers to use the library in the implementation of software switches and other similar applications that leveraged the fine-tuning that DPDK offers. DPDK is generic to any software that wants to leverage it, but it has found its most profound use in OVS. OVS finds significant improvement in performance by using DPDK—the combination is often referenced as accelerated OVS or OVS-DPDK.

DPDK replaces the built-in data plane of the Linux kernel with its own libraries. DPDK's lightweight library functions bring performance improvement through their very efficient memory handing by using a ring-buffer for transferring packets back and forth between the physical NIC and the application that is using DPDK (for example, OVS). To reduce the number of CPU interrupts that are required for packet reads, DPDK uses a periodic poll mechanism where the kernel polls for new packets periodically. If the packet rate drops to very low values, it can switch to the interrupt mode instead of periodic polling. With efficient buffer management, minimized and optimized CPU interruption, and other enhancements, DPDK has been shown to enable OVS to achieve near-native performance. DPDK, however, doesn't bring a rich set of features. It doesn't have a networking stack of its own and is meant entirely for packet processing and forwarding functions. Its combination with application implementing networking functions, such as OVS-DPDK, gives both features and forwarding performance.

Vector Packet Processing (VPP)

The previous section discussed DPDK's packet forwarding performance implementation. Through DPDKs optimized CPU and memory usage, it treats the data in a serial stream. Each of the packets go through the networking stack functions in a sequence, processing one packet processed at a time. This is referred to as scalar processing. Vector Packet Processing (VPP) brings enhancements on top of DPDK and processes the data in a batch rather than one by one. This parallel or batch processing is referred to as vector processing. Packets that are part of same stream are highly likely to be processed and forwarded in the same way. Vector processing leverages this possibility and achieves additional performance improvements by processing the packets simultaneously in batches.

The technique used in VPP has been proprietary information by Cisco, and used in its high end routing platforms such as a CRS and ASR9000 series devices. In early 2016, Cisco made the VPP technology available as open source under the FD.io (Fido) banner. VPP is closely coupled with DPDK and complements it, and is capable of running on any x86 system. Since VPP offers a very decent networking stack, primarily for Layer 2 to Layer 4 functions, it can be considered and used as a high-performance virtual router or virtual switch. It works with higher-level applications to offer network functions such as a firewall, full-fledged router (with routing protocol support), and load balancer. In fact, VPP claims to the first user-space line rate packet forwarding switch with networking capabilities.

How VPP Works

Though the details of VPP's implementation and optimization are beyond the scope of this book, it is useful to study it at a high level. In scalar processing of packets, as the packet moves through the forwarding stack, it may get de-capsulated, validated, and fragmented. Most importantly, it gets matched against a forwarding table to determine if it should be forwarded, sent to a higher level for additional processing, or simply dropped. Figure 6-19 shows an example for two different types of flows going through some processing stages that a packet may need to flow through. Each time a processing code is invoked, say Ethernet encapsulation, label swap, or forwarding decision, the CPU is invoked to work on the packet. This happens for every packet while it is going through the pipeline. VPP refers to these processing stages as a Packet Processing graph. This graph processing is applied to an entire group of packets.

> **Note**
>
> VPP is highly modular and allows for additional packet processing graph functions to be easily added and integrated into a flow through the use of plug-ins. Since it works in user space, any such plug-in or change doesn't require modification at the kernel level and is easily implemented and added.

VPP and FD.io

When VPP was released as open source, the proprietary code from Cisco was adopted by the Linux Foundation and named FD.io, or the Fido project. Aside from Cisco, other founding members of FD.io include 6WIND, Intel, Brocade, Comcast,

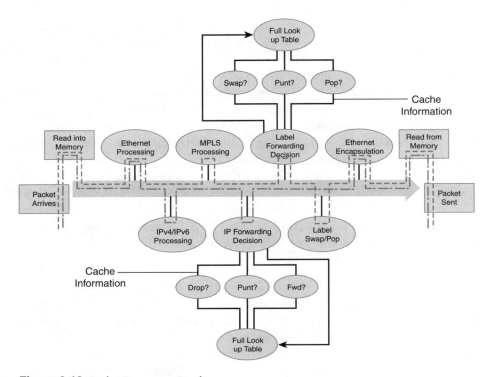

Figure 6-19 *Packet Processing Pipeline*

Ericsson, Huawei, Metaswitch Networks, and Red Hat. FD.io inherited contributions from other members as well, most notably the DPDK code that was already released as open source under the Berkeley Software Distribution (BSD) License. Many management, debugging, and development tools were also packed together with FD.io through these contributions. This makes FD.io a ready-to-use virtual switch or router with debugging and development capabilities while utilizing DPDK and VPP's enhancements for forwarding [7]. Note that in many places, including this book, FD.io is loosely referred to as Open-VPP or simply VPP, because of the pivotal importance of VPP in its code.

Interfacing with VPP

VPP's networking stack can be accessed using its published low-level APIs, which can be called by an application performing a networking function. Since the application is using and managing VPP for data forwarding, the term Data Plane

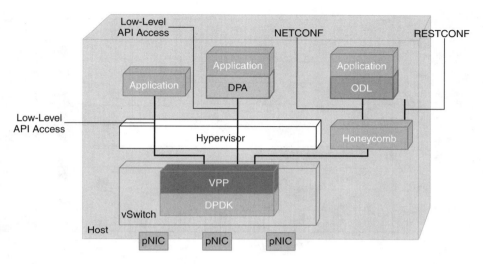

Figure 6-20 *VPP Northbound Interfacing*

Management Agent (DPA) is sometimes used for the application. One of the offerings by FD.io is an agent called Honeycomb that acts as a DPA while offering RESTCONF and NETCONF interfaces northbound. Applications and controllers, notably ODL, then talk to VPP using the Yet Another Next Generation (YANG) data models over NETCONF interfaces. Figure 6-20 shows these different possibilities of using VPP.

VPP Benefits and Performance

VPP has already been promoted and described in this text. That's because it's the first user-space high-performance open source switch with forwarding and networking stacks built in. Lab tests performed by independent organizations have shown VPP to bring significant performance improvement compared to OVS-DPDK, and it achieves close to near-native performance in a virtualized environment. Figure 6-21 shows the results of the impact of forwarding table size and packet size on throughput and latency respectively. These two comparisons alone suffice to justify the promotion of VPP.

VPP is written to run as an 64-bit application. It also supports service chaining and metadata header fields, which makes it an ideal switch to use in an NFV-based environment.

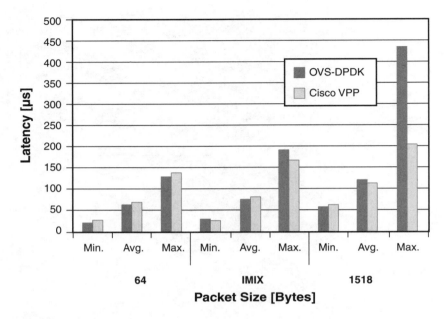

Figure 6-21 *VPP versus OVS-DPDK [8]*

Data Performance Considerations

Virtualization adds another layer of overhead and imposes a tax on the achievable throughput. Recall that the virtualization layer takes the CPU, memory, and NIC resources of the hardware and creates a virtual pool that the VNFs use. The VNFs that are usually in the data path need to be highly optimized for their packet performance. The previous section discussed how high packet performance is achieved for the virtual switch and vNICs. That alone is not sufficient to achieve high performance for the VNFs. The efficiency of the methods for utilization of CPU, storage, and memory resources in the virtual environment play an important part in the overall data path performance of the virtual environment. The VNF must be able to read, process, and write back the packets without becoming a bottleneck in the packet path. This section briefly introduces some of the options that can be used to optimize a virtual machine's performance for CPU and memory usage. Readers interested in a more extensive study of these and other parameters for tuning VNF performance should refer to books and websites specifically written on this topic. [9]

Before diving into the performance knobs, it must be emphasized that a virtual environment cannot outperform the resources that are allocated to it. Sometimes, the only way to increase performance is to allocate additional resources to the virtual machine (elasticity), or use multiple copies of the virtual machine (elasticity and clustering) that share the traffic load. Elasticity is managed and implemented by the NFV Management and Orchestration (MANO) block or a higher-level applications. The optimizations being discussed here are directed towards a means of enabling a virtual machine to use the virtual environment more efficiently and minimize the virtualization tax. These techniques play an important role in determining the overall performance that VNF is able to achieve for both throughput and latency.

CPU Usage Optimization

Most high-performance servers use multisocket, multicore CPUs. As explained in Chapter 2, "Virtualization Concepts," when the CPUs are virtualized, you can theoretically allocate all of the cores to the VNF. Another virtual machine using this host can be also be assigned the same number of cores without any issue, because the hypervisor takes care of managing the use of these CPU cores across the virtual machines. This can result in unpredictable CPU availability, especially if one virtual machine momentarily consumes most of the CPU resources. For time-sensitive applications relaying on CPU availability, such as packet processing, this can result in a high jitter value or even packet drop.

The following CPU terminologies would be useful when discussing CPU optimization

Multi-Socket: A CPU socket is simply the electrical connector on the motherboard that the CPU is plugged into. Multi-socket systems allow the use of multiple physical CPUs on the same physical host hardware.

Multi-Core: Physical CPUs today have multiple independent processing engines or processing units within them. These processing units are referred to as cores, and these cores multiply the number of instructions the CPU can execute simultaneously. These cores are often compared to separate pipelines for processing of CPU instructions required by one or multiple operating system processes.

Multithreading (or simultaneous multithreading): This technology allows each CPU core to process instructions from different application threads at the same time. Increasing the utilization of the CPU cores through SMT generally results in a performance boost for the applications. Intel uses a proprietary way of achieving SMT, which it calls hyper-threading (HT).

A utility available in Linux to check the number of available CPUs, sockets, and cores is lscpu (which is part of the util-linux package). Example 6-1 provides sample output from this tool.

(continued)

Example 6-1 *Viewing Information about available CPUs in Linux*

```
Linux:~$ lscpu
Architecture:          x86_64
CPU op-mode(s):        32-bit, 64-bit
Byte Order:            Little Endian
CPU(s):                32
On-line CPU(s) list:   0-31
Thread(s) per core:    2
Core(s) per socket:    8
Socket(s):             2
NUMA node(s):          2
<snip>
```

As the output shows, this system is viewed as a 32 CPU system because it has 2 sockets, 8 cores per socket, and the ability to multitask, running two threads on each core simultaneously.

> **FYI:** *A system with 8 cores and 2 sockets can offer a total of 16 dedicated cores. The host OS or hypervisor can choose to take this capability of the processor to multitask into account and increase the total number of virtual CPUs the system offers to an even higher count. If these CPUs are capable of dual-threading, then the system may be viewed as being capable of providing up to 32 virtual CPUs (2 sockets x 8 cores/socket x 2 threads/core) to the virtual machines.*

For VNF performance, some techniques that can contribute significantly are the following:

Disable Hyper-Threading

Enabling hyper-threading (HT) or simultaneous multithreading (SMT) can result in inconsistent performance, because the physical core is being logically shared across threads. In general, disabling SMT or HT can cause a smoother packet processing performance by the VNF because the CPU doesn't have to shuffle between the VNFs and other applications use. This technique reduces the system's scalability (decreasing the number of logical CPUs). However, implementation of HT or SMT is not always possible because it has to be done in the Basic Input/Output System (BIOS) of the server and that means a restart for the entire server. A possible workaround is for VNF to isolate CPU cores (using namespace or similar techniques) and prevent other applications from using any CPU threads that are being used by a VNF.

CPU Pinning or Processor Affinity

By pinning a process to a physical process, the hypervisor thread doesn't move between CPUs, therefore ensuring smooth performance as well as better utilization of the memory cache. If this technique is used, care must also be taken that the threads of a process are pinned to CPUs that are on the same socket.

Using Tickless Kernel

The Linux kernel can be compiled using flags that allow certain CPU cores to execute their tasks without getting slowed down by interrupt processing. This obviously requires recompiling a kernel recompile and can't be performed on a running system. However, if implemented, then use of a tickless kernel can result in performance improvement for a VNF applications.

Optimized Use of Memory

CPU processing requires frequent memory reads and writes. A high-speed memory ensures that a CPU doesn't spend cycles waiting for data to be retrieved from or stored into the memory. Memory access times are also critical when performing searches and matches against stored data, as well as queuing data that has been read and is waiting for processing. For example, some physical routers use specialized high-performance memory types such as ternary content-addressable memory (TCAM) to store the searchable data (such as routing information), but the same privilege cannot be assumed when the VNF is working on generic hardware and sharing memory allocation with many other processes.

In older systems, a single memory bank was accessed by the processors. This was referred to as uniform memory access. In multi-socket, multi-processor servers with large amounts of memory, the memory is divided into zones (also called nodes) which are then paired with CPU sockets. In this technique, referred to as non-uniform memory access (NUMA), each CPU accesses its local memory (faster to fetch and write) before working across the NUMA boundary to access shared memory. By confining an application to work within a NUMA boundary, performance improvement is achieved.

Programmability in a Virtualized Network

It has been emphasized throughout this book that to reap the full benefits of NFV and SDN, the network must be provisioned, managed, and maintained with maximum use of network programmability. These technologies, along with increasing adoption of open software framework, pave the way for a programmable network. Methods and protocols used for this have also been covered in detail. This section combines those pieces of information in the full context of an NFV-based network using SDN. It illustrates how the network is managed by applications and programs that boost its efficiency. while contributing to achieve the goals of SDN and NFV.

To paint the complete picture, let's walk through the development and use of programmability in the stages of the NFV network's deployment and operations. We start with the assumption that the NFV infrastructure components (computing, storage, and networking), along with underlay network that provides connectivity, are already deployed and available. Figure 6-22 shows the flow of events in the back-drop of the NFV, SDN, and application. The figure and the steps listed are meant to demonstrate the application's involvement and include a comprehensive set of steps.

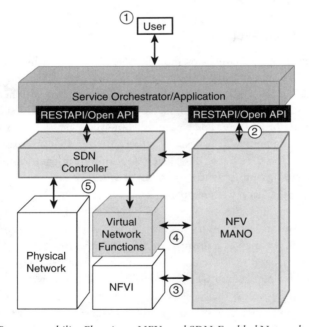

Figure 6-22 *Programmability Flow in an NFV- and SDN-Enabled Network*

The steps are as follows:

Step 1. The network design and implementation flow are initiated from the application layer. The application layer sits on the top the hierarchy and talks to the NFV-MANO and SDN controller.

The application layer may consist of a single application or a group of sep-arate applications working coherently These applications take on the role of service orchestrator as well as network monitor and manager. The application may be written in any language as long as it can communicate using the northbound protocol of the MANO and SDN blocks. Popular choices for this are Python, C++, Java, and the Go language. The northbound protocols are typically RESTAPI or Open APIs published by the developer of the SDN and MANO tools.

Step 2. Based on the service description, the application communicates with MANO to instantiate the virtual machines and VNFs that are needed for the network service. The functional blocks within MANO have already been discussed in depth previously in Chapter 5, "Software Defined Networking (SDN)"; for example, VIM works with the infrastructure to create the virtual machines, and VNFM helps bring up the VNFs, etc. These blocks use the ETSI-defined reference points for communication between them.

Step 3. Once the VNFs are created, they are interconnected using the Virtual Link Descriptor information. This interconnection of VNFs involves the programming of the virtual switch.

Step 4. The VNF is provisioned and connected, creating a topology for the Virtual Network Service that forms the data-plane of the network. The data plane may be a pure Layer 2 network, a VXLAN-based network, a Layer-3/IP-based network, or an MPLS-based network. The network is ready for performing the functions, such as firewall, load-balancing, NAT, etc. that are all in place. Though this network is using the actual physical network (forming NFVI) as its underlay, this network itself may be used as an underlay for the service layer which uses service function chaining methods to provision a service overlay.

Step 5. The application involves the SDN/SF controller at this point and uses it to provision the service path for the traffic based on the defined policies. This communication from the controller to the VNFs uses the SDN southbound protocols that were introduced in Chapter 5, "Software Defined Networking." Network Configuration Protocol (NETCONF), RESTCONF, and gRPC are the most popular choices. Other protocols, such as XMPP used by Juniper's Contrail, PCEP, OpenFlow, or Open APIs may also be used.

This completes the initial deployment stages of the network. At this point, the network layers are fully available to offer their services. The application can now take up the role of monitoring the network. The monitoring can be at different levels, for example the monitoring the VNFs for the states and parameters related to the functions, monitoring of the VNF and virtual machine states, and monitoring of the infrastructure. This application can be programmed to take autonomous decisions based on information in the monitoring data. Consider the following use cases to demonstrate how this arrangement could benefit:

- A traffic path change may be required to handle a certain traffic stream, a bandwidth demand surge, or a network fault. This decision to change the traffic path can be made by the logic in the application, and it can then be propagated to the device through the SDN controller.

- An increase in demand (expected or unexpected) that overloads the VNFs resources can be detected by the NFV MANO, and this information can be then used to trigger VNF elasticity. This can be done by the MANO's functional blocks, but can also involve the application implementing this decision based on a global policy defined to deal with these situations.

- A fault in the VNF's (or host's) code can result in a potential impact to the network. If the application is programmed with the intelligence to identify and fix the fault, it can automatically remediate the error condition and restore or protect the network.

The application could also allow the user, operating support system/business support system (OSS/BSS), or other applications to interact with it and request changes to the network service, scale, or topology. These inputs could result in the application translating the request to the exact change needed and then send the instructions to MANO or SDN for implementing the changes.

While the steps previously mentioned demonstrate the role of the application and use of programmability in this deployment and operations of the network, they also demonstrate how the stages result in the network being built in multiple logical layers. Figure 6-23 elaborates on this logical layering and also highlights the relationship between the topology layers to the six phases illustrated. As shown in Figure 6-23, the physical infrastructure gives a topology view and serves as the original underlay for NFV. The NFV network is created on this infrastructure and presents the virtual network topology view that is a fully functional network with all the VNFs interconnected in the desired topology to offer a service. To the end user, the interconnection of the VNFs is not significant, but it is more useful to know what this service offers—which is shown as virtualized network service view. Finally, when SFC is implemented, the service topologies are seen as logical networks that offer a different set of services to the traffic depending on traffic type, metadata, and other higher-level information. This is implemented as

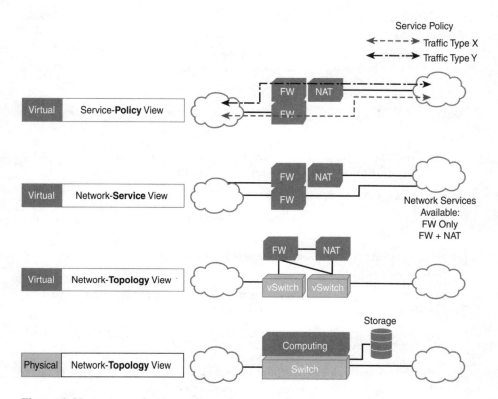

Figure 6-23 *Layers in the Network Based on Perspective*

a policy for traffic forwarding and processing and can be referred as a virtualized service policy view.

Summary

This chapter brought together the concepts discussed in the previous chapters and integrated them into a complete picture of the conjoined worlds of NFV, SDN, and applications for a programmable, open, and highly efficient network. The chapter covered details of service chaining and the NSH standards for its implementation. It also laid out the foundations of some advanced topics, such as NFV security and NFV performance optimizations, as a basic knowledge of these is imperative to the design and deployment on an NFV network.

References

Please refer to the following for additional information.

[1] https://tools.ietf.org/html/draft-ietf-sfc-nsh-05

[2] https://tools.ietf.org/html/draft-rijsman-sfc-metadata-considerations-00#-section-3

[3] http://media15.connectedsocialmedia.com/intel/12/14088/Enabling_NFV_Deliver_its_Promise_DPDK_solutions_Brief.pdf

[4] http://www.linux-kvm.org/images/e/e8/0.11.Nahanni-CamMacdonell.pdf

[5] http://arantxa.ii.uam.es/~vmoreno/Publications/BookChapters/dorado-TMABOOK2013.pdf

[6] http://www.intel.com/content/www/us/en/communications/nfv-packet-processing-brief.html

[7] http://www.linuxfoundation.org/news-media/announcements/2016/02/linux-foundation-forms-open-source-effort-advance-io-services

[8] http://img.lightreading.com/downloads/Cisco-Validating-NFV-Infrastructure-Pt1-and-2-SH-Edits.pdf

[9] https://access.redhat.com/documentation/en-US/Red_Hat_Enterprise_Linux/6/html/Virtualization_Tuning_and_Optimization_Guide/index.html

Review Questions

Use the questions here to review what you learned in the chapter. The correct answers are found in Appendix A, "Answers to Review Questions."

1. In NFV design with SDN, what are the different domains that require consideration of security?

   a. VNF

   b. CPU

   c. NFVI

   d. OSS/BSS

   e. MANO

2. In SFC architecture, who is responsible for attaching the SFC header?

   a. Service Function Forwarder (SFF)

   b. DPDK

   c. Service Function (SF)

   d. SFC classifier

3. What is the difference between NSH metadata options of type 1 and type 2?

   a. Context header with metadata is mandatory and of fixed size in type 1, while in type 2 it can be of arbitrary size and is optional.

   b. Context header with metadata is optional and of fixed size in type 1, while in type 2 it can be of arbitrary size and is mandatory.

   c. Context header with metadata is mandatory and of arbitrary size in type 1, while in Type 2 it can be of fixed size and is optional.

   d. Context header with metadata is optional and of arbitrary size in type 1, while in Type 2 it can be of fixed size and is mandatory.

4. What are the inner layer protocols supported by NSH?

   a. IPv4, IPv6, GRE, NSH, and MPLS.

   b. IPv4, Ethernet, VLAN, NSH, and MPLS.

   c. IPv4, IPv6, Ethernet, NSH, and MPLS.

   d. IPv4, IPv6, Ethernet, NSH, and GRE.

5. True or False? Service function chaining is applicable only to NFV-based networks and not on traditional physical networks.

   a. True

   b. False

6. True or False? VPP replaces DPDK as a packet performance technology.

   a. True

   b. False

7. True or False? The use of SR-IOV for a virtual machine requires that the virtual machine and host support this functionality. True/False?

   a. True.

   b. False

8. What are three methods discussed for interface virtualization?

   a. virtual switch

   b. virtual machine

   c. VPP

   d. DPDK

   e. shared memory

   f. SR-IOV

9. What are two common choices for communication between applications and SDN?

   a. REST API, Open API

   b. REST API, NETCONF

   c. OpenFlow, NETCONF

   d. Python, Java

10. Management of the infrastructure is the role of which of the following?

   a. SDN Controller

   b. SFC Controller

   c. MANO functional blocks

   d. all of the above

Appendix A

Answers to Review Questions

Chapter 1

1. a
2. c
3. b
4. b
5. d
6. a, c, and d
7. c

Chapter 2

1. a
2. b, d, f, and g
3. b
4. a, c, and e
5. a, b, and c
6. c
7. d
8. c

Chapter 3

1. c
2. a, b, and d
3. a, c, d, and f
4. b
5. a
6. c
7. a

Chapter 4

1. a
2. c
3. b
4. b
5. b
6. d
7. a
8. b
9. c
10. c
11. a

Chapter 5

1. a
2. a
3. b
4. d
5. c
6. b
7. b
8. a
9. a

Chapter 6

1. a and c
2. d
3. a
4. c
5. b
6. b
7. a
8. a, e, and f
9. a
10. c

Index

REGISTER YOUR PRODUCT at informit.com/register
Access Additional Benefits and SAVE 35% on Your Next Purchase

- Download available product updates.

- Access bonus material when applicable.

- Receive exclusive offers on new editions and related products.
  (Just check the box to hear from us when setting up your account.)

- Get a coupon for 35% for your next purchase, valid for 30 days. Your code will be available in your InformIT cart. (You will also find it in the Manage Codes section of your account page.)

Registration benefits vary by product. Benefits will be listed on your account page under Registered Products.

InformIT.com—The Trusted Technology Learning Source

InformIT is the online home of information technology brands at Pearson, the world's foremost education company. At InformIT.com you can

- Shop our books, eBooks, software, and video training.
- Take advantage of our special offers and promotions (informit.com/promotions).
- Sign up for special offers and content newsletters (informit.com/newsletters).
- Read free articles and blogs by information technology experts.
- Access thousands of free chapters and video lessons.

Connect with InformIT—Visit informit.com/community

Learn about InformIT community events and programs.

the trusted technology learning source

Addison-Wesley • Cisco Press • IBM Press • Microsoft Press • Pearson IT Certification • Prentice Hall • Que • Sams • VMware Press